IDEALS AND IDEOLOGIES OF MODERN POLITICS

Mark N. Hagopian

American International College

Longman
New York and London

IDEALS AND IDEOLOGIES OF MODERN POLITICS

Longman Inc., 1560 Broadway, New York, N.Y. 10036
Associated companies, branches, and representatives
throughout the world.

Developmental Editor: Irving E. Rockwood
Editorial and Design Supervisor: Jennifer C. Barber
Production Supervisor: Ferne Y. Kawahara/Karen Lumley
Composition: The Composing Room of Michigan
Printing and Binding: The Alpine Press

Library of Congress Cataloging in Publication Data

Hagopian, Mark N.
   Ideals and ideologies of modern politics.

   Bibliography: p.
   Includes index.
   1. Comparative government   2. Ideology.   I. Title.
JF51.H26   1985   320.3   84-15442
ISBN   0-582-28528-3 (pbk.)

Manufactured in the United States of America
Printing: 9 8 7 6 5 4 3 2 1   Year: 93 92 91 90 89 88 87 86 85

To the memory of
Vahe H. Aghababian
and
Jerair N. Hagopian

CONTENTS

PREFACE

In recent years the number of "ideologies" books has increased markedly. Although all such books necessarily display certain family resemblances, this one, I hope, has certain distinctions. First is the contrast I make between political ideals and ideologies, which is reflected in the book's organization and argument. This contrast follows if one employs, as I do, a "tight" definition of ideology. Whereas "loose" definitions of ideology attach the label "ideology" to belief systems regardless of content and coherence, tight definitions require that a full-fledged political ideology interrelate philosophical, programmatic, and propagandistic elements in a more or less coherent manner.

Ideals, on the contrary, tend toward vagueness and incompleteness, at least when compared to genuine ideologies. Thus, notions like democracy, socialism, or nationalism have a chameleon-like variability that qualifies them as ideals rather than ideologies. More systematic belief systems such as anarchism, communism, liberalism, fascism, and the like, however, manifest a richness and historical specificity that mark them off as ideologies.

There is, of course, room for legitimate disagreement as to where the line between ideals and ideologies should be drawn or whether a particular idea falls into one or the other category. Nonetheless, even if people dispute the categorization of this text, they might still find value in the specific expositions. For example, someone who prefers to call socialism an ideology might nevertheless concur with much of the text's specific analysis of socialism.

While many authors of ideologies books, for good reasons of their own, choose to be highly selective in their treatment of ideals and ideologies and give emphasis to the more "important" positions, I have tried to be comprehensive, and have given a number of ideals and ideologies separate chapters. This naturally results in a larger book, but the trade-off in broader coverage demands this.

Specifically, a comprehensive approach allows me to include separate discussion of ideals such as utopia and revolution or "neoindividualism" or ideologies such as Christian Democracy and Populism that often get short shrift in other books. I find these lesser known doctrines both important and instructive.

Beyond these methodological choices, there is the problem of ideological bias and fairness. My conscious intention was to produce a book that surveys the various ideals and ideologies *sine ire et studio.* In other words, my objective was not to provide ideological instruction to aid students in making their personal ideological commitments.

Having said this, I must admit that I am not a computer—some of the specific notions discussed I consider false, harmful, or alien; others seem true, beneficial, and congenial. Nonetheless, the student of political ideas should have enough respect for his subject matter and his audience to be able to minimize, if not entirely suppress, any missionary zeal that might animate him. If I have not succeeded in presenting a fair account of the varying doctrines, it was not for want of trying.

Finally, I would like to say a word of thanks to my main editor Irv Rockwood for his strong personal interest in this project, which has materially improved the final result. Also, the hard work of David Estrin and Jennifer Barber of the Longman team should not go without my grateful recognition.

Mark N. Hagopian

1

INTRODUCTION

IDEALS AND IDEOLOGIES

This book makes much of the contrast between political ideals and ideologies. As the notion of ideology itself is most controversial, the distinction we draw between it and ideals will not be accepted by all. When we identify a certain expression as an ideal rather than an ideology we suggest, at the very least, that it has an elasticity of meaning, a variety of connotations suggesting different things to different people. An ideal is thus a vague symbol that is positively evaluated by large numbers of different people for somewhat different reasons—opponents of the ideal, of course, may have a similar notion of it in mind, but they evaluate it negatively.

In this book we consider democracy, socialism, capitalism, nationalism, utopia, revolution, and individualism as ideals rather than ideologies. This is so because each can be defined in an abundant variety of ways. As a result, each ideal can surface at various points of the ideological spectrum. How many divergent conceptions of democracy, socialism, and nationalism can we encounter? The almost boundless possibilities suggest the seriousness of the problem.

In our century, for example, democracy is a term rejected only by the extreme right wing of the ideological spectrum. Indeed, even the Fascists and the Nazis sometimes claimed—perhaps cynically—that their own dictatorships best embodied "organic" or "true" democracy. How can democracy be an ideology if it weds itself to the beliefs of Marxist–Leninists, Social Democrats, Christian Democrats, modern liberals, and others? The fact of the matter is that democracy is an ideal, remaining vague until we explore exactly how a given ideological system interprets it. Naturally, each ideological system claims that it monopolizes the "true" rendering of the meaning of an ideal such as democracy. Accordingly, each ideology tends to deny that others use the terms—democracy, socialism, nationalism, revolution—correctly or honestly. The greater the distance between the ideological systems, the more numerous and fundamental the differences in how the ideals are interpreted.

We have suggested, for example, that both modern liberals and communists use and cherish the ideal of "democracy." The former, however, would deny the democratic character of any regime that did not allow free and open political competition. Communists, on the other hand, have generally felt that their conception of democracy was not only compatible with, but actually demanded, a regime ruled by a single party where other parties are outlawed or kept in a wholly subservient position.[1]

With disagreements so fundamental as these in mind, we might go to the opposite extreme and conclude that even though the term democracy is found throughout the ideological spectrum, there is no common substantive ideal involved. Thus, the democratic vision of the liberal and the communist would possess virtually nothing at all in common. But this extreme conclusion goes too far. At the most general level, communists and modern liberals construe democracy in some sense as "rule of the people," and favor some sort of "equality of rights."

The issue lies in the precise institutional format that would allow the people to express and exercise their rule, and in what precisely equality of democratic rights involves for the citizenry. In these more specific areas, ideology enters the picture and causes the modern liberal and communist notions of democracy to diverge more and more. The possible consensus at the most general level of the commonly held ideal begins to shatter once we ask more specific and concrete questions on how to make the ideal work in the real world. Ideologies help to answer this latter type of question, but, as in our example, the modern liberal and communist answers are dramatically different.

Another way of grasping the differences between ideals and ideologies is to say that ideologies are far more *systematic* than ideals. A political ideal is a broad symbol that entails values and goals that make it worthy of notice and acceptance. But the very vagueness of the ideal prevents its developing an accompanying doctrine that follows a certain logic and displays a high level of coherence.

Ideologies, on the other hand, attempt to follow their own logic and reach a level of coherence that constitutes a *system*. As we will see later, a system can be analyzed in terms of its structure and its functions. The analysis of structure deals with how the various parts of the system (in this case the "principles" of the ideology) relate to each other and to the system as a whole. The analysis of functions asks what specific roles are played by ideologies in political life. What do ideologies do? How much do they count? And is their political significance fundamental or derived from other still more basic factors or forces?

We will examine three structural components of ideologies (philosophy, program, propaganda) and three functional components (legitimation, mobilization, and interpretation). Analysis of structure and function is far easier with ideologies than with ideals. Their diffuseness and ambiguity prevents our pinning ideals down as nicely and neatly as we can with full-blown ideologies.

We can see this better when we view the problem historically. Political ideals through their vagueness and generality have a certain timelessness about them, or, at the very least, they are difficult to relate exclusively to any specific time, place, and thinker. Democracy is a term developed by the ancient Greeks two-and-a-half millenia ago, and it has been enriched and amplified over the ensuing centuries. Nevertheless, the original Greek conception of democracy still retains much relevance for us today.

With an ideology it is different: we can often trace its origins and evolution with great precision. Because the contributors to any ideological system express ideas current in a given time and place, ideologies often retain clear birthmarks. Furthermore, we can identify specific turning points in the evolution of an ideological system, when given ideologists, spurred by events and crises, strive to convey what these events and crises mean in ideological terms. Thus, these historical birthmarks and turning points stand out far more clearly with ideologies than they do with political ideals.

Even if we were to grant provisional approval to the basic contrast between ideals and ideologies, we will encounter disagreements on whether a particular notion amounts to an ideology or an ideal. In the long run we can only appeal to each reader's verdict after reviewing what is covered as ideals in Part 1 and what is covered as ideologies in Part 2. But one possible dispute can be raised now to illustrate the overall problem: why, for example, is socialism treated as an ideal and social democracy as an ideology? Is this what the philosophers call a distinction without a difference?

Our answer must be in the negative. Our decision to treat socialism basically as an economic conception—naturally, with a number of political ramifications—makes it relevant to ideas that go back deep into history. Socialism in this sense has to do with public or common ownership of the basic means of production and exchange. Social democracy, however, is little better than a century old and reflects some specific historical events and crises. First, there is the question, in the last two decades of the nineteenth century, of whether capitalism could be replaced peacably. Next, the same issue was pressed more strikingly still in the debate over the "socialist" merits of the Russian Revolution of 1917. Finally, after World War II, social democrats faced the issue of whether ownership or control of modern industry was the more decisive factor for the contemporary working class. For some the net result of this debate was to question whether the social democratic agenda for reform really involved "socialism" at all.

Clearly, social democracy and socialism are not the same. The former has a historical preciseness that the broad notion of socialism necessarily lacks. Socialism (with its stress on common or public ownership) can be found in antique utopias, the "millenial dreams" of countless religious cults inspired by all the higher religions, as well as in a host of contemporary movements and regimes. At any rate, it is this sort of contrast between the conceptual vagueness and historical imprecision of ideals and the conceptual clarity and historical exactness of ideologies that governs how we cover the subject matter of this text.

The Role of Ideology

In contrasting ideals and ideologies we maintained that the precision and systematic nature of ideologies lent itself to structural and functional analysis. "Structure" refers to the organization of anything: what component parts are and how they relate to each other. The three main structural components of ideology are philosophy, program, and propaganda. "Function" refers to how the system in question works both on the inside and with respect to the outer world. The three main functions of ideology are legitimation, mobilization, and interpretation.

Knowledge of both the structural dimension and the functional dimension of ideologies is crucial for a full understanding of political life, though the main body of this book is concerned with structural analysis. When functional analysis gains the upper hand, we often find historical narratives of certain periods or descriptions of political institutions that supposedly embody ideological principles. Although there is nothing inherently wrong in these approaches, they generally downplay analysis of the ideas and principles involved. This text concentrates on the ideas and principles to ensure they get the attention they merit.

The Structural Element of Ideology

Philosophy

Ideology is not philosophy. Rather, an ideology makes an open or hidden appeal to philosophical notions. However, only rarely does an ideology utilize philosophical principles completely. Its use of them is often careless and incomplete; the presentation often fuzzy and hazy. The reason for this sloppiness is that metaphysical subtleties and abstruse doctrines would soon lose most of the audience an ideology is supposed to reach. To be politically effective, an ideology must unavoidably abridge, simplify, translate, and thus transform the relevant philosophical notions.

Nevertheless, ideologies somehow take sides on the issues that have divided philosophers over the centuries and still do so today. Does God exist or not? Is the world material or spiritual? Does knowledge come from the senses or from the powers of the human intellect? Is there a stable foundation to reality, or is change the very essence of things? Are human values objective, or are they merely a matter of personal tastes or peculiarities? Does history have a "meaning," or is it a vast mass of separate events or "facts?" Does man have a nature, or is he a creature of free choice or of complete social conditioning? What is justice?

This list of issues is only partial, but it gives a sense of what is at stake. Thus, the "materialism" of Marx's dialectical materialism, the "rationalism" of classic liberalism, and the "vitalism" associated with fascism all have a definite philosophical pedigree. Philosophical puzzles have always been dear to intellectuals; and intellectuals, most will agree, are intimately involved in the origin and spread of modern political ideologies

Program

Whereas the philosophical assumptions of an ideology will vaguely suggest desirable goals, the program must spell out more specifically "what is to be done." The program tries to apply general philosophical principles to the problems of this or that society or civilization. The ideology's judgments about man, society, and history help determine whether it will preach keeping things intact, moderate reform, or total reconstruction of society. In this sense every ideology has a picture of an ideal society, to which it compares the existing society. The radicalism of the ideology is a function of how different the two pictures are.

Ideological criticism can naturally find all sorts of evils in the present culture and organization of society. Usually it is the *mode of social stratification* that becomes the bone of ideological contention. Societies tend to be stratified in three distinct, though interrelated, ways. One is political stratification, in which we generally find a sharp contrast between the powerful and influential elite and the rest of the population. Another is economic stratification, which divides society into unequal groupings (classes) based upon wealth or control over the means of production. The third is status stratification based on birth and involving serious gaps in social privilege and prestige. The programatic aspect of ideologies aims at these modes of stratification and attacks or defends them.

Strategy is the second aspect of an ideology's program. Once it is determined whether to preserve, reform, or overthrow the status quo, the obvious question is how best to do this. With the apparent exception of anarchist ideologies, the central strategic problem is how to achieve enough political power to accomplish the goals dictated by the ideology. Debates over strategy emerge most clearly in revolutionary ideologies of the left, where those separated by different schools of thought argue over the best way to overthrow the "capitalism" they all reject.

Their arguments concern such issues as: should the revolutionary movement develop a rural or an urban base? If rural, should the movement embrace vast peasant masses or remain a small cadre of highly mobile professional revolutionary fighters? If urban, should the strategy involve a secret organization of urban guerrillas or instead use the weapon of the mass general strike of workers? More broadly, strategy involves questions of violence or nonviolence, alliance or aloofness, immediate action or gradualism, participation in elections or boycott, and so on.

Propaganda

Propaganda is perhaps the most elusive structural aspect of ideologies. It is directly linked to the mobilization function (i.e., arousing people to political action). Traditionally, propaganda was viewed as spreading opinions so as to get people to change their minds. Jacques Ellul, however, thinks that modern propaganda differs fundamentally from the traditional approach because its aim

> is no longer to modify ideas, but to provoke action. It is no longer to change adherence to a doctrine, but to make the individual cling irrationally to a process of action. It is no longer to lead to a choice, but to loosen the reflexes. It is no longer to transform an opinion, but to arouse an active and mythical belief.[2]

Though Ellul has put his finger on an important change of tactics in progaganda, traditional-style propaganda is still very important.

How does propaganda contribute to political mobilization? One key way is the use of certain rhetorical techniques to gain converts and spur on the desired action. Ideologies try to do this by distorting reality in order to trigger certain emotional reactions. It seems clear that philosophical themes and social ideals are not enough in themselves to mobilize a mass of enthusiastic followers. These concerns may energize small bands of intellectuals, but something more is necessary if one hopes to expand the base of the movement.

An early attempt to sort out this missing ingredient is Georges Sorel's theory of the "political myth." For Sorel a myth is not a primitive legend about gods and heroes, nor is it a fully elaborated ideological system or blueprint for utopia. Instead, the Sorelian myth is a vague but effective symbolization of the hopes, aspirations, and dreams of a group of people. It is a thing of passion, not of reason. Sorel claimed that great religious movements like the Protestant Reformation or political movements like the French Revolution of 1789 changed history because the participants thought and acted with boundless passion.

Thus, it is the myth that unleashes the inner emotional forces of the group it animates. Once the movement is launched people leave their ordinary lives behind and experience and exhilarating sense of freedom. Some students of myth have even discerned the remnants of archaic mythical themes in the Aryan racism of the Nazis or in the world-redeeming role of the "proletariat" in Marxism.[3]

In addition to exploiting the mythical dimension of certain ideologies, ideological propaganda uses exaggeration and sometimes crude oversimplification. This is especially true because most ideologies operate at both the elite and the mass level. The former level concerns intellectuals and others willing and able to study the teachings of the ideology in some depth. However, exaggerations and oversimplifications are essential if the ideology is going to succeed with the mass public.

Every ideology has its own cast of "good guys" and "bad guys," determined on a social, racial, or religious basis. Mass-level ideology pictures the bad guys in the ugliest possible terms. Furthermore, whereas the elite-level ideology may explain historical events and trends as the result of complex and deep social forces, the mass-level doctrine will probably speak in terms of a "conspiracy" of evil-doers.

We have broken down ideologies into the three structural elements of philosophy, program, and propaganda. Different ideologies, of course, will lay a different weight on each of these three things. In all, however, the program serves as the connecting link between the philosophical abstractions and the highly concrete imagery of the propaganda.

The Functions of Ideology

We must now look more closely at what ideologies actually do in political life. Their three main functions are *interpretation, legitimation,* and *mobilization.*

Interpretation

The previous section was somewhat critical of ideologies. We argued that ideologies tend to distort reality by using mythic themes, exaggerations, oversimplifications, and hypercharged rhetoric. Now we must balance things a bit and ask whether the ideologue always possesses less knowledge and understanding than the nonideologue. Our answer must be that this is not necessarily so. If a nonideologue has inaccurate and primitive political notions, if his "belief system" is vague, incoherent, and unstable—hardly a "system" at all, then the ideologue may be his superior in intellectual terms. In other words, if the ideologue is somehow "closed-minded," the nonideologue can turn out "empty-minded" rather than truly "open-minded."

The ideology of the ideologue provides him with a gridwork of concepts, through which he can bring some order to the otherwise chaotic complexity of political life. Ideologies, then, do help some people see some political objects more clearly than they might otherwise. They are like eye glasses: the right prescription can improve our vision considerably, whereas the wrong lenses can reduce us to near blindness.

Thus, we can appreciate that specific ideologies enlighten some political objects and obscure others. Different ideologies will understandably provide their own peculiar insights and blind spots. For example, one need not be a Marxist to concede that before Marx political ideologies tended to underestimate the importance of economics. Similarly, anthropologists, who themselves might be atheists or agnostics, might find little to quarrel with when Christian Democrats expound on the religious foundation of human societies. Other examples could show still further that political insights, however partial, are strewn across the whole spectrum of ideologies.

Legitimation

Another function of political ideologies is the legitimation of political regimes. Why are regimes supported and laws, rules, and regulations complied with? Brute force is one answer, and illegitimate or alien rule is no rarity in the modern world. Legitimation, however, relates to support and compliance based on convictions of the rightfulness of the regime or of the ruler's commands. As Gaetano Mosca (1858–1941) pointed out a century ago, "No political class, however constituted, ever admits that it commands for the sole reason that it is composed of elements which are—or have been to that historical point—fittest to govern. It always finds justification of its power in an abstract principle, in a formula. . . ."[4] Mosca called this the *political formula*.

Political formulas run the gamut from the "divine right of kings" to the "will of the people." They serve both to explain and to justify the rule of the minority ruling class. There is a connection between the type of ruling class and the specific content of the political formula. This latter will reflect whether the ruling class is based primarily on wealth, birth, military power, or knowledge. Thus, change in the political formula is a barometer for changes in the actual composition of the ruling class. Mosca, however, shows himself a political "realist" when he cautions that "it is not the political formula which determines the mode of formation of the political class, but rather the political class always adopts the formula which is most useful to it."[5] We would only suggest that relationship between ruling class and political formula is less one-sided than Mosca seems to think. Ideas have a more powerful impact and are less easy to manipulate than Mosca's realism suggests.

Mosca's political formula embraces both the ideals and ideologies of this text. He sensitizes us to the manipulations of political elites, who drum up support for their domination by invoking ideological principles. However, he underestimates the force of these principles, which have been known, like Frankenstein's creature, to turn against their creators. Moreover, legitimation is not just for mass consumption: ruling groups themselves need reassurance that their dominant position reflects some sort of justice. Clearly, many modern regimes, especially revolutionary regimes, seek legitimation in and through ideology. Others make do with vaguer formulas woven out of our ideals.

Mobilization

A third function associated with modern political ideologies is political mobilization. This involves three related, though distinct, processes. The first involves the recruitment of political militants who will spearhead the activities of a political party or social movement. The problem is to attract people willing to work hard and make sacrifices for the party or movement. A second sort of political mobilization reawakens groups that have become politically inactive, at least temporarily. Finally, there is the "politicization" of previously apolitical elements. Ideology can help to do all these things.

As suggested earlier, the mobilizing force of an ideology can work at both the elite and mass level. In the former case an ideology can mobilize intellectuals, some of whom are almost always alienated from the status quo. To explain this, Edward Shils has argued that intellectuals, however nonreligious, are in fact the cultural heirs and counterparts of the priestly castes prevalent in ancient societies. "Intellectual work arises from religious preoccupations. In the early history of the human race it tended, in its concern with the ultimate or at least with what lies beyond the immediate concrete experience, to operate with religious symbols."[6]

Intellectuals are concerned with the life of the mind, which they consider a "sacred" realm. Actual societies, however, may be governed or otherwise dominated by businessmen, soldiers, bureaucrats, or professional politicians. Intellectuals are prone to view money making, war, administration, or partisan politics as merely "profane" activities. As custodians of the "sacred" realms of philosophy and beauty, they look down on profane activities and those engaged in them. Ideologies that attack or slight these things are likely to find adherents among the intellectual elite.

At the mass level ideologies can mobilize "the man in the street" in a somewhat different way. Mass discontent is more visceral than cerebral insofar as feelings of outrage or despair or of blocked hopes do not translate easily or directly into philosophical disquisitions or utopian schemes. Social psychologists have long maintained that "frustration" leads to "aggression." Frustration results when someone is balked in his attempt to do something. That something can be something quite tangible and simple or quite abstract and complex. Frustration is not a tolerable state of mind and some release is necessary. This is where aggression enters the scene, because it allows the frustrated person or group to strike out at something and thus gain some relief.

Thus, we find that mass-level ideologies serve to explain the frustration that comes from desperate conditions or unachieved aspirations. In this way ideologies can strike the exposed nerve of mass publics. Moreover, frustrated people do not want complex analyses or sophisticated diagnoses of their plight. Rather, they want simple answers to what is wrong as well as short-order solutions to their woes. They demand some sort of remedial action and punishment of those responsible for the dismal situation. Mass-level ideology can select targets for immediate aggression as well as hope for the not-too-distant future. In this way the ideology brings a clear focus to the previously discordant discontents.

CONCLUSION

Our introductory chapter has done two basic things. First, it has elaborated a contrast between political ideals and ideologies. Ideals, we found, are broad, diffuse political symbols that appeal to different people situated at rather diverse points in history. The very vagueness of ideals means that they must be incorporated into specific ideological systems before we can sense what precise interpretation is made of them. Ideologies not only display a greater degree of systematic coherence than ideals, but they are much easier to pin down to certain specific periods in history, because they respond more clearly to definite historical events and developments.

Our second major task was to concentrate on ideologies and analyze their structure and functions. The structural aspect involves philosophical, programmatic, and strategic factors in the content of given ideological systems. The functions are concerned with what political use is made of ideologies by political movements and regimes. Ideologies legitimize by providing moral justification for political power; they help interpret reality by organizing the complexity of the political world into more readily manageable categories of thought; finally, they mobilize the masses by fanning discontents into full political conflagrations.

Although we will return to this point in a final chapter, the guiding assumption of this chapter and those following is that political ideals and ideologies matter. In other words, they are forces that operate with real impact in determining the course of modern history. Now we must look at ideals and ideologies from the inside.

NOTES

1. This, of course, may not be true of "Eurocommunism." Western European communist parties, especially in France, Italy, and Spain, appear to have renounced revolutionary strategies and to have embraced the rules of the game of constitutional democracy. Skeptics, however, say that this change-over is superficial and temporary.
2. Jacques Ellul, *Propaganda: The Formation of Men's Attitudes* (New York: Vintage Books, 1973), p. 25.
3. Mircea Eliade, *Myth and Reality* (New York: Harper & Row, 1968), p. 183; and *Myths, Dreams, and Mysteries* (New York: Harper & Row, 1967), p. 25.
4. Gaetano Mosca, *Teorica dei governi e governo parlamentare*, in *Ciò che la storia potrebbe insegnare* (Milano: Giuffre Editore, 1958), pp. 52–53.
5. Ibid., p. 53.
6. Edward Shils, *The Intellectuals and the Powers and Other Essays* (Chicago: University of Chicago Press, 1972), p. 16.

SUGGESTIONS FOR FURTHER READING

Almond, Gabriel and Verba, Sidney. *The Civic Culture.* Princeton: Princeton University Press, 1963.
Apter, David, ed. *Ideology and Discontent.* New York: Free Press, 1964.
Barth, Hans. *Truth and Ideology.* Berkeley: University of California Press, 1976.
Ellul, Jacques. *Propaganda: The Formation of Men's Attitudes.* New York: Vintage, 1973.
MacIver, R. M. *The Web of Government.* New York: Macmillan, 1963.
Seliger, Martin. *Ideology and Politics.* New York: Free Press, 1976.

PART 1

IDEALS

Part 1, including Chapters 2 through 7, is concerned with the major political ideals of modern times. Here we need point out once again that the ideals covered—democracy and elitism, socialism, capitalism, nationalism, utopia and revolution, and neoindividualism—are too broad to be considered in themselves as ideologies. Many of the specific ideologies covered in Part 2 invoke several of these ideals but define them in ways that are highly peculiar and hard to reconcile with alternative usages. Our goal in Part 1 is not only to suggest diverse interpretations of such notions as democracy, socialism, or nationalism but to impose some order on that diversity. Although there may be an infinite number of possible variations on any theme, it is important to stay with original theme.

2

DEMOCRACY
AND ELITISM

CLASSIC DEMOCRATIC THEORY

Democracy is one of the most diffuse and pervasive ideals in all of history. The term entered the political dictionary early, with the ancient Greeks. It meant quite literally the rule of the people (*demos* = people). The premier political thinkers of ancient Greece, strange to say, were highly critical of this form of government, largely because of the stormy history of the supposedly democratic regimes in the city-state of Athens in the fifth century B.C. Save for the interlude under the great democratic leader Pericles, the Athenian democracy behaved high-handedly towards its allies, provoked a disastrous war with its rival Sparta, and executed its most illustrious teacher and citizen, Socrates.

These events and others made thinkers such as the great historian Thucydides and the philosophers Plato and Aristotle into critics of democracy. As a system of government, Greek democracy involved the direct policymaking role of all adult, male citizens. (These in fact were a minority due to the large slave and resident alien population.) Because the Greek polis was small in size and numbers, it was easy enough to gather the citizens in one assembly to debate and decide policy. Greek democracy extended beyond the legislative functions, as many judicial decisions were also made by panels of ordinary citizens. Moreover, the principle of choosing "administrative" officials by lot followed the Greek view of rule by the people themselves. Thus, there was no true *bureaucracy* in the modern sense of the term.

The ideal of Athenian democracy resembles modern liberal democracy more than does its institutional set-up. The classic statement of this ideal comes in the famous Funeral Oration of Pericles as reported, with poetic license, by Thucydides:

> Our constitution is called a democracy because power is in the hands not of a minority but of the whole people. When it is a question of settling private disputes, everyone is equal before the law. When it is a question of putting one person before another in positions of public responsibility, what counts is not membership of a particular class, but the actual ability which the man possesses. No one, so long as he has it in him to be of service to the state, is kept in political obscurity because of poverty.[1]

Pericles's faith in the common man is reflected in his pride in the free political atmosphere of Athens. Clearly contrasting the open society of Athens to the closed society of enemy Sparta, he exults that "our city is open to the world, and we have no periodical deportations in order to prevent people observing or finding out secrets. . . . This is because we rely, not on secret weapons, but on our own real courage and loyalty."[2] Finally, Pericles celebrates a keynote of all classic democratic theory, mass participation: "We do not say that a man who takes no interest in politics is a man who minds his own business; we say that he has no business here at all."[3]

The critics saw it rather differently. Thucydides himself attributed the temporary success of Athenian democracy to the towering presence of Pericles: "So, in what was nominally a democracy, power was in the hands of the first citizen." When Pericles died, no supreme leader emerged and lesser competing leaders "adopted methods of demagogy, which resulted in their losing control over the actual conduct of affairs. Such a policy, in a great city with an empire to govern, naturally led to a number of mistakes."[4]

Plato was still more vehement. In the *Republic* he describes democracy as the worst form of government short of tyranny—the oppressive rule of one man. In Plato's ironical view democracy is a "charming form of government, full of variety and disorder, and dispensing a sort of equality to equals and unequals alike."[5] In a democracy freedom degenerates into license and equality into insolence. There "the master fears and flatters his scholars, and the scholars despise their masters and tutors; young and old are all alike." Democracy destroys rank and other differences, including those based on sex. Plato's ire over the rebellious democratic spirit comes out when he reports that even "the horses and asses have a way of marching along with all the rights and dignities of freemen. . . ."[6]

Aristotle, as usual more moderate than Plato, distinguishes between two types of democracy. One, which he simply called "democracy," was the rule of the poor, regardless of whether the poor were a minority or a majority. Such a democracy was a defective form of government since it violated the true purpose of all government, which lies in pursuing the interest of the whole community. Democracy, along with oligarchy—rule of the rich—favors special groups over the whole.

"Polity," on the other hand, is a blend of democracy and oligarchy. It is a sort of middle–class democracy characterized by political stability. This stability results because the middle class holds the balance of power in the state. If stability is menaced by the rich who want an oligarchy, or the poor who want pure democracy, the middle groups can throw their weight in either direction. This prevents or defeats sedition.

Theorizing about democracy did not stray far from Greek ideas for over two millenia. It was considered by theorists to be a rather volatile regime suitable in any case for small states. The shady reputation of democracy even influenced the Founding Fathers of the American Constitution, who studiously avoided the label "democratical" for the new system of 1789. Thus, James Madison in the famous Federalist Paper No. 10 points out that "such democracies have ever been spectacles of turbulence and contention; have ever been found incompatible with personal security or the rights of property; and have in general been as short in their lives as they have been violent in their deaths."[7]

Madison, however, by no means rejected popular participation in government, when he preferred "republican" government to classic democracy. What basically distinguished these two forms of government was the momentous eighteenth century contribution to democratic theory—the idea of representation. Not all democrats were willing, however, to abandon the ancient view of democracy. Rousseau, whom we will shortly discuss, denied the possibility of democratic representation by maintaining that "every law the people has not ratified in person is null and void—is, in fact, not a law."[8]

Rousseau notwithstanding, the notion of representative democracy has enjoyed tremendous influence over the last two centuries. Disputes have raged, however, over the precise nature of representation in a democratic state. This debate is called the mandate–independence controversy. On the one side is the mandate or "mandated delegate" theory, which conceives the representative as the passive instrument of his constituents. The representative is simply an "agent" or "mouthpiece" for those he represents. The idea behind these terms is that the representative is supposed to reflect faithfully the express wishes of his constituents. He thus has a –"mandate" or set of instructions that he is obliged to observe to the letter. Should he depart significantly from these instructions, there should be some mechanism to "recall" him from office.

Although the mandate theory seems at first glance to fit in best with the fundamental democratic tenet of rule by the people, many sincere democrats have doubts. The difficulty involves determining what is good and effective government.[9] From this critical perspective the mandate theory reduces the role of the representative to that of a glorified errand boy. Supporters of the independence theory find grist for their mill in the writings of the eighteenth-century British statesman and thinker, Edmund Burke. Though much of Burke's conservatism is unacceptable to modern democrats, many would accept his statement that:

> Parliament is not a *congress* of ambassadors from different and hostile interests; which interests each must maintain, as agent and advocate, against other agents and advocates; but *Parliament* is a *deliberative* assembly of *one* nation, with *one* interest, that of the whole; where not local purposes, local prejudices, ought to guide, but the general good resulting from the general reason of the whole.[10]

Burke is convinced that any attempt to tie the representative's hands with mandatory instructions would contradict the overarching function of a representative assembly—to discover the common good by free deliberation.

The representative's role then is to engage freely in the search for the common good. This role demands that he maintain his independence and discretion. He must examine his conscience, consult his wisdom and experience, and cast his judgment farther than the limits of any electoral district. He must hear the wishes of his constituents, heed them if he can, but clearly reject them if he must. The voters should choose a representative not on the basis of his blind submission to their transitory wishes, but because he has qualities of heart and mind necessary for his difficult and delicate calling.

At any rate, all forms of classic democratic theory since the eighteenth century share certain key notions. First, they advocate "majority rule" in the sense that public policy should somehow reflect the will of the majority of citizens. Second, they advocate "political equality" or "one man (person), one vote" with each to count as one and none for more than one—to paraphrase Jeremy Bentham. Third, they stress "maximum public participation" in the sense that it is the right and duty of all citizens to get involved in elections, public discussions, and other aspects of the political process.

Beyond these three general principles of majority rule, equality, and participation, important disagreements appear about the moral justification and conditions of majority rule. On these issues we can roughly divide classic democratic theory into two main schools: liberal (or individualist) democracy and nonliberal (or collectivist) democracy.

Liberal Democracy

One major school of classic democratic theory espouses liberal or individualistic democracy. This does not mean that all forms of liberalism or individualism favor democratic government. Indeed, as Chapter 12 will show, early liberalism feared democracy largely on the grounds of its threat to individualism. In the last century or so, however, the convergence of liberalism and democracy has been based on two alternative doctrines: the theory of *natural rights* and the moral philosophy of *utilitarianism*.

According to the doctrine of natural rights—sometimes called "human rights" today—people as people possess certain rights that do not derive from or depend upon their membership in specific human societies. On the contrary, the legitimacy of these societies themselves depends upon how well they protect the rights of individuals. One of the earliest to argue in this manner was the great liberal philosopher John Locke (1632–1704).[11] As Locke saw it, God has endowed man with reason and the ability to know the basic principles of morality or "natural law." In fact, these principles operate in the prepolitical society of mankind that Locke and many others called the "state of nature."[12] For Locke natural law dictated that each rational person possesses three fundamental natural rights: the rights to life, liberty, and private property (or "estate" in Locke's language).

The state of nature (i.e., society without government) starts out quite auspiciously, but because each person is both "judge and executioner" of the natural law, the original harmony turns into conflict. People interpret natural law, which is rather general, to suit their own interests and these inevitably clash and cause violence. There is a clear need for a more settled interpretation and application of the precepts of natural law. Locke actually speaks of an "umpire" to enforce the rules and to arbitrate and settle disputes. This umpire function he assigns to "civil society" or what we might today call the "state."

In the Lockean theory, the state is thus a limited-purpose organization, the whole rationale of which lies in protecting the people's original natural rights. If a government violates this basic commission and acts arbitrarily by violating equality before the law, or by seizing private property, or passing laws contrary to the public good, or by unilaterally transferring law-making power to unrepresentative bodies, a basic right to revolution may be invoked. In such a "revolution" only the government is dissolved. Society remains intact and there is no reversion to the state of nature. Society is in a kind of intermezzo before a new government truly respectful of the people's rights is set up.

The basis for viewing Locke as an "extreme majority-rule democrat"[13] comes forth in the following passage:

> For when any number of men have, by the consent of every individual, made a community, they have thereby made that community one body, with a power to act as one body, which is only by the will and determination of the majority; for that which acts any community being only the consent of the individuals of it, and it being necessary to that which is one body to move one way, it is necessary the body should move that way whither the greater force carries it, which is the consent of the majority. . . .[14]

Locke's defense of majority rule is thus based on a physical analogy. Just as a physical mass will move where its vast bulk goes, the political community must follow its own political bulk, the majority. Thus, when the individual commits to membership in the political community— through the so-called "social contract,"[15]—he subscribes to majority rule as well.

While apparently categorical, Locke's defense of the principle of majority rule can be termed a "weak" one. It comes close to saying that the *de facto* political weight of the majority means that democracy is a matter of right. It just seems foolish to try to move society in a direction contrary to the majority. Since all citizens are individuals with their natural rights, there is no principle available to override that of the numerical majority.

The justification for democracy may follow from very different moral and philosophical grounds than natural or God-given rights. For the great English reformer and publicist Jeremy Bentham (1748–1832) "natural rights," "states of nature," and "social contracts," are unhistorical, purely metaphysical fantasies. Bentham wished to base personal morality and public policy on a realistic, even scientific, foundation. He thought he found this basis in the principle of "utility" and his less-than-orthodox disciple, John Stuart Mill, christened the whole doctrine "utilitarianism."

Bentham claimed to have found the key both to describing actual human behavior and to prescribing the "principles of morality and legislation." The starting point was a psychological one, to the effect that "nature has placed mankind under the governance of two sovereign masters, *pain* and *pleasure*. It is for them alone to point out what we ought to do as well as to determine what we shall do. On the one hand the standard of right and wrong, on the other the chain of causes and effects, are fastened to their throne."[16]

All ethics and all ethical terms, if they have any real meaning at all, are related to the two primitive notions of pleasure and pain. Happiness, good, right, justice refer in the final analysis to pleasure; unhappiness, bad, wrong, injustice are in the final analysis reducible to pain.

The science of ethics thus has two parts: (1) private ethics, which teaches how each person can work toward his own happiness; and (2) "the art of legislation," which "teaches how a multitude of men, composing a community, may be disposed to pursue that course which upon the whole is the most conducive to the happiness of the whole community, by means of motives to be applied by the legislator."[17] In other words, the goal of policy and legislation is "the greatest happiness of the greatest number."

Although Bentham's early ideas were by no means fully democratic, they contained a germ of equality that would blossom later. First of all, his conception of society was staunchly individualistic. He called the community a "fictitious body" and held that its interest is "the sum of the interests of the several members who compose it."[18]

Another egalitarian feature is Bentham's refusal to acknowledge any qualitative difference between pleasures. They differ only in quantity: how long they last or how strong and intense they are. To suggest this Bentham once opined that "pushpin is as good as poetry," thus suggesting that a silly child's game can be equal to the most refined pursuits, provided the amount of pleasure is the same. In this outlook, no social group can claim that its happiness or pleasure is of a higher or nobler nature and thus merits special treatment. The pleasure-pain principle is a great leveller.[19]

Bentham's egalitarianism became more clearly democratic when he concluded that in both voting and summing up pleasure each individual counts no more and no less than one. He came to see the democratic franchise as essential to the goal of the greatest happiness of the greatest number. This is first of all true because the individuals who make up the community are the best judges of their own interests. Accordingly, the problem becomes how to make certain that the government follows the wishes and interest of the community in matters of law and policy.

Bentham found the solution in a representative democracy which would achieve a "community of interest between governors and governed." This relationship will work only if public officials "are subject to the superintendence and control, or check, of the representatives of the people; such representatives speaking and acting in conformity to the sense of the people."[20]

In Bentham's mature thought, then, democracy is the only sure safeguard of the "greatest happiness" principle. He perhaps sensed that an individualistic utilitarian democracy could conceivably carry beyond liberalism. To avert this he distinguished between the realm of economics where laissez-faire was enough to produce a "natural" harmony of interests and the realm of criminal justice where government had to construct an artificial harmony of interests by legislation. Government economic intervention would upset a natural balance that was socially useful, whereas its activity elsewhere would produce social utility.

Even though many modern liberal democrats think Bentham's pleasure-pain psychology crude, the utilitarian defense of liberal democracy is alive and well. The idea that the individual is the best judge of his own interest, and that the public interest is the sum of individual interests, remains very strong in western countries.

Nonliberal Democracy

Nonliberal democracy also believes in majoritarianism, equality, and participation. However, the justification for democracy and the conditions necessary for its success differ substantially in the two democratic traditions. Whereas liberal democracy focuses on the political order and plays down social and economic institutions somewhat, these latter assume paramount significance in nonliberal democratic theory. Moreover, nonliberal democracy either rejects individualism outright or redefines individuality as far more intimately involved in the social community.

Many would agree that the great Swiss-French political philosopher Jean-Jacques Rousseau (1712–78) first or best raised many of the concerns of nonliberal democracy. Certain problems occur because Rousseau sometimes denied that true democracy can be put into practice. His early writings involved a radical social criticism that indicted the corruption, immorality, inequality, and oppression of eighteenth-century society. The harshness of his critique has led some to consider him an anarchist preaching a romantic retreat to the primeval forests.

That this was not Rousseau's main message is clear enough from his major work, *The Social Contract*. There he hopes to resolve his famous paradox that "man is born free, yet everywhere he is in chains." What it is to be free in society cannot be separated from democratic rule. Rousseau advocated a "positive" conception of freedom, whereby freedom is not just an absence of restraint and coercion. Still less is freedom and ability to indulge momentary passions and whims. Quite the contrary, for "the impulsion of mere appetite is slavery and the obedience to a law that one has prescribed to himself is liberty."[21]

How can we obey a law that is in some sense "our own" law? On the surface Rousseau's answer is simple enough: obedience to self-prescribed law is only possible in a community where my good and the common good are inseparable. Such communities are not only rare; they are supremely difficult to achieve. The reason, to some extent, is man himself. He has a potential for two very different types of conduct. He can act selfishly and think narrowly of "number one" with no consideration of the broader community. To Rousseau this means that we each have a *particular will*. When the members of society look only to their particular wills, the collective selfishness that results is called the *will of all*.

Neither the particular will nor the will of all egotistic citizens is a solution to the problem of true freedom. This false sort of individualism would produce a caricature of true democracy. In clear contrast to Bentham, however, Rousseau assigns to man the potential for non-egotistic, non-pleasure-seeking conduct. His interests can merge with those of the broader community that includes him. The individual thus has a second will that aims at the good of his whole community, the "general will." And when a collective decision is reached by citizens with a sincere desire to uncover the common good, that decision also manifests the general will.

Man is thus free in a moral, spiritual way only in a community where the general will regularly prevails. Rousseau takes the term "general" quite seriously because it only applies to law and the "sovereign." Law is general as it never can be applied to particular cases, persons, or instances. Rules so applicable he considers mere "decrees." Lawmaking is the unique prerogative of the sovereign people, whereas decrees may be issued by the "government" in the narrow sense. Sovereignty, people, and general will are inseparable.

How can we create a community that will produce the general will? For Rousseau this issue has both a moral and a social side. Morally, a community where the general will prevails requires that its members shed their egotism and devote themselves to the common good of the whole. Like Locke, Rousseau uses the notion of the social contract to symbolize the moral transfiguration that membership in a moral community produces. In essence the social contract means that "each of us puts in common his person and all his power under the supreme direction of the general will; and we receive again each member as an indivisible part of the whole."[22] The result of this pact is that "in place of the particular person of each contractor, this act of association produces a moral and collective body, composed of as many members as the assembly has votes, which receives from this same act its unity, its common self, its life and its will."[23]

Rousseau's community evidently requires the highest possible degree of unity and integration. Causes of disunity and conflict must be removed or neutralized. The three things that fragment social unity most are unequal wealth, religious cleavages, and special interest groups—for Rousseau "partial societies." There is no hope for a unified community if rich and poor, orthodox and dissenters, and various narrow associations are at each other's throats.

Rousseau's remedies for social disunity are rather simple: (1) wealth differences should be reduced to a minimum; (2) divisive religions should be banned and perhaps an official or "civil" religion should be established; and (3) groups between the citizen and the state should be eliminated or, if this is too extreme, groups should be kept small, numerous, and weak.

Having countered the danger of disunity, the last problem is the political mechanism of expressing the general will. This is accomplished through the act of voting itself, and it is here that Rousseau's democratic leanings seem strongest. In a morally and socially unified community the decision of the majority is a *virtually infallible guide to the general will.* To manifest the general will through voting, all must vote though they do not have to agree. This raises the ticklish question of the minority. Rousseau's handling of this issue involves another of his paradoxes as well as points of contrast with liberalism. He argues that to make the social contract more than a vain "formula," it tacitly includes the fundamental commitment that "when one refuses to obey the general will, he will be constrained to it by the whole body. This means nothing else than one will *force him to be free.*"[24] It is, of course, the forced-to-be-free business that alarms liberals and others. It seems at first blush to deny minority rights and to promote the tyranny of the majority.

Nevertheless, before passing judgment we should consider a few points. Recall that all members of Rousseau's unified community are mutually committed to the prevalence of the general will. If we assume further, as Rousseau does, that the majority is the incorruptible source of this general will, then forcing the disagreeing individual or minority to go along with the majority is not coercion or duress in the usual sense. Such "constraint" is merely the indispensable means to achieve a purpose that all share. The disagreeing individual or minority is merely in error: he or they have simply strayed from the path that leads to the true destination.

Thus, Rousseau offers us a strong defense of democracy understood as majority rule. If the general will is the sign of a free, just, and legitimate society, we can appreciate the importance of majority-rule democracy. Later nonliberal theories of democracy have essentially embroidered the arguments made by Rousseau. They have stressed the importance of the community for the individual's self-development, implying that the "privatism" of liberal democracy places a barrier between one man and his fellows. Whereas liberal democracy inherits a fear of concentrated power and majority tyranny from liberalism, nonliberal democracy considers such notions as undemocratic.

The nonliberal democrat has almost total faith in the will of the people. It should prevail over all obstacles as quickly and completely as possible. From this viewpoint, notions like "separation of powers," "checks and balances," and other limits on governmental power can be harmful or at least superfluous. If all power comes from the people, and the people manifest the general will, there is no need to disperse, divide, and balance public power. All of these devices simply impede the enactment of the popular will. If we cannot resurrect classic direct democracy, then there should be a single legally sovereign legislature that reflects and represents the politically sovereign people.

Modern nonliberal democracy has moreover laid greater stress on certain points that were less outstanding to Rousseau. Nonliberal democrats doubt very much that true democracy can flourish in a society characterized by social classes and serious inequalities of wealth. How can the poor majority control the rich minority? How is the pauper the political equal of the millionaire? The social conditions underlying democracy are far more important than the institutional mechanisms through which it is expressed.

This is why almost all nonliberal conceptions of democracy are associated with some version of socialism. Socialism takes industry and gigantic sources of wealth out of the hands of a few private individuals and administers them for the sake of the whole community. Only thus will the few be kept in check and the many be raised to where one man, one vote, and majority rule mean something. If we want to have democracy in the political sense, we must first have it in the social sense.

The Elitist Challenge

There are two main currents of "antidemocratic" thought.[25] One maintains the "undesirability" of democracy when measured against some aristocratic or authoritarian standard. We have already had an inkling of such doctrines in our discussion of Plato, and will discover more in later chapters. A second current preaches instead the "impossibility of democracy" (i.e., that majority rule cannot work under any circumstances). This thesis can be split into the twin arguments of the "ruling class as organizational necessity" and the "ruling class as conspiracy of power." David Spitz has assigned Gaetano Mosca to the first school and Vilfredo Pareto to the second.

Here we will only consider Mosca, since he and Pareto are close on many important issues. These two and their younger disciple, Roberto Michels, make up the "classic elitist" school of political theory.[26] Mosca published the first full statement of elitist political theory in 1884 at the age of twenty-six. He continued to write almost to his death in 1941. It is no surprise that his thought evolved, which led to a considerable softening of his initially hostile view of democracy.

The young Mosca began his new theory by attacking the traditional doctrine of the forms of government. From the time of the ancient Greeks, this classification first divided governments according to the number of rulers (one, few, many). Then came the question of the good or bad ethical quality of regimes, and we end up with three good regimes (kingship, aristocracy, democracy) and three bad ones (tyranny, oligarchy, mob rule).

In regard to this classification, Mosca objects that neither the rule of one nor the rule of many are realistic alternatives in political life. The idea that one person could hold all the levers of power in his hands is an illusion. This "sovereign" in reality is no more than the titular head of a much more extensive ruling minority. On the other hand democracy or the rule of the many runs up against an iron law of politics. This law states that whatever the formal name of the system, "the governers (i.e., those who possess and exercise the public power) are always a minority."[27]

As we saw in Chapter 1, this dominant minority or "ruling class" defends or disguises its position by appealing to a *political formula*. But its monopoly power position results less from ideology than from its representing a predominant "social force." Mosca points to wealth, birth, military prowess, and knowledge as the social foundations of historical ruling classes. Wealth has been the passport to the ruling class both in the "oligarchies" of ancient Greece and in the modern capitalist societies of the west. Birth in the sense of inherited status gives access to the circle of the ruling class in other societies, especially those with a hierarchy of "estates" capped by a hereditary aristocracy.

In times of disorder, as in the time after the fall of the Roman Empire in the fifth century, military prowess can become the main social force. Leaders with a band of armed followers are able to dominate vast numbers of weak and vulnerable people. When this relationship becomes settled, it can follow the course of serfdom and vassalage, as in medieval European feudalism. The military nobility is the ruling class.

Finally, "knowledge" understood as the possession of some technique or, more commonly, mastery of some moral or religious lore can also justify the position of the ruling class. Although such "knowledge" may appear to be myth or superstition, what counts is how the particular societies see it. To become an official of the Chinese Empire, for example, one had to pass examinations on the writings of the sage Confucius and his chief disciples. The scholars who passed were known as Mandarins and administered China's affairs for many centuries.

Mosca was well aware that the forces of wealth, birth, military force, and knowledge were not exclusive. Wealth can sometimes buy military force, entry into a ruling aristocracy, or the leisure and education to gain the "knowledge" so esteemed in a specific society. Moreover, he was fond of pointing out that all ruling classes tend to become closed and hereditary and pass power from parents to children. Thus, a given ruling class can actually blend several or all of his four primary social forces. This would be more likely, of course, in periods of rapid social change.

Also contributing to the "antidemocratic" reputation of Mosca is his critique of parliamentary government. The young Mosca had harsh things to say of the "government by assembly" found in late nineteenth-century parliamentary systems. By lowering or dropping restrictions on the right to vote, the resulting broadened electorate tended to choose parliamentary representatives of mediocre talent and demagogic behavior. To make the legislative branch supreme, as the current democratic theory demanded, was in Mosca's view to open the door to bad government and worse legislation.

While Mosca never gave up the theory of the ruling class, his attack on extreme parliamentarism shows that political institutions themselves were enormously important for him. He saw alternatives to the runaway government-by-assembly of so-called democratic regimes. One was "absolutism," but this was obsolete or otherwise unacceptable to the classic liberal Mosca. Indeed, as time went on he became as much a defender as a critic of parliamentary institutions. Similarly, his concept of the ruling class began to change. Originally it was of a monolithic entity, a closed and uniform clique of rulers immune to outside influence and infiltration.

Later, Mosca said that whereas some ruling classes were virtual castes sealed off from the rest of society, others were far more open to elements from below. In fact, there were two contrasting principles at work. One was the "aristocratic principle," which "aspires to maintain power and the means of obtaining it always in the same hands." The other, the "democratic principle," favors "the rights of merit and of individual abilities against hereditary advantages."[28] Mosca felt that the battle between these two principles was the "pivot" of contemporary history.

Still further complexity entered Mosca's conception of the ruling class when he expanded his notion of "social forces" beyond the initial four of wealth, birth, military force, and knowledge. Social forces included new religions, economic transformations, and so on. All social forces, he felt, are driven to seek political preeminence, and when one of them succeeds it is called "despotism." Conversely, freedom results when a large number of social forces can compete for a share of power. Indeed, Mosca went one step further and concluded that "the state is nothing more than the organization of all the social forces that have a political significance."[29]

Although Mosca came close to leaving the strict elitist approach in favor of a more pluralistic or group vision of politics, he never abandoned his view that majority rule in the literal sense was a myth. Whereas Mosca became more favorable to democracy, the other two classic elitists, Pareto and Michels, went the other way. These latter became sympathetic to fascism, though Pareto died before the true features of Mussolini's regime had emerged. Both these men were so repelled by what they felt was the fraud of democratic rule that they welcomed an openly antidemocratic movement. Nevertheless, as the later Mosca shows, and as we shall see in the next section, the challenge of classic elitist thought can lead to a rethinking of democratic theory, not just to a rejection of it.

SYNTHESIS OR CONFRONTATION

Democratic Elitism

Democratic elitism emerged precisely as a response to the alleged naivete of classic democratic theory. This theory is deeply influenced by classic elitism, especially by Mosca. In the English-speaking world the name of Joseph Schumpeter (1883–1950) is the one most associated with democratic elitism. Schumpeter found the chief failing of classic democratic theory in its poor handling of the "vital fact of leadership."[30]

For Shumpeter a realistic conception of democracy would define it as "that institutional arrangement for arriving at political decisions in which individuals acquire the power to decide by means of a competitive struggle for the people's vote."[31] Such a revised notion of democracy gives up some of the values and assumptions of classic democratic theory in favor of a more narrow concern with how to select governments.

Democracy is no longer seen as a system of popular sovereignty, in which the majority discerns the common interest—whether along Rousseauan or Benthamite lines. Rather it takes the aspect of a kind of market place where competing elites display their wares to the consuming public. The people select between the rival elites just as they choose different brand names and products, but the actual "product" (i.e., public policy) is made by the elites. Schumpeter frankly admitted that in terms of policymaking, democracy is to all intents and purposes the "rule of the politician."[32]

For democratic elitism the "rule of the politician" changes one's attitude toward the democratic need for maximum public participation in politics. Indeed, this change can go so far that political *apathy* could even play a positive role in politics. Some democratic elitists see this insofar as apathy can act as a sort of ballast preventing rapid and destabilizing shifts to the far left and the far right. They charge that classic democratic theory missed this point because it made unrealistically high demands on the level of political knowledge and interest of the average citizen.

This same lack of realism in classic democratic theory led it to neglect the "functional prerequisites" of the democratic polity as a whole. For democratic elitists, such prerequisites demand that "the intensity of conflict must be limited, the rate of change must be restrained, stability in the social and economic structure must be maintained, a pluralistic social organization must exist, and a basic consensus must bind together the contending parties."[33] When these conditions are not met, democracy will meet the fate of brevity and violence that James Madison spoke of. Apathy helps to mitigate conflict, limit change, stabilize the policy, and reflect consensus. People do not get very agitated about politics unless things are going very badly for them.

Participatory Democratic Theory: A Restatement of Classic Democracy?

Democratic elitism seems to argue that if universal suffrage, freedom of organization and communication, and real political competition prevail in a political system, the system is democratic. A number of recent theorists, however, have raised strenuous objections to this view. To such critics, democratic elitism's preoccupation with elite competition and its positive view of political apathy represent a false and emaciated view of democracy. Indeed, they charge that democracy, which was historically the most radical of political ideas, functions in its new democratic elitist garb as a clearly "conservative" ideology. It works to support the social and economic status quo in a number of western countries.

This critique of democratic elitism involves a participatory notion of democracy. This ideal suggests that

> the productive effort of the state, the effort of declaring and enforcing a system of law, should be a process in which, and through which, each member of the state is spurred into personal development, because he is drawn into free participation in one of the greatest of all our secular activities.[34]

With such an ideal in mind, "participatory" theorists usually find that contemporary societies do not do enough to "spur" the personal development of the vast majority of citizens.

Participatory theorists complain that democratic elitism's concern with democracy at the "system" level loses the vital significance of democracy at the individual level. Participatory theorists wish to restore the classic democratic emphasis on mass participation, and what it does to and for the democratic citizen. They charge that existing channels of participation seem clogged and that apathy, far from registering confidence in the existing system, reflects alienation and frustration over its lack of responsiveness. The apathetic are convinced that they and others like them do not make a difference in the political process. Apathy is disillusionment, sullen and surly resignation.

For this sorry state of affairs, participatory theorists propose a variety of cures. If the old channels of participation through old-line parties and interest groups are clogged, then new ones must be opened. The "politics of confrontation" with mass demonstrations and deputations represent a sort of "direct action" democracy designed to impress both elites and the general public. Voter registration drives and automatic registration of voters would sustain the participatory theorists' hopes for reinvigorating democracy.

As some participatory theorists embrace a nonliberal conception of democracy, they may view the political reforms just mentioned as " a drop in the bucket." The ultimate causes of the shortcomings of contemporary democracy are not political, but economic. C. B. Macpherson represents this tendency when he ponders whether meaningful liberty can much longer be had without a much greater measure of equality than we have hitherto thought liberty required.

We should not shrink from either the populist teaching of Rousseau or the radical teaching of Marx. Neither will suit us, but we may have more to learn from them than we think.[35]

Until capitalism gives way to socialism, true participation of the masses in making their own destiny will remain illusory.

Still other participatory theorists would extend the principle of democratic participation to the governance of all sorts of formal organizations. "Self-management," a term hitherto associated with the "workers' councils" in Yugoslavia, is to be applied to workplaces, educational institutions, and the like. Participation would come in the end to characterize all systems of collective decision making throughout modern society.

CONCLUSION

This chapter has surveyed the major renditions of the powerful ideal of political democracy, and we can now put it into a more historical perspective. We saw how the term originated with the ancient Greeks and signified the rule of the people. Such antique democracy required the direct vote of the assembled citizenry to function and the service of the ordinary citizen in posts of high responsibility. The stormy history of the Athenian democracy made a philosopher like Plato into a rabid anti-democrat and his disciple Aristotle into a more constructive, but still critical, commetator on democracy.

With the seventeenth- and eighteenth-century broadening of the notion of representation beyond its originally feudal origins, democracy was freed from its long-time association with small-scale polities. Democrats now debated whether the role of the representative should involve broad discretion (independence theory) or strict control by constituents (mandate theory). In the nineteenth century and after, democratic thought was polarized into nonliberal and liberal schools—the former stressing community as with Rousseau, the latter stressing the individual as with Bentham.

Whereas conservatives, aristocrats, and authoritarians had long attacked democracy because of its elevation of the "common man," at the turn of this century, the classic elitists challenged the very possibility of majority rule. Because of the partial correctness of their arguments and the evident strong role of minorities, some democrats used part of the elitist message to redefine democracy as "democratic elitism." In turn, critics of democratic elitism labelled it "democratic revisionism" as it "revised" the classic democratic principles of equality, majority rule, and mass participation in a weaker direction. Insufficient emphasis on popular participation is what troubled these critics and they became known in the 1970s as theorists of participatory democracy.

At any rate, the existence of so many schools of thought suggests the breadth and historical variability that we associated with political ideals. The specific visions of democracy are themselves influenced by definite ideological systems.

NOTES

1. Thucydides, *The Peloponnesian War*, trans. R. Warner (Baltimore: Penguin Books, 1959), p. 117.
2. Ibid., p. 118.
3. Ibid., p. 119.
4. Ibid., p. 135.
5. Plato, *The Republic*, in *The Dialogues of Plato*, vol. I, trans. B. Jowett (New York: Random House, 1937), p. 816.
6. Ibid., p. 822.
7. James Madison, "Federalist No. 10," in James Madison, Alexander Hamilton, and John Jay, *The Federalist Papers* (New York: New American Library, 1961), p. 81.
8. Jean-Jacques Rousseau, *The Social Contract and Other Writings*, trans. G. D. H. Cole (New York: Dutton Everyman, 1913), p. 83.
9. For a good survey of these issues with special reference to the British tradition, see A. H. Birch, *Representative and Responsible Government* (Toronto: University of Toronto Press, 1969).
10. Edmund Burke, "Speeches at Mr. Burke's Arrival at Bristol, and at the Conclusion of the Poll," in *Burke's Works*, vol. I (London: Bohn's Libraries, 1893), p. 447.
11. How far Locke's political philosophy was truly democratic is controversial. For the affirmative view see Willmoore Kendall, *John Locke and the Doctrine of Majority Rule* (Urbana: University of Illinois Press, 1965); for the negative see C. B. Macpherson *The Political Theory of Possessive Individualism* (New York: Oxford University Press, 1962).
12. There is some dispute as to whether the seventeenth and eighteenth century thinkers who spoke of a "state of nature" had in mind a real period of human prehistory or simply a fictitious device to help them explain complex ideas.
13. Kendall, *John Locke*, p. 112.
14. John Locke, *Two Treatises of Government* (New York: Hafner, 1969), p. 169.
15. As with the "state of nature" idea, the social contract theme raises the issue of actual history versus a historical fiction. In fact, the social contract theorists could skirt the issue by maintaining that a contract can be "tacit" and thus does not actually have to be signed. This tacit contract simply reflects one's choosing to remain a member of the state.

16. Jeremy Bentham, *A Bentham Reader*, ed. M. P. Mack (New York: Pegasus Books, 1969), p. 85.
17. Ibid., p. 139.
18. Ibid., p. 86.
19. This is precisely what John Stuart Mill could not accept. There is some hierarchy of pleasures: human pleasures rank higher than subhuman pleasures; intelligent pleasures rank higher than stupid ones.
20. Quoted in Elie Halevy, *The Growth of Philosophic Radicalism* (Boston: Beacon Press, 1955), p. 262.
21. Jean-Jacques Rousseau, *Du Contrat social* (Paris: Garnier, 1962), p. 247.
22. Ibid., p. 244.
23. Ibid.
24. Ibid., p. 246.
25. David Spitz, *Patterns of Anti-Democratic Thought* (New York: The Free Press, 1965).
26. They are because of their Italian background also called Machiavellians; the best survey remains James Burnham, *The Machiavellians: Defenders of Freedom* (New York: John Day, 1943).
27. Gaetano Mosca, *Teorica dei governi e governo parlamentare*, in *Cio che la storia potrebbe insegnare* (Milano: Giuffre Editore, 1958), p. 27.
28. Gaetano Mosca, *Partiti e sindacati nella crisi de regime parlamentare* (Bari: Laterza, 1949), p. 22.
29. Gaetano Mosca, *The Ruling Class* (New York: McGraw-Hill, 1939), p. 168.
30. Joseph Schumpeter, *Capitalism, Socialism, Democracy* (New York: Harper & Row, 1962), p. 270. To Schumpeter the classic conception of democracy assumed that the "democratic method is that institutional arrangement for arriving at political decisions which realizes the common good by making the people decide issues through the election of individuals who are to assemble to carry out its will." (p. 250).
31. Ibid., p. 269.
32. Ibid., p. 285.
33. Bernard Berelson, "Survival Through Apathy," in *Frontiers of Democratic Theory*, ed. H. S. Kariel (New York: Random House, 1970), p. 70.
34. Ernest Barker, *Principles of Social and Political Theory* (New York: Oxford University Press, 1967), p. 208.
35. C. B. Macpherson, *Democratic Theory: Essays in Retrieval* (Oxford: Oxford University Press, 1973), p. 184.

SUGGESTIONS FOR FURTHER READING

Kariel, Henry, ed. *Frontiers of Democratic Theory*. New York: Random House, 1970.

Macpherson, C. B. *Democratic Theory: Essays in Retrieval*. Oxford: Oxford University Press, 1973.

Pennock, J. Roland. *Democratic Political Theory*. Princeton: Princeton University Press, 1979.

Plamenatz, John. *Democracy and Illusion*. New York: Longman, 1977.
Sartori, Giovanni. *Democratic Theory*. New York: Praeger, 1965.
Spitz, David. *Patterns of Anti-Democratic Thought*. New York: Free Press, 1965.

3

SOCIALISM

In this chapter and the next we will contrast the two major economic–political ideals of the century: socialism and capitalism. No two terms excite more controversy. Both socialism and capitalism have been defined in exclusively political terms—as with the strange expression "our capitalistic form of government." Also, defenders and critics of both ideals have seen them basically as systems of morality. While politics and morality always are involved with economic concepts, there are strong reasons to envisage both socialism and capitalism primarily as ideal economic systems.[1]

To begin with, any viable notion of capitalism features *private ownership of the basic means of production and exchange*, whereas socialism reduced to its bare essence involves *public ownership of the means of production and exchange*. Means of production are such things as land, mines, machines, and techniques, while the means of exchange are the wholesale and retail outlets, transportation and communication facilities, financial institutions, and so on. In short, capitalism and socialism require fundamentally different principles of ownership in a country's economic system. The problems of control, organization, production, and distribution in the two economic ideals give us much of the work of the next two chapters.

In stressing the economic dimension of socialism in this chapter, we, of course, acknowledge that socialists defend their economic ideal on the moral grounds that socialism alone can end the *exploitation of man by man*. We also find, as in Chapter 2, that political thinkers say that political democracy without "economic democracy" (i.e., socialism) is false or incomplete. Still again, the socialist economy is sometimes represented as the truest rendition of Christian brotherly love or equality before God. In the end, however, what all twentieth century varieties of socialism aim at is an economic system without private ownership in the key sectors of the economy.

Such an economic ideal spreads itself across the ideological spectrum; anarchists, communists, social democrats, some Christian Democrats, and even a few fascists and Nazis have demanded "socialism" in some sense of the term. Nevertheless, we can best study the socialist ideal by examining two variants, *statist socialism* and *self-managed socialism*, which form the opposite ends of a continuum running from high to low centralization.

STATIST SOCIALISM

The Justification

In the ideal of statist socialism the central government owns and operates the major segments of a country's economic system on behalf of the people as a whole. The process of transferring industries from private to public ownership is called *nationalization*. Taking ownership and management of industry into public hands is justified on two basic grounds. The first is justice: socialists generally contend that the private ownership of capital produces massive inequalities of wealth, status, and power. These inequalities go far beyond those warranted by possible human differences in talent, intelligence, and industry. Most forms of socialism embrace an egalitarian ethic, which judges the class system of capitalism as hopelessly beyond redemption.

Yet, more than a wish for greater social equality underlies the socialist demand for public ownership. The socialist idea of community contradicts the notion that private individuals should be allowed to employ vast resources for their own "selfish" purposes. Men are not only equals in the abstract; they are equal members of an entity larger than themselves. Some socialists view the larger community as having a real moral existence; others feel that it is simply an association of separate individuals. In either case, private ownership is condemned because it makes impossible a society where the needs of all members can be truly met.

The second major critique of capitalism has been part of the socialist tradition since the early nineteenth century. It concerns the efficiency of the capitalist system. Karl Marx, for example, admitted that in the past capitalism had produced technological wonders, but maintained that it had become a drag on further progress by the mid-nineteenth century. The inefficiency of capitalism, most socialists charge, stems from two key factors. First of all capitalism spends an enormous amount of time and resources producing goods that nobody really needs. These are the various luxuries and playthings of the rich and super rich and more recently the mass-produced and mass-consumed baubles of the "affluent" or "consumer" society. This is inefficiency on a colossal scale as it diverts resources away from the alleviation of human misery and the building of a just society.

The other chief cause of capitalist inefficiency is the market. Socialists traditionally do not concede that uncontrolled supply and demand works beneficially. In the classic days of "laissez-faire" in the nineteenth century, socialists, with Karl Marx in the lead, maintained that the market system was a form of "anarchy." They saw no way in which a socially useful allocation and distribution of resources could spontaneously emerge from a system that was buffetted by human ignorance, whim, and irresponsibility.

Later socialists, recognizing economic changes around the turn of the twentieth century, sensed that the market was no longer so anarchical or chaotic as their forerunners had charged. The growth of monopolies with their power to control markets and fix prices had changed things dramatically. Under the new conditions the trouble became not so much anarchy as control of the market by the wrong people for the wrong purposes. As a contemporary socialist puts it, capitalism

> cannot deal adequately, no matter how sophisticated it has become, with either poverty or affluence. Left to itself the system produces a welfare state that provides some benefits for all, yet favors the rich and discriminates against the desperate; it generates problems, like those of the urban environment, that demand comprehensive planning; and even when it functions to produce the highest standard of living the world has known, the social consequences of that achievement are so apalling as to vitiate much of it.[2]

As this statement suggests, for socialists the inefficiency and immorality of capitalism go hand in hand.

A Planned Society

Statist socialism has a simple enough solution for the inadequacies and injustices of capitalism. The government must take over and run the economy for the benefit of the whole society. This involves centralized economic organization and planning. This type of socialism is found in the USSR and other "socialist" countries, and our examination of it will use certain of their experiences to aid understanding.

In undiluted statist socialism, market features are almost entirely eliminated. The basic allocation of goods and resources is accomplished by central planning. Such planning is called "imperative planning."[3] Its most outstanding trait is its very comprehensiveness: ideally, all of a country's productive efforts would be prescribed by the plan. No segment of industry, agriculture, or trade will be left out. Clearly, even in an age of computers this is no mean task.

Such a plan must be drawn up and administered in a highly centralized manner. This involves a central planning agency, as with the famous Soviet Gosplan or State Planning Commission, entrusted with the task of formulating both long-term and short-term plans. On this general point most socialist thinkers agree. There is, however, disagreement about the desirability and amount of input and consultation from below. Some maintain that the central planning agency should be highly autocratic and make major decisions in a purely administrative manner with little or no feedback from subordinate units.

Other socialists favor a more flexible set-up that would allow for opinions to filter up to the architects of the central plan. There would be negotiations and give-and-take over the final shape of the plan. Moreover, such a "democratic" form of central planning would also require that the planning agency be ultimately responsible to the elected representatives of the people. (Although this is technically true in the USSR, political reality shows that the planners are really subordinated to the leaders of the Communist Party).

One way of implementing the central plan would involve a bureaucratic approach. In this framework, the central planning agency would issue separate plans to various ministries, each in charge of a given segment of national economic activity. Such ministries might exist for agriculture, metallurgy, electronics, transportation, petrochemicals, textiles, fisheries, forestry, foreign trade, and the like. Each ministry is in charge of all the various enterprises that fall within its subject area. The result is a three-tiered system such as shown in Figure 3.1. This three-tiered structure could, in theory, be altered to take note of the federal structure of the state or other administrative features, such as grouping a number of separate enterprises into a "trust." But such complicating features have not generally aroused much enthusiasm with traditional statist socialists.

The experience of the USSR and other socialist countries suggests that centralized planning can become rigid and insensitive to the actual needs and productive possibilities of enterprises situated far from the capital city where the planning agency and the various ministries have their headquarters. At any rate, it is a serious challenge to the ingenuity of both central planners and individual factory managers to see to it that production quotas are realistic and the right resources are allocated to the right places.

For this reason, many socialists have suggested that statist socialism can be modified and improved by several types of decentralization. One

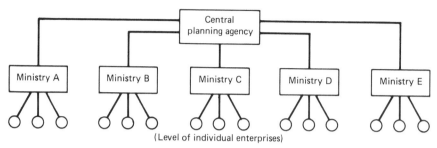

(Level of individual enterprises)

Figure 3.1.

type—which was tried in the USSR in the late 1950's under Nikita Khrushchev—is regional decentralization. Under such a system the central economic ministries in the capital city are trimmed down or abolished outright, and many of their functions are transferred to regional administrative agencies situated throughout the country.

As these centers would have a certain measure of autonomy, they could be more responsive to the concrete needs and problems of their own districts. Some of the bottlenecks that emerge because all major decisions have to be cleared with the relevant central ministries or even the central planning agency would be eliminated. Instead, decisions would be made in the multiple regional centers that would by physically closer to the actual farms and factories involved.

Still another sort of decentralization would modify statist socialism by allowing a somewhat greater release of the market forces of supply and demand. Statist socialists had originally thought that planning would make the supply and demand of the market utterly superfluous in a socialist economy. The planners could accurately estimate what the authentic needs and projected demands would be for all goods and services. Nevertheless, some statist socialists have always argued the opposite: socialism would not abolish the market, but bring it to perfection.

For these thinkers a socialist market bears a strong family resemblances to a capitalist market. This is the case because

> the rules of consistency of decisions and of efficiency in carrying them out in a socialist economy are exactly the same as those that govern the actual behavior of entrepreneurs in a purely competitive market. Competition forces entrepreneurs to act much as they would have to act were they managers of production in a socialist system.[4]

Differences would involve such things as more equal income distribution. Moreover, the prices set for commodities under socialism would include costs for social expenses left out in capitalistic prices. That is, certain sums would help pay for certain government services, even though they were not involved in making the goods in the first place. These sums are known as the "turnover tax" in the USSR and make up a key source of government revenue.

One implication of more reliance on the market and less on central planning would be to use "profit" as an indicator of efficiency. Such socialist profitability differs from capitalist profit making because it would not go to private persons such as owners, stockholders, or investors. Thus, if a socialist manager showed a decent profit, it might indicate that he was meeting a real demand in a real market at a reasonable price. As Peter Drucker points out, this may have little to do with the formal ownership structure of the economy, for "profit is needed for an expanding economy regardless of political beliefs or economic structure. This is surely not Karl Marx; but it is also not Adam Smith."[5]

Nonetheless, there are definite limits as to how much regional or market decentralization a socialist economy can undergo and still be called "statist socialism."

SELF-MANAGED SOCIALISM

When the socialist ideal crosses these limits, we can generally speak of some type of "self-managed" socialism. An early version of this is "guild socialism," while the "self-management" of Yugoslavia dates only from the 1950s.

Guild Socialism

The link between central planning and bureaucracy has always been deeply troublesome to certain currents of socialist thought. In the years around World War I, guild socialism enjoyed a vogue among some English socialists who feared the huge modern state and rejected the strategy of a revolutionary transition to socialism. Guild socialism's foremost thinker was G. D. H. Cole (1889–1959), even though he moved beyond it in the early 1920s to a more standard view of democratic (statist) socialism.

Cole's early guild socialism reflects not only the traditional anticapitalist concerns of socialism but also the "pluralist" attack on the modern state, which was also strong in the decades around World War I.[6] Such a view is evident in his contention that the "omnicompetent State, with its omnicompetent Parliment is . . . utterly unsuitable to any real democratic community and must be destroyed or painlessly extinguished as it has extinguished its rivals in the sphere of communal organization."[7]

From this perspective, statist socialism with its inevitable bureaucratic overgrowth was not a suitable successor to the dying capitalist system. Guild socialists looked instead to the guild organization of the middle ages for inspiration. At that time the guilds were made up of those involved in the various crafts and trades of the medieval urban economy. Actually, the medieval city held a certain attraction for other socialists, who were fearful of the state (i.e., anarchists) or of large-scale organization in general. The medieval guilds grouped the master craftsmen, journeymen, and apprentices of a given art and controlled production, distribution, prices, and conditions of labor in their city or town. They also performed a list of civic and religious functions.

As Cole was less enamored of the medieval system than other guild socialists, he did not simply wish to resurrect a supposed golden age. Modern guilds were to emerge from present-day trade unions and would assume the management of industry in local or regional areas. There would be a three-tiered system with local and regional guilds, at the summit of which would be a National Guild. The National Guild was seen as "an association of all the workers by hand or brain concerned in the carrying on of a particular industry or service, and its function would be actually to carry on that industry or service on behalf of the whole community."[8]

However, to give the National Guilds too much power would violate the decentralizing spirit of Guild Socialism. Accordingly, Cole was at pains to stress that the various national guilds would be essentially "coordinating rather than directly controlling bodies, and would be more concerned with adjustment of supply and demand than with the direct control or management of the several industries."[9] As much initiative and authority must be kept at the lowest levels as possible, beginning with the individual factory organized on a democratic basis.

But the guild socialist organization sketched thus far is one-sided. It only represents the producing aspect of society. Yet men are not only producers in a given activity, they are also the consumers of the goods and services produced by others. Each of us thus has a dual interest, which should be reflected in the structure of the new society. To begin, Cole rejected the traditional idea of representative democracy. One cannot represent the individual as a whole living being; one can only represent him in and through his "functions," and these amount to his roles as producer and consumer. Thus, Cole maintained that "all true and democratic representation is therefore *functional* representation."[10]

Clearly, the individual should be represented once through the guild set-up and again through the consumers' organization. In addition, the guild system will provide for "joint consultation and action between the Guilds and the consumers' organizations at every stage, local, regional, and national."[11] Such a joint consultative body Cole originally called the "Commune," and it was to coordinate rather than directly run things. At the top was a National Commune, embracing representatives of various national guilds, national councils, and regional communes. The National Commune itself would "pass constitutional laws determining the respective spheres of the various functional bodies" and could thus be called the "Constituent Assembly and the constitutional legislature of Guild Democracy."[12]

In his guild socialist scheme Cole thought he had avoided the unpleasant dilemma between "collectivism" (i.e., pure statist socialism) and "syndicalism" (i.e., "absolute ownership of the means of production by the unions").[13] Syndicalism was wrong because even though the workers should "control the normal conduct of industry," they should not arbitrarily set prices or force consumer choices. This high-handedness would "exploit the community as the individual profiteer exploits it today."[14]

The solution of the collectivist versus syndicalist dilemma was to have the state serve as the "representative of the organized consumers" whereas the trade unions (or bodies emerging out of them) would represent the workers. The key to this approach would involve an appropriate "division of functions" and balance between the producer and consumer networks.

Yugoslav Self-Management

While guild socialism is an interesting theory of a self-managed socialism—with the "self" being the workers themselves—"self-management" in the narrow sense refers to the theory and practice of Yugoslav socialism. The Yugoslav experience has reinvigorated the debate about the "true" nature of socialism. From 1945 to 1948 Yugoslavia was a rigid communist dictatorship led by the late Josip Broz Tito. Indeed, in those early days Yugoslavia was probably the most Stalinist of all the East European "satellite" countries. The Yugoslav Communist Party had squashed all rivals, and the economy was largely nationalized and followed the Stalinist recipe of collectivized agriculture and a tight planning system.

Nevertheless, by the spring of 1948, Soviet–Yugoslav relations had reached a breaking point. As did the Chinese, the Yugoslav Communists had essentially liberated the country from the Axis occupiers on their own. Thus, these two Communist parties had come to power without being installed by the Soviet Army as was true elsewhere. In any case, long before the Chinese split with the Soviets, Tito led the Yugoslavs out of the Soviet orbit. People naturally began to speak of "national communism" and "Titoism" to describe the new reality. However, the break with Stalin was so sudden that it took some years for a new theory of Yugoslav communism to emerge.

From our perspective, the most important result of this ideological crisis is the concept of a self-managed socialism that opposes not just capitalism, but the bureaucratic centralization of statist socialism. (The backdrop of all this is, of course, disillusionment with the Soviets.) In the theory of self-managed socialism, bureaucracy and centralization are two sides of the same coin. A French theorist sees two crucial defects in statism: first, it is very sluggish in adapting to "the new scientific and technological revolutions, which require the widest participation, creative initiatives, and the responsibility of all." Second, it fails to accomplish the "major objective of socialism," which is "disalienation," because in statist socialism "the worker is transformed once more into a wage earner, no longer of a private employer, but of the state."[15]

In other words, bureaucracy even in a nationalized economy suffers from the defects that its critics have attacked for more than a century: *rigidity* and *elitism*. Bureaucracy, so the criticism goes, is addicted to established methods and plays a basically conservative role with respect to social change. This again runs counter to socialism's claim to promote technological and social development.

Elitism refers to the emergence of an antidemocratic caste spirit that effectively suppresses the movement towards the participatory democracy that socialism is supposed to bring about. In the perspective of Yugoslavia, this means that "political bureaucracy is a permanent and coherent social group which occupies itself professionally with politics, which has escaped the control of the masses, and which . . . secures lesser or greater material privileges to itself."[16]

Clearly this attack on centralization and bureaucracy also strikes at the type of imperative planning that goes along with them. This is why Yugoslavs have eliminated that sort of planning and refer to their economy instead as "market socialism." The market replaces the central plan as the basic way of determining society's priorities. As a French admirer puts it:

> in contrast to the etatist and centralist (Soviet) model, in this model these needs will not be defined 'from above' by central directives of the Party and the State, but by the play of the *market* and of the demands that emerge from it. If one remembers that it is socialist enterprises, and not private owners, that are confronting each other on this market, then one cannot consider this market economy a capitalist economy.[17]

The market itself provides the guidance to policymakers that central planning does in statist socialism, but without the gargantuan bureaucracy and its alleged dangers. Planning will be much weaker and will allow the government to influence the economy generally and indirectly rather than administering it specifically and immediately.

This allows for decentralization instead of centralization, which in turn opens the doors to genuine participation of the worker at the individual workplace. This is still socialism insofar as there is no private ownership in the basic industries. Such developments were reflected in the new Yugoslav Constitution of 1958, which contained two expressions that became trademarks of Yugoslav socialism. The first was "socially owned means of production" or, more simply, "social ownership." The Yugoslavs preferred this to the traditional "public ownership" because the latter suggested government ownership and hence the detested centralized bureaucratic administration.

The second noteworthy expression of the 1958 Constitution was "self-management." This system was to be introduced in "organizations of associated labor, local communities, self-managing communities of interest and other self-managing organizations and communities, and also in sociopolitical communities and society as a whole."[18] Social ownership and self-management are connected in the sense that the people who band together and collectively manage an organization do not really own it. They run it, share in its profits and other benefits, but in this way they operate as trustees of society as a whole.

Self-management can thus be viewed from within individual firms or from the perspective of the whole economic order. From within, the self-managed organization is intended to embody the true principles of democracy. The ultimate decision maker is thus the collective body of all those (workers) associated with the organization. This does not mean, however, that each and every decision must come up before that body along the lines of antique Greek democracy. Such a proviso would leave too little time for actual work.

For this reason, self-management means that workplace democracy is representative rather than direct.[19] The basic elective body is a "workers' council" in charge of the broad determination of policy. Its powers include approval of such vital policies as the determination of basic pay and work conditions, and how much of the firm's earnings are to be "ploughed back" for expansion, and how much workers should get as bonuses and other fringe benefits. This is why some see an analogy between the role of this council and that of the board of directors in an American corporation. Further, the membership of the workers' council is to be rotated rapidly so as to prevent permanent control by a narrow clique.

However, the self-managed firm need not necessarily dispense with more traditional types and aspects of management. In Yugoslavia there are enterprise directors or general managers in nearly all self-managed organizations. In the theory of self-management, however, this official is far from the old-fashioned "boss." Instead, he is the representative of the whole firm and is chosen and removed by the council. He supervises operations on a day-to-day basis; other professional managers can be found at lower levels of the firm.

The link between this "democratization" of the workplace and the broader concerns of the socialist tradition is expressed by a Yugoslav theorist in the following terms:

> placing the associated producer in the position of directly and jointly controlling the social conditions of his labor and his material existence, self-management *ipso facto* removes the principle social causes and roots not only of authoritarian forms of political organization but also all forms of rule and 'bossing' by aloof political forces above the working man and the social conditions of his existence.[20]

In the long-run the transformative powers of self-managed socialism present society with the "prospect of such consistent democratization of managing society's affairs, of the merger of self-managed organization of labor with the global organization of society, as will logically lead to the withering away of the state, that is, to the complete socialization of policy-making."[21]

As we will see in Chapter 9, this connection of self-management with the ultimate "withering away of the state" completes the link with the classic ideas of Karl Marx. The Soviet approach of statist socialism is far harder to reconcile with a gradual phasing out of the state. Here certain theorists of self-managed socialism can claim to be purer Marxists than their Soviet counterparts.

CONCLUSION

In this chapter we have tried to explore only the main currents of the broad ideal of socialism. Making a choice that some will dispute, we envisage socialism essentially as a type of economic system. Naturally, the argument of those who prefer to view socialism in basically political, moral, or even religious terms is not to be lightly dismissed. Our point is rather that political, moral, or religious concerns provide the rationale or motive for embracing some rendition of the socialist economic ideal.

Our primarily economic focus also has a strong historical support to it. Though "primitive communism" dates back through the ages, modern theories of communism emerge in the period after the French Revolution of 1789. This is also the period of the Industrial Revolution, which propelled the capitalist economic order to ever greater heights of technological achievement. In most western countries this meant the end or decline of whatever "precapitalist" economic relationships had survived into the early nineteenth century.

Moreover, the rapid industrialization involved created sprawling urbanization laced with widespread poverty—the things that moved the early socialists to demand a radically different economic order on humanitarian grounds. The precise arguments involved take us into specific ideological systems, and thus will be found in Part II of this book. Here, we can only maintain that modern socialism is an anticapitalism, that attacks capitalism at its jugular vein—private ownership of the means of production and exchange.

This is why our treatment analyzed two main ways in which socialists tried to envisage an ideal economic system premised upon public ownership of the means of production and exchange. Statist socialism entrusts the central government with the administration of the publicly owned economy. This would entail an imperative planning system to ensure appropriate production and equitable distribution of goods and services.

Various socialists that we group together as advocates of "self-managed" socialists have feared that the centralization and bureaucratization of statist socialism would make quick work of both freedom and democracy. Thus, they have developed schemes that emphasize radical decentralization of authority and "workers' control" as with guild socialism before World War I, and Yugoslav self-management after World War II.

NOTES

1. Of course, as the eighteenth-century notion of "political economy" and the recent revival of the term suggest, politics and economics are interconnected. Economic systems have political implications and vice versa. Indeed, it is often the political dimensions that critics of this or that economic system are trying to discredit. Our primarily economic approach to socialism in this chapter (and to capitalism in Chapter 4) should not obscure this.
2. Michael Harrington, *Socialism* (New York: Bantam Books, 1977), p. 356.
3. Imperative planning is so called because it involves a kind of command— thus the critical expression "command economy." Imperative planning has the force of law as is the case with governmental decrees and regulations. A much weaker type of planning is known as "indicative" planning. Practiced by many capitalist countries, it involves forecasting current economic trends and selective action to encourage "good" trends and counteract "bad" ones. We will discuss it at some length in Chapter 4.
4. Oscar Lange, "The Economist's Case for Socialism," in *Essential Works of Socialism*, ed. I. Howe (New York: Bantam Books, 1971), pp. 699–700.

5. Peter F. Drucker, *The Age of Discontinuity* (New York: Harper & Row, 1978), pp. 146–47.
6. Pluralism in one form or other surfaces at various points across the spectrum of ideologies. The common core of these different ideological expressions is the idea that the social or economic *group* is the basic unit of society, not the separate individual or the society taken as a whole.
7. G. D. H. Cole, *Guild Socialism: A Plan for Economic Democracy* (New York: F. A. Stokes, 1920, p. 23.
8. Ibid., p. 38
9. Ibid., p. 40.
10. Ibid., p. 23.
11. Ibid., p. 79.
12. Ibid., pp. 133–34.
13. Ibid.
14. G. D. H. Cole, "Collectivism, Syndicalism, and Guilds," in *Self-Management: Economic Liberation of Man*, ed. J. Vanek (Baltimore: Penguin Books, 1975), p. 64.
15. Roger Garaudy, "The Possibility of Other Models of Socialism," in *Self-Governing Socialism*, Vol. II. ed. B. Horvat, M. Markovic, and R. Supek (White Plains, N.Y.: International Arts and Sciences Press, 1975), p. 31.
16. Mihailo Markovic, "Socialism and Self-Management," in Horvat, *Socialism*, vol. I., p. 422.
17. Garaudy, "Other Models of Socialism," p. 33.
18. "The Constitution of the Socialist Federal Republic of Yugoslavia," in Vanek, *Self-Management*, p. 72.
19. Here a word of caution is needed. Recall that we are giving an idealized picture of Yugoslav self-management based largely upon the views of enthusiastic admirers. Idealization usually diverges somewhat from the reality of a system.
20. Nadjan Pasic, "The Idea of Direct Self-Managing Democracy and Socialization of Policy-Making," in Horvat, *Socialism*, vol. II, pp. 34–35.
21. Ibid.

SUGGESTIONS FOR FURTHER READING

Berki, R. N. *Socialism*. New York: St. Martin's, 1975.
Glass, S. T. *The Responsible Society: The Ideas of Guild Socialism*. London: Longman's, 1966.
Harrington, Michael. *Socialism*. New York: Bantam Books, 1977.
Howe, Irving, ed. *Essential Works of Socialism*. New York: Bantam Books, 1971.
Lichtheim, George. *The Origins of Socialism*. New York: Praeger, 1969.
Vanek, J., ed. *Self-Management: Economic Liberation of Man*. Baltimore: Penguin Books, 1975.

4

CAPITALISM

As with the last chapter on socialism, the capitalism we are concerned with here is an "ideal." This means that we are not really describing how any economic system actually works, but how defenders of a system think it works and why it is so beneficial to society. Twentieth-century defenders of capitalism fall generally into two basic schools. The first or neoclassical school defends capitalism and its virtues in a way that recalls the "bible" of capitalism, Adam Smith's *The Wealth of Nations* (1776).

The second school, defenders of *managerial capitalism*, have no single prophet and sometimes use ideas from thinkers who themselves had no great fondness for the capitalist system. Both schools defend modern capitalism but disagree rather sharply on how it actually works, why it is better than other economies, and what can be done to improve it.

NEOCLASSICAL DEFENDERS OF CAPITALISM

Neoclassical defenders of the capitalist ideal share a rough consensus on the nature and workings of capitalism. It is a system where individuals, groups of individuals (i.e., stockholders), or families own and operate (or have their employees operate) the various firms or businesses in the economy. The overriding motivation for business activity is profit. This motivation is as strong as it is because men are both selfish and rational. They therefore generally pursue their "rational self-interest." Other motives can be found in noneconomic activities perhaps, but when they infiltrate economic life the results are usually poor. The individual businessman or "entrepreneur" suffers, and so does the whole economy.

What links the various businesses together, forms the division of labor between different economic activities, and allows exchange between buyers and sellers is the *market*. The market involves buying and selling not only of goods or commodities, but also of labor, shares in business ownership (i.e., the stock market) as well as money itself (loans and interest). Because neoclassical defenders of capitalism endow the market with many beneficial "self-regulating" functions, they wish to minimize government interference with the market mechanism. This is where the French term "laissez-faire" comes in to suggest that government should leave the market economy alone. Similarly, "free enterprise system" implies that the government's economic role should be minimal.

Neoclassical defenders of capitalism, though they usually avoid the term "capitalism,"[1] argue its benefits in terms of arguments about (1) capitalism and the common good; (2) capitalism and human nature; and (3) capitalism and freedom.

Neoclassical arguments Capitalism and the Common Good

Hearkening back to Adam Smith, the first argument maintains that the capitalist economy works for the good of society as a whole. Smith assumed the general capitalist rule that everyone is out to maximize his own self-interest, to "buy cheap and sell dear" in the old maxim. Businessmen thus hope to charge as much for their wares "as the traffic will bear" according to another maxim. Customers likewise run to a bargain. There thus reigns a sort of universal selfishness.

Up to this point it is no mystery why some—those who profit—opt for the competitive workings of the capitalist system. But Smith said more: the interest of the community is best served by such a system. He escapes from the dilemma between selfish individual behavior and a publicly beneficial result through his famous metaphor of the "invisible hand." He says that the individual usually

> neither intends to promote the public interest, nor knows how much he is promoting it. By preferring the support of domestic to that of foreign industry, he intends only his own security; and by directing that industry in such a manner as its produce may be of the greatest value, he intends only his own gain, and he is in this, as in many other cases, led by an invisible hand to promote an end which was no part of his intention. Nor is it always the worse for society that it was no part of it. By pursuing his own interest he frequently promotes that of society more effectually than when he really intends to promote it.[2]

Smith's "invisible hand" imagery suggests that he is really at a loss as to why ultimate results are so different from intentions. It just happens. Such unintended consequences are today often considered bad side-effects of certain actions; Smith more optimistically saw the positive side.

It is thus the market that transforms selfishness into public benefit. Smith's strong defense of the "natural system of liberty" has sometimes been read as a plea for extreme laissez-faire (i.e., for reducing the role of government to virtual disappearance). Smith, however, assigned the "sovereign" or government three basic duties. The first is to protect against foreign foes and dangers. The second is to preserve domestic law and order. The third task is more complex.

This third task involves the "duty" of erecting and maintaining certain public works and certain public institutions, which it can never be for the interest of any individual, or a small number of individuals, to erect and maintain."[3] Smith included in this nonprofit area such things as educational and religious institutions and certain activities to "facilitate commerce." Here he may have included certain governmental functions that strict laissez-faire doctrinaires would balk at.

Nonetheless, it is limited government, if not minimal government that allows the market mechanism to convert the selfish strivings of each into the good of all. The general prosperity, the "wealth of nations," is increased by allowing everyone to do his best to advance himself. This does not mean that everyone benefits equally from the "natural system of liberty." Smith was not an egalitarian: like most theorists of his day he assumed that society naturally disposed itself into a hierarchy of "ranks."

This meant that wealth would inevitably be distributed unequally. To balance this off somewhat, Smith argued that growing prosperity produced by the market economy would eventually reach the masses. Such a "trickle-down" effect was the consequence of the division of labor. This principle furthered the "great multiplication of the productions of all the different arts," which means "in a well-governed society, that universal opulence which extends itself to the lowest ranks of the people."[4] Smith's modern-day disciples still speak in pretty much the same terms when they extol the American "standard of living."

Capitalism and Human Nature

A second neoclassical argument for capitalism pleads the "naturalness" of the capitalist system. In social and political theory the term "natural" is one of the most difficult and controversial. Usually it suggests that some sort of "human nature" exists and that it should guide our judgments about what is desirable and workable in social and political organization. Moreover, we often sense the clear implication that what is "natural" is good, real, solid, and even close to God. In a different view, the "natural" is what is inevitable, with the warning that going "against nature" is futile and self-defeating.

We have already seen Adam Smith use "natural" in his "natural system of liberty." In particular he derives the division of labor, so crucial to prosperity, from human nature itself. It is, he says, the "necessary, though very slow and gradual consequence" of man's "propensity to truck, barter, and exchange one thing for another."[5] Man, in other words, is a born wheeler-dealer, and capitalism, with its market economy, is tailor-made for such a creature.

Another variant of the naturalness of capitalism argument that still finds support was well-formulated by the American Social Darwinist,[6] William Graham Sumner (1840–1910). Unlike most Social Darwinists, he did not stress the connection between the capitalist economy and long-term social progress. Why worry about progress, taught the gloomy Sumner, when we have our hands full preventing humanity's relapse into barbarism! Especially fearsome to Sumner was the rise of socialism and other versions of what he attacked as the "sentimental philosophy." The chief error of the sentimental philosophy was naively to think that the defects of the present (capitalist) order could easily be remedied by reform or revolution.

In this case the cure would be far worse than the disease, because, in Sumner's view, socialists and other sentimentalists have confused two radically different types of problems. These are "social ills" and "natural ills." The first result from defective aspects of the social order that conceivably could be changed or improved. Natural ills, on the contrary, are the product of "laws of nature," as these work in and through human society. According to Sumner, the "social order is fixed by laws of nature precisely analogous to those of the physical order. The most that man can do is by ignorance and self-conceit to mar the operation of social laws."[7]

Perhaps the supreme law of nature is the "struggle for existence," which first of all involves

> the struggle of individuals to win the means of subsistence from nature, and secondly there is the competition of man with man in the effort to win a limited supply. The radical error of the socialists and the sentimentalists is that they never distinguish these two relations from each other. They bring forward complaints which are really to be made, if at all, against the author of the universe for the hardships which man has to endure in his struggle with nature.[8]

In other words, reformers mistake natural ills for social ills. Their delusion that they can change things that really depend on the natural laws of society will simply produce more social ills and suffering.

The virtue of capitalism is thus its realism: its economic competition reflects the natural competitiveness that comes from the struggle for existence. Competition in nature leads to the "survival of the fittest" (i.e., those best adapted to the given environment). Capitalist competition leads to the survival of the most industrious and skillful businessmen and workers. To attempt to lessen the harsh results of this competition by social legislation and state interference is to rush headlong against the workings of nature.

Laissez-faire capitalism is thus the most "natural" and fairest possible type of economic system. The reformist movement to expand the role of the state in order to aid the poor and weak is in reality the move of some people to gain an unfair advantage over others. As Sumner laments, "History is only a tiresome repetition of one story. Persons have sought to win possession of the power of the state in order to live luxuriously out of the earnings of others."[9] While socialism and sentimentalism suggest to Sumner that lower groups would use the state to fleece the higher ones, he was aware that the well-off could use the state to line their own pockets. He called individual cases of such dishonesty "jobbery" and referred to a political system based on this as "plutocracy" (rule of the rich).

Sumner poses simple and stark alternatives: either we can have the benefits of our present civilization along with the rigors imposed by nature or we can have socialism or welfarism at the price of eventual calamities and the loss of our individual freedom. There is no in-between; all versions of the sentimental philosophy amount to just one more "absurd effort to make the world over." Capitalism follows the laws of nature; its alternatives attempt quixotically to deny them. We may as well ask Congress to repeal the law of gravity.

Capitalism and Freedom

The third basic argument of neoclassical defenders of capitalism maintains that it is the only economic system truly and lastingly compatible with political freedom. The classic expression of this doctrine is Friedrich A. Hayek's, *The Road to Serfdom* (1944). Virtually the same position was taken by the Nobel prize-winner Milton Friedman in his *Capitalism and Freedom* of 1962. Both men agree that freedom is the right of individuals to choose their own course of action so long as they do not interfere with the like freedom of others. Society is composed of individuals, and their freedom includes the chance that they will make wrong and harmful decisions.

Neither Hayek nor Friedman thinks that the individual is necessarily selfish in the sense that he or she is ruthlessly egotistic or manifests unbridled greed. He can include the welfare of others, individuals or humanity at large, in his projected activities. Such altruism, however, must not be imposed upon him from the outside, for in Friedman's words "a major aim of the liberal is to leave the ethical problem to the individual to wrestle with."[10]

As individual freedom is the highest good, any threat to it must be strenuously opposed. One such threat is posed by the massive growth of governmental economic activities in the twentieth century. Freedom is of a piece, so there can be no political freedom without economic freedom. Even though government expands first in the area of regulation of industry, the necessary progression is through some type of "welfare state" and ends up, following Hayek, in some sort of "totalitarianism."

> The various kinds of collectivism, communism and fascism, etc. differ among themselves in the nature of the goal toward which they want to direct the efforts of society. But they all differ from liberalism and individualism in wanting to organize the whole of society and all its resources for this unitary end and in refusing to recognize autonomous spheres in which the ends of the individuals are supreme.[11]

The reason collectivism necessarily leads to totalitarianism and the end of individual freedom is seen most forcefully in the problem of economic planning.[12] In order for planning to work at all, it must be mandatory and all-inclusive. That you can draw up a plan for *a* society implies that you know it has *a* single overriding purpose. Planning demands unity and uniformity, and since these do not "naturally" characterize society, they must inevitably be imposed at the planners' behest. More specifically, comprehensive planning "presupposes that every one of our needs is given its rank in an order of values which must be complete enough to make it possible to decide among all the different courses which the planner has to choose."[13]

For Hayek central economic planning is incompatible with both individual freedom and democratic government. Because planning seems to presuppose everything in its place and a place for everything, it runs up against the diversity, complexity, and uncertainty found in human societies. In a free society individuals inevitably go off in many different directions. The convergence of outlooks and consensus on basic values necessary to make planning a smooth and painless operation will be wholly lacking. This means that one will never get a majority to agree freely on enough specific points to make the plan a true expression of their will. They might agree, of course, on a vague "need" for planning, but not on the actual priorities, the nut and bolts, of the plan itself.

Planning presupposes not only artificial unity, but also judgments based on it that reward some and not others, that favor some interests and not others, that promote some purposes and not others. Its claims to full knowledge fall far short of the mark. For this reason there will be massive conflict if any freedom is allowed and stalemate if majority rule is tried. Democracy will have to go sooner or later because

> it is the price of democracy that the possibilities of conscious control are restricted to the fields where true agreement exists and that in some fields things must be left to chance. But in a society which depends . . . on central planning this control cannot be made dependent on a majority's being able to agree; it will often be necessary that the will of a small minority be imposed upon the people. . . .[14]

Thus, some sort of minority dictatorship will eventually emerge, if we are serious about central economic planning.

Hayek denies the possibility that dictatorial control of this elite of planners can be limited to narrow economic concerns. Although economics is by no means the whole of life, it is a unique area that preconditions all spheres of social life. "The authority directing all economic activity would control not merely the part of our lives which is concerned with inferior things; it would control the allocation of the limited means for all our ends."[15] Such an economic strategy would have so much control that all else would fall under its sway—thus the totalitarian culmination of even half-hearted moves toward planning.

The lesson of all this is a simple one. If we wish to preserve individual freedom, to go beyond the market economy of traditional capitalism is to court the utmost danger. The planned economy assumes a set moral code and perfect knowledge of all needs of all members of society. The free market economy when conjoined to a liberal democratic political system makes no such assumptions. It assumes instead that morality cannot be reduced to a formula and that human needs are complex and ever changing.

The liberal and democratic solution is to admit ignorance and cherish diversity and to permit all individuals to choose what they do and what they want by themselves. The free market registers the freedom of discrete individuals to buy and sell as they so choose. If one man's meat is another man's poison, there is no getting away from it. The market will allow one man to choose the meat for himself, and if he sometimes errs and chooses poison instead, this is the price of freedom. Freedom is something of a gamble, but a planned economy avoids this only by stacking the deck.

MANAGERIAL CAPITALISM

Theories of managerial capitalism defend capitalism on rather different grounds from its neoclassical advocates. They see the capitalist system quite differently and thus point out different virtues. The core of these different views lies in the significance of the so-called "divorce of ownership and control." For theorists of managerial capitalism this change has many important consequences that have transformed traditional capitalism almost beyond recognition. To managerialists the neoclassical theorists seem almost quaint in their glorification of a capitalism that passed away many decades ago.

The Coming of the Managers

Ironically, much of the case for a distinctive managerial type of capitalism originally came from thinkers who thought that capitalism was on its very last legs. One of these was the brilliant, if bizarre, American critic of capitalist civilization Thorstein Veblen (1857–1929). Veblen produced a harsh indictment of the "conspicuous consumption" and "ostentatious wealth" of the "leisure class" in his *Theory of the Leisure Class* (1899). It was two decades later, however, in his *The Engineers and the Price System* (1921), that he outlines the forces making for the death of the capitalist system.

Veblen did not deny that businessmen in the early days of capitalism had done yeoman work in promoting industrial and technological development. But by the late nineteenth century businessmen with actual mastery of the technical aspects of their enterprises were an endangered species. The old-time "captains of industry" had been replaced by the new-time "captains of finance."

This change meant that the new breed of business leaders were motivated solely by the financial considerations of profit. Such captains of finance are "unremittingly engaged in a routine of acquisition, in which they habitually reach their ends by a shrewd restriction of output, and yet they continue to be entrusted with the community's industrial welfare, which calls for maximum production."[16] Such restriction of output (i.e., limiting production) seems to Veblen a virtual "sabotage" of business. This is done obviously to keep the supply of goods down so that prices and hence profits will be kept artificially high. As this maintains scarcity and the suffering that derives from it, we can see why Veblen condemned financial capitalism.

Veblen thought he saw the beginning of the end of this sorry state of affairs. Hope springs from the fact that " industrial experts, engineers, chemists, mineralogists, technicians of all kinds, have been drifting into more responsible positions in the industrial system and have been growing up and multiplying within the system because the system will no longer work at all without them."[17] This means that the financial manipulations of the legal owners of industry ("the captains of finance") count far less in the actual work of the firm than the activity of experts and technicians ("the engineers"). There is thus a true divorce between ownership and control.

The engineers are strongly interested in overall efficiency and expanding production. Thus, their basic outlook favors the masses. Indeed, Veblen saw the end of finance capitalism coming from the revolt of technicians, rather than from the insurrection of the working masses.

> Right lately these technologists have begun to become uneasily 'class-conscious' and to reflect that they together constitute the indispensible General Staff of the industrial system. Their class consciousness has taken the immediate form of a growing sense of waste and confusion in the management of industry by the financial agents of absentee owners.[18]

Veblen speculated that eventually finance capitalism would be overthrown and a "soviet of technicians" would handle the running of a planned economy.

Veblen thought he saw early signs of capitalism's downfall; James Burnham later (1941) felt himself in the midst of a truly "revolutionary transition." In the late 1930s Burnham had been a disciple of the exiled Soviet Communist leader Trotsky. By 1940 he had broken with Trotsky partly on the grounds that his mentor still considered the USSR a "workers' state." In his *The Managerial Revolution,* there remain traces of this Marxist-Trotskyite background in the ideas that capitalism is doomed and that economics has a primacy over politics.

Burnham left Marxism when he argued that capitalism will not be replaced by a "workers' state" leading to the "classless society." Instead, a new *managerial* society will prevail. It will have a new ruling class, the managers, and will adopt ideologies suitable to this new social reality. As Veblen did before him, Burnham maintained that divorce between ownership and control was the central fact of the time. The capitalist owners were simply irrelevant and obsolete in the modern economic system. The managerial "revolution" was simply the overall process that replaces the capitalists with a managerial ruling class.

This transition occurs in various ways and at different tempos in different places. Thus, one might miss the common nature of certain political regimes if one looks only at surface differences. This could happen, for example, with Stalinism, Nazism, and New Deal doctrines in the United States. These ideologies of the 1930s are, despite rhetorical differences, variations on the theme of the coming of managerial society. Burnham was convinced that "under Nazism, Stalinism, and New Dealism, the group in society which has done better (however well or badly) than any other group is the managers; above all, the managers who have had sense enough to be integrated in the state."[19]

More specifically, the ideological reflex that registered emerging managerialism was the decline of individualistic capitalist ideologies and

the rise of various "collectivist" doctrines. Instead of the individual the new stress was placed on things like " 'the state,' the people, the folk, the race."[20] Ideas like socialism, planning, and duty were forcing out older ideas like private enterprise, freedom, and rights.

In their prognosis of the not-too-distant future, both Veblen and Burnham proved mistaken or highly premature. Burnham argued, for example, that the basis "of the economic structure of managerial society is governmental (state) ownership and control of the major instruments of production."[21] Although this characterization fits most communist countries, capitalism has stood up rather well in most of the rest of the world.

If a Veblenite "soviet of technicians"—later the term "technocracy" was associated with his ideas—or a Burnhamite "managerial society" have not as yet displaced capitalism, are their ideas just another case of false prophecy? Not really, because contemporary observers argue that many of the ideas of the two thinkers describe changes *within* capitalism, changes that are fundamental and irreversible. Changes at the level of the firm have transformed the dynamics of the economic system as a whole.

The Transformation of Capitalism

The insights of Veblen, Burnham, and others are reflected in John Kenneth Galbraith's theory of the "mature corporation." Galbraith maintains that the legal structure of the mature corporation (i.e., the modern big business) does not accurately describe its real power and decision-making structure. This legal structure, inherited from classic capitalism, would have the corporation's stockholders as the ultimate control body and the board of directors as the representatives of the stockholders. In this view the board exercises a direct control over the top management people—the president, vice-president(s), department heads, etc. who run the corporation on a day-to-day basis.

Although this picture may have once described big business and may still do so for small business, Galbraith maintains that the stockholders and the board of directors are usually of secondary importance in the mature corporation. Even top management is too far removed from the actual process of decision making to be a significant influence. The real policymaker is rather the "technostructure" of the firm. This grouping includes "all those who bring specialized knowledge, talent, or experience to group decision making. This, not the management is the guiding intelligence—the brains of the organization."[22]

Rather than a hierarchy or pyramid organization, this new organizational set-up suggests that a series of concentric circles better captures different degrees of involvement with decision making of the mature

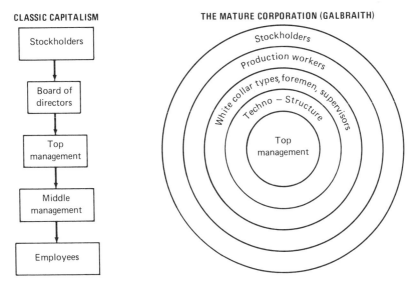

Figure 4.1.

corporation. Fig. 4.1 depicts the contrast between the classic and Galbraithian views.

Because the technostructure shapes the basic decisions of the largest firms, its aims and tastes help explain the workings of the modern capitalist economy. While the neoclassical view teaches that profit maximization is the overriding goal of businesses, this is clearly not the case with the technostructure. It would be if the stockholders and their boards really dominated the scene, but Galbraith and managerial theorists deny this. Instead of the highest possible profit, what the technostructure is after is first, a *secure minimum of earnings,* and second, *maximum corporate growth in terms of sales.*

The secure minimum of earnings is necessary to preserve the "autonomy" of the technostructure. In other words, the technostructure wants to avoid a "stockholders' revolt" by keeping them content with a reasonable return on their investment. Similarly, secure minimum earnings will prevent those financial problems that lead to banks or the government coming to the rescue. Such rescue operations have definite strings attached. If the banks are to foot big loans or the government is to come in to "bail out" the troubled firm, they will want a strong say on how the firm is to be run.

The technostructure wants maximum growth, measured in sales rather than profits, for a somewhat different reason. Growth of the firm in size and complexity creates enticing opportunities for members of the technostructure. Quite simply, there will be more money, more promotions, more responsibility, and more "perks" around. In short, a corporation dominated by the technostructure is very different from the corporation in classical capitalism.

Because the goals of the technostructure are far more complex than simple profit maximization, Galbraith would include things like "technical virtuosity" and a "rising dividend." Furthermore, there are "subordinate" goals such as "building a better community; improved education; better understanding of the free enterprise system" as well as other humanitarian, political, and religious goals. According to Galbraith such goals of "social responsibility" are not "irrelevant window-dressing." On the contrary, they are a "perfectly plausible expression of the goals of the individual members of the technostructure and, thus, collectively of the mature corporation."[23]

This last point, of course, is a bone of contention between the neoclassical and the managerial theorists. Representative of the former school is Milton Friedman who pithily remarks that the "social responsibility of business is to increase its profits." He argues thus because "in a free-enterprise, private-property system, a corporate executive is an employee of the owners of the business. He has direct responsibility to his employers. That responsibility is to conduct the business in accordance with their desires, which will generally be to make as much money as possible while conforming to the basic rules of the society . . . . "[24]

Friedman seems to say that the *business of business is business!* The imposition of an extra duty of trying to solve society's problems upon the corporate executive is to sidetrack him from what he does best. We must recall here the underlying assumption that goes back to Adam Smith: when businesses strive to maximize profits, everyone ultimately benefits.

What then about the problems of hardcore poverty, pollution, discrimination, the quality of life, and so on that still plague society? Friedman's and the neoclassical answer would be, in part, that a capitalist economy, freed of troublesome government regulations and irrelevant demands on the social responsibility of business to do this or that, would of itself make many of these problems disappear or shrink. For those that remained another approach, harnassing the very life force of capitalism, should be tried. That is, if there is truly a need for something to be done, there will surely be someone to pay for it. Thus, the trick will be to convert the activity from an added burden on business activity to a profitable undertaking.

Among the managerial theorists Daniel Bell denies Friedman's argument. In his view we are moving into a "post-industrial society," where theoretical knowledge and basic research become more important than traditional manufacturing. Indeed, the business corporation may lose its socially predominant role to the universities and other knowledge-producing organizations. Nevertheless, corporations are and will remain of vital importance. This is especially so in view of the long-term weakening of the social role of the small town, the church, and the family. In place of these, "new kinds of organizations, particularly the corporations" have grown, and these have become "the arena in which the demands for security, justice, and esteem are made. To think of the business corporation, then, simply as an economic instrument is to fail totally to understand the meaning of the social changes of the last half century."[25]

Bell, Galbraith, and managerialist theorists in general agree that for businesses to do things that make no sense from a purely economic, that is, profit-maximizing, perspective is no scandal. The people in charge, whether professional managers or Galbraith's technostructure, are a different breed from the entrepreneurs of the neoclassical theory. Furthermore, business is a part of the general society, and, as such, cannot afford to play the ostrich. It cannot close its eyes to society's problems because these directly effect the "environment" within which business operates.

Business and Government

In the neoclassical version of the capitalist ideal there is a problematic relationship between business and government. We have already seen Hayek's and Friedman's strong aversion to governmental intervention in economic life. In contrast, theorists of managerial capitalism see some real changes in this relationship. Not only is government accepted as a fixed feature of the economic landscape, but there can also be a harmonious, even symbiotic, relationship between modern business and modern government.

One result of this view is that most theorists of managerial capitalism accept what is called the "Keynesian revolution" in economic theory and practice. John Maynard Keynes (1883–1946) was one of the premier economists of the modern age. His most important work is *The General Theory of Employment, Interest, and Money*,[26] the technical details of which can only be suggested here. Coming out in the Great Depression of the 1930s, Keynes's message was that the classical capitalists and their modern-day disciples had misunderstood the workings of the capitalist economy. The massive unemployment of the 1930s seemed an ever-present confirmation of Keynes's charge.

Keynes's ultimate vision was of a modified capitalism characterized by full employment, a levelling out of wealth differences, economic growth, and, to a degree, a rise in the level of inflation. According to Keynes, serious downturns of the business cycle like the Depression came from lack of investment funds. Classical economics had taught that such funds came basically from savings, so that when these went down economic troubles followed. This problem in turn was caused by an oversupply of goods due to overproduction.

Keynes challenged these and other principles of the classical economists head on. He held that the key to business downturns and hence unemployment was lack of "aggregate demand." In other words, people did not have enough money available to purchase what they wanted and so businesses found a smaller market for their products. Whereas the classical economists said that such troubles were necessary readjustments that in time would correct themselves, Keynes demanded a more active approach. Government would have to assume greater responsibility for the overall course of the economy.

He suggested that the "fiscal" (spending and taxing) and "monetary" (money-supply and interest-rates) policy of government, what we now call "macroeconomics," be used to steer the economy in the direction of growth and full employment. Taxes, for example, traditionally thought of mainly as a way to finance the government, could be manipulated to stimulate economic growth or cool it down if inflation got out of hand. On interest rates, Keynes basically favored low ones, though these too could be readjusted to fit the current economic situation. Direct government spending, sometimes called "pump-priming," could also be used to get a sluggish economy moving again. The basic idea was to push the level of aggregate demand up to a point where business activity was assured.

However, these policies could result in a government deficit, and this is precisely where Keynes most brashly challenged classical economic orthodoxy. The balanced government budget was almost an "Eleventh Commandment" to most classical economists. To Keynes, however, "deficit spending" was no great calamity. The important thing was a healthy economy. If promoting economic growth or recovery meant that government finances went temporarily into the red, increased revenues from an expanding economy would soon put things into the black again. The supposedly mild inflationary push involved with these policies was a very small price, Keynes and his disciples felt, for society to pay for the ostensible benefits.

Theorists of managerial capitalism naturally were far friendlier to Keynes than were the neoclassical school.[27] The loose form of (indicative) planning associated with Keynesian macroeconomics is far more acceptable to managers of modern business (and the technostructure) than to their grandfathers. Big business, which Galbraith even calls "the planning system," may work more like government than was ever the case in the past. Government, thus, is no longer the enemy, since it is government contracts, tax credits, and direct supports that help to keep many businesses, large and small, prosperous today. Even government regulations are viewed with scepticism rather than fear by Galbraith's mature corporation.

CONCLUSION

In this chapter we have examined capitalism as an economic ideal directly counterpoised to the ideal of socialism. Our stress on the question of ownership should not cause confusions about actual economic systems. As an ideal, socialism certainly features public ownership, whereas capitalism involves private ownership. Actual economies, however, may lie somewhere on a continuum between pure public and pure private ownership systems (see Fig. 4.2.). In the "socialist" USSR, for example, even if we leave aside a massive illegal underground economy of black marketeering and smuggling, there is a strong "private sector" in agriculture.

Soviet collective farmers can sell the produce of small plots that they till, but do not own, on the open market. Likewise, capitalist America not only runs a massive public defense establishment, it also runs the Post Office as a "public corporation" as well as a whole array of government services and activities.

Similarly, the association of socialism with planning and capitalism with the market must not be overdone when we look to real economies. We have already mentioned market aspects coexisting with the Soviet planning system and have suggested that managerial capitalism does resort to (indicative) planning in order to compensate for market weaknesses. In other words, as with the ownership issue, the planning problem is not a choice between all and nothing at all. As Fig. 4.3 shows, it is a matter of degree.

That conceptual differences are generally sharper than observed differences is no surprise to social scientists. Ideals need to be marked off as clearly as possible from competing ideals. This makes them appear more clear-cut and extreme than they are in practice.

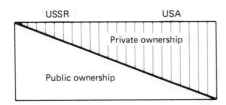

Figure 4.2 Public and private ownership in actual economies.

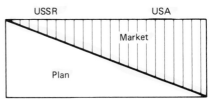

Figure 4.3. Market and plan in actual economies.

Our examination of the capitalist ideal contrasts the neoclassical version and the managerialist version. With the former, the virtues of capitalism such as prosperity, freedom, and naturalness derive from the premise that owners are the highest authority in the firm and that all they want is maximum profit. In the managerialist version the divorce between ownership and control has lessened some of the harshness of old-fashioned capitalism. This results in less of an antagonism between business and government and a greater business commitment to social responsibility.

NOTES

1. Adam Smith spoke instead of the "natural system of liberty." The term "capitalism" was popularized by Marxists and other critics of capitalism. Most defenders of the capitalist ideal generally prefer "free enterprise system" or "market economy."
2. Adam Smith, *The Wealth of Nations* (New York: Modern Library, 1937), p. 424.
3. Ibid., p. 651.
4. Ibid., p. 11.
5. Ibid., p. 13. Smith did not wish to determine whether this propensity represented an ultimate feature of human nature or was itself derived from still more basic traits.
6. "Social Darwinism" refers to late nineteenth-century attempts to apply certain interpretations of the doctrine of evolution to social and political affairs. Some of these ideas were inspired by Charles Darwin, who published his epoch-making work, *The Origin of Species* in 1859.
7. William Graham Sumner, *Social Darwinism* (Englewood Cliffs, N.J.: Prentice-Hall, 1963), p. 85.
8. Ibid., p. 16.
9. William Graham Sumner, *What Social Classes Owe To Each Other* (Caldwell, Ida.: Caxton Printers, 1954), p. 27.
10. Milton Friedman, *Capitalism and Freedom* (Chicago: University of Chicago Press, 1962), p. 12.
11. Friedrich Hayek, *The Road to Serfdom* (Chicago: University of Chicago Press, 1958), p. 56.
12. Hayek, for one, either denies the distinction between indicative and imperative planning, which we developed in the last chapter, or thinks that the first is simply the prelude to the second. Likewise planning and socialism seem so inseparable to him that Yugoslav "market socialism" must appear like an economic unicorn.
13. Hayek, *Serfdom*, p. 57.
14. Ibid., p. 69.
15. Ibid., p. 91.
16. Thorstein Veblen, *The Engineers and the Price System* (New York: Holt, Rinehart, Winston, 1963), p. 64.

17. Ibid., p. 66.
18. Ibid., pp. 83–84.
19. James Burnham, *The Managerial Revolution* (Bloomington, Ind.: University of Indiana Press, 1960), p. 194.
20. Ibid., p. 190.
21. Ibid., p. 118. Burnham's preface of 1960 acknowledged that he had exaggerated certain key points.
22. John Kenneth Galbraith, *The New Industrial State* (Boston: Houghton Mifflin, 1971).
23. Ibid., p. 177.
24. Milton Friedman, "The Social Responsibility of Business is to Increase its Profits," in *Issues in Business and Society*, ed. G. A. Steiner and J. F. Steiner (New York: Random House, 1977), p. 168.
25. Daniel Bell, *The Coming of Post-Industrial Society* (New York: Basic Books, 1976), p. 289.
26. John Maynard Keynes, *The General Theory of Employment, Interest, and Money* (New York: Harcourt, Brace, Jovanovich, 1964).
27. For the growth of Keynesianism in the public policies of Western countires, see Andrew Shonfield, *Modern Capitalism* (New York: Oxford University Press, 1968).

SUGGESTIONS FOR FURTHER READING

Friedman, Milton. *Capitalism and Freedom*. Chicago: University of Chicago Press, 1962.
Hayek, Friedrich, *The Road to Serfdom*. Chicago: University of Chicago Press, 1958.
Hofstadter, Richard. *Social Darwinism in American Thought*. Boston: Beacon Press, 1955.
Schonfield, Andrew. *Modern Capitalism*. New York: Oxford University Press, 1968.
Schumpeter, Joseph. *Capitalism, Socialism, Democracy*. New York: Harper & Row, 1962.
Veblen, Thorstein. *The Engineers and the Price System*. New York: Holt, Rinehart, Winston, 1963.

5

NATIONALISM

Ours is an age of nationalism. In saying this we say both much and little. We say much because we directly contradict the confident hope of many leading nineteenth-century thinkers that our own century would bring about a decline of national feelings. The nineteenth-century optimists felt that such feelings served only to bar the way to a world civilization where common humanity would overcome past divisions.

On the other hand, to speak of our age as one of nationalism adds little to our understanding, particularly when we stretch the meaning of nationalism so much that a wide variety of highly distinct regimes, movements, and ideologies are all reduced to a simple common denominator of "nationalist." This risks ignoring or at least underestimating the force of other ideals or even ideologies that may be at work. The interesting issue is *how the presence of these ideals or ideologies can influence and transform nationalism in a given circumstance.* These problems, however, will be insoluble unless we do some very careful conceptual spadework in the next few sections.

NATION AND STATE

Despite its obvious importance and the vast scholarly attention devoted to it, there is little consensus today as to what nationalism really is. A good place to begin is to dispel the widespread confusion between "nation" and "state." This muddle is found in the press as well as in more scholarly works. In simple terms, a nation is *a group of people,* whereas a state is a *form of political organization.* A nation is a mass of men and women who collectively feel that they belong together. Their association marks them off from outsiders and aliens. The state, however, is something of an abstraction: it is a structure that emerges out of certain political relationships.

Unfortunately, when the term "nation" is used, what is often really meant is "state." In this strict sense even "United Nations" is a misnomer. It would be an accurate name if all member states were true *nation-states*, but they are not. Another example of our problem is the USSR—the Union of Soviet Socialist Republics. We often and misleadingly call the USSR "Russia" and its people the "Russians." But Russia, properly speaking, is but one, though the largest, of the sixteen union-republics that make up the USSR. Moreover, true or "Great" Russians are a slight minority in a country that includes nationalities such as the Ukrainians, Belorussians, Jews, Georgians, Azerbadjanis, Armenians, Turkmens, Kazakhs, Usbeks, and others. Some of these peoples do not speak Russian as a first language, and they certainly do not consider themselves Russians. The USSR must be considered a "multinational" state.

In other states the situation is complex, but in different ways. Quite often, we find a state containing one or more full-fledged nations plus several more primitive formations or *ethnic groups.* In this situation the dominant nation tries, often in vain, to assimilate the resisting ethnic minorities into an expanded nation. A most serious problem in a host of Asian and African countries, the rise of "ethnonationalism" is also a factor in certain western European countries (e.g., with the Basques in Spain). At any rate, the distinction between nation and state is not only a matter of concepts; the dynamics involved are also productive of serious political conflicts. We will see this more clearly in the following discussion.

THE FACTORS OF NATIONHOOD

Some obvious questions are why do nations and nation-states exist at all? Why has consciousness of belonging to one nation been found with some populations and not others? Why do some nations have their own state and not others? Good answers have been found for these and related questions in specific cases. A harder nut to crack is whether some identical set of traits is always at the heart of viable modern nations. We will see, as the saying goes, that nationhood is more a product of history than of nature.

Language naturally comes to mind as the premier factor in the development of nationhood. One of the earliest German nationalists J. G. Fichte (1762–1814) made extreme claims for the link between language and nationhood. According to Fichte German unity and cultural superiority were foreshadowed by the possession of a "primitive" language, which was close to nature and expressed the spiritual essence of the German people. Other peoples, especially the "neo-Latin" ones like the Spanish, French, and Italians, were culturally handicapped. This was so because their secondary Romance languages were derived from the dead Latin.

German cultural uniqueness and superiority were largely a result of language:

> What an immeasurable influence on the whole human development of a people the character of its language may have—its language, which accompanies the individual into the most secret depths of his mind in thought and will and either hinders him or gives him wings, which unites within its domain the whole mass of men who speak it into one single and common understanding. . . .[3]

Unfortunately for Fichte's grandiose claims, language is not quite so omnipotent.

In the first place there are speakers of the same language who do not consider themselves members of the same nation. English-speakers north of the US border consider themselves Canadians; and the French-speakers there do not consider themselves members of the French nation. The various states and peoples in which Spanish or Arabic is the dominant language further confirms the frequent dissociation of language and nationhood.

But what of the opposite and more telling point: can members of the same nation speak different languages? Again, contrary to Fichte, the answer is yes, and Switzerland is the classic example. There is no Swiss language—the Swiss speak German, or French, or Italian, or Romansch (a local dialect) in different parts of the country. This linguistic diversity has at times hampered, but not prevented, an overarching Swiss nationality. History has overcome nature.

Such examples in no way detract from the importance of language in the growth of many nations. They simply suggest that the language base is not absolutely essential. Although language has often been of decisive importance, loss of a distinct language has not necessarily led to the full-scale absorption of one group by another. Long ago Gaelic ceased to be the main tongue of the Irish, but this did not lessen their sense of nationhood. They did not, that is, become Englishmen. Some nineteenth-century Irish Nationalist leaders failed to see this and felt that a full return to Gaelic was essential to their cause.

Territory is also associated with nations. This seems self-evident. Must not the nation have a homeland? But the problem is a bit more complex than this. Both Israelis and Palestinians claim the same area as an ancestral homeland. Before fastening on Palestine early Zionists gave serious attention to parts of Africa and czarist Russia for a Jewish homeland. This seems strange in the 1980s; it was not so strange a century ago. Thus, in certain nationalist movements territory is as much a matter of dream and choice as it is of latitude and longitude. The modern African state of Ghana takes its name from an ancient kingdom whose borders were by no means coterminous with present-day ones.

The problem of territory is focused on in the views of a great student of nationalism, Hans Kohn, who suggested that

> the most important outward factor in the formation of nationalities is a common territory, or rather, the state. Political frontiers tend to establish nationalities. . . . The condition of statehood need not be present when a nationality originates; but in such a case it is always the memory of a past state and the aspiration toward statehood that characterizes nationalities in the period of nationalism.[4]

But Kohn also suggests that state and territory along with other "objective" factors are not really essential to the existence or "definition" of nationality.[5] This is so because the "most essential element is a living and active corporate will. Nationality is formed by the desire to form a nationality."[6]

Ethnicity is another apparently objective factor that has served both nationalists and social scientists as the key to nationhood. And here too the historical record is mixed. For every instance where ethnic homogeneity provided the backdrop for emergent nationhood, we find an instance where distinct nations spin off from the same ethnic base. Moreover, there are plenty of cases of nations with ethnic pluralism.

Religion can be another source of nationhood. This usually involves a broad region that contains distinct religious groups. Religion thus generates that we-versus-they sentiment essential to any genuine national feeling. We can see this in 1947 with the formation of India and Pakistan out of old British Imperial India. India emerged as a predominantly Hindu state, while Pakistan was mainly Muslim. That religion itself can be counteracted by other factors was shown in 1973 when east Pakistan seceded and formed the new country of Bangla Desh. The dispute between Pakistan's two halves was ethnic. People in east Pakistan felt with considerable justification that they were second class citizens oppressed by the westerners.

Common culture is frequently brought up to explain nationhood. In one sense this is a foolproof explanation, because it is so broad as to always cover the case. Because nationhood is a type of political culture, it is not great surprise to find out that the evolution of culture has sometimes produced nations. If we define culture more narrowly, we confront the problem of why only certain subcultures and not others become nations.

Our general conclusion must be that despite the influence of factors like language, territory, religion, ethnicity, and culture, there is no precise formula or set of necessary conditions for the emergence of nationhood. Various combinations of these factors have been decisive in different cases. As Hans Kohn reminds us, a nation is a group of people who think they are a nation.

NATIONAL SENTIMENT AND NATIONALISM

If we are to understand the ideal of nationalism and its relationship to various other ideals and ideologies, we must first distinguish between national sentiment and nationalism proper.[7] National sentiment characterizes a nation that has already "grown" or been "built." It is the feeling of a nation whose very sense of nationhood is strong and secure. Nationalism on the other hand involves a movement that represents weakness and insecurity. It either comes before full achievement of nationhood and national sentiment or it reflects a fear of their decline or disappearance.

In the first case there is only a potential nation, an array of separate groups still beset by ethnic, tribal, religious, regional, or other cleavages. In this case it is the hope of the nationalist movement to join together what is separate and to create a loyalty to the nation that overwhelms all other loyalties. In the second case, nationalism is a kind of "revitalization movement" responding to a real or imagined threat to the nation. We can call the first sort of nationalism a "nation-building" movement and the second a "nation-preserving" movement. Historically, nation-building movements have often shown an affinity for communism, while nation-preserving ones often incline toward fascism.

Nationalist movements whose ideal is to build a nation have been widespread since World War II. Their success is something else again. To understand this problem, let us recall that the older European nations "grew" and were not really "built." In other words, the development of nationhood and national sentiment was usually a long and drawn-out affair. It was not the conscious, controlled process that the term "nation-building" implies. The growth of European nations was often a side-effect of complex social, economic, and political trends.

If there was any "building" involved, it was "state-building" rather than "nation-building."[8] State-building, more specifically, involves the development of a central bureaucracy, an efficient system of collecting taxes, and a standing or mercenary army under central command. In Europe this meant the victory of "absolute monarchy" over the feudal or semifeudal institutions of the past. While successful state-building often provided the framework for emergent nationhood, this was not the original goal. Indeed, if most modernizing monarchs—usually called "enlightened despots"—could have seen the ultimate fruits of their labor, they would have thought twice about their policies. This is the case because nationalism was later involved in many revolutions that overthrew monarchies.

Nation-building means to build a nation, that is, to infuse a motley array of sociological groupings with a sense of common overriding community. In a brief time, people are supposed to consider as brothers those whom they up to now viewed as incurably alien, hostile, unclean, heretical, inferior, oppressive or just plain different. This is no easy task; and, if the time-frame is too short, it is impossible.

Let us take as an example a newly independent state, most likely in Asia or Africa. This state contains several large ethnic groups, with one of them the predominant force in the post-independence government. This prevalent group wishes to lead the process of creating a strong state and to unify the other ethnic groups under its leadership. It thus proclaims a new encompassing nationhood. The ruling groups' state-building efforts and the drive for autonomy or independence of the dissident ethnic minorities are clearly on a collision course.

Something close to this scenario was enacted in Nigeria in the late 1960s. There, the Hausa people appeared to be the leading force in the country. The Ibo people decided that this sort of future was not for them and attempted to set up an independent state in Iboland called Biafra. After several years of a bloody civil war, the Biafran secessionist movement was crushed.

Now, in much of the "nation-building" or "political development" literature, the Biafran tragedy would be written off as merely a "tribalist" or "subnational" eruption of "primordial sentiments." In other words, this sort of episode figures as a backward, parochial revolt against modernization and modern nationalism. But such an estimate is valid only if genuine nationalism is tantamount to loyalty to the state. However, this is to confuse two very different things, for nationalism proper refers to people and not to political organization.[9]

Let us summarize our findings about nationalism thus far. First, a nation is a group manifesting national sentiment. It is not a state, which is a political formation sometimes coinciding with a nation (the "nation-state") and sometimes not. Accordingly, nation-building is not at all the same thing as state-building; indeed, if state-building efforts are ruthlessly pushed in a situation of competing ethnic nationalisms, the result will not be nation-building, but "nation-destroying."[10] Nationalism proper is a movement with the ideal of building or preserving a nation which would possess true national sentiment.

NATIONALISM AND IDEOLOGY

Up to this point our discussion has been very sparing of the term "nationalism"—the supposed subject of our investigation. Because it was first necessary to get a sense of key ideas like nation, national sentiment, and nation-building, it is only now that we can procede to nationalism proper. A close-to-useful definition of nationalism comes from Anthony D. Smith, who sees it as an "ideological movement for maintenance of autonomy, cohesion, and individuality for a social group, some of whose members conceive it to be an actual or potential nation."[11] In fact, the only thing wrong with this approach is the word "ideological." Smith considers nationalism an ideology because he uses a loose definition of ideology that contrasts with the more rigorous usage of this book.

The reason why nationalism must be considered more of an ideal than a true ideology has been implied above. While an ideology can be placed in a definite place in the ideological spectrum, nationalism, like most ideals, cannot. It is sometimes on the right; it is sometimes in the center; it is sometimes on the left. As an ideal that inspires a movement to create or revamp a nation, the historical circumstances involved are highly variable. This is why nationalism will wed itself to practically all political ideologies.

Nationalism, therefore, is ideologically promiscuous. Certain anarchists, despite their hatred of the state, are nationalists. The expressions "national communism" and "communist nationalism" are commonplace today. Social democrats, especially the "Austro-Marxists" before World War I, have often tried to show that socialism was not antinational. Christian Democracy may be a partial exception, but strong nationalist currents are found in liberalism, conservatism, populism, and fascism.

A very important consequence of this ideological promiscuity is that *the nation itself may be defined ideologically*. In other words, we frequently find that some groups are included while others are excluded in the present or future nation. The determining test of who is inside and who is outside the nation comes from the ideology associated with that specific nationalist movement. Such a principle of exclusion usually involves class or race, and it is especially utilized in epochs of revolution.

A case in point is the English Revolution of the 1640s and 1650s, which Hans Kohn called the "first example of modern nationalism, religious, political, and social at the same time . . . ."[12] One aspect of this complex ideological scene involved the idea of the "Norman Yoke." This referred back to 1066, when the Normans under William the Conqueror crossed the English Channel and defeated and subjected the Anglo-Saxon population in England. William's military leaders were rewarded with vast landed holdings throughout England and they rapidly developed into a hereditary aristocracy. For a time they kept their French language and ways, but long before the English Revolution they had become Englishmen.

Nevertheless, the Norman Yoke idea or myth served certain revolutionary factions as an ideological sledge to knock down the legitimacy of the English nobility. In 1646 members of Oliver Cromwell's New Model Army asked, "What were the Lords of England but William the Conqueror's Colonels? or the Barons but his Majors? or the Knights but his Captains?"[13] This rhetoric implied that both monarchy and aristocracy rested not on right, but on violence and usurpation. This meant that the existing social and political order was alien. Thus the nationalist demand was to restore the rights of true Englishmen (i.e., Anglo-Saxons) as they existed before 1066. Henceforth, the nation could dispense with the alien Norman aristocrats.

Similar developments are seen in later revolutions. In the French Revolution of 1789, one of the most influential tracts was Sieyes's *What is the Third Estate?* In the old regime of France there were three "estates" or status groups: the first estate was the clergy; the second estate was the nobility; and the third estate was the other 95 percent of the population. The three estates had unequal privileges and prerogatives. In fact, when the Estates General—a kind of consultative semi-legislature convened by the monarch—was summoned in 1789, each full estate, regardless of size, had one vote.

Earlier defenders of the French aristocracy had argued that their superior position derived from the right of conquest of the Frankish invaders over a thousand years before. Sieyes turned this argument on its head to prove the illegitimacy of the aristocratic order. Indeed, he went further and asked

> Who is bold enough to maintain that the Third Estate does not contain within itself everything needful to constitute a complete nation? It is like a strong and robust man with one arm still in chains. If the privileged order were removed, the nation would not be something less but something more.[14]

With the Norman Yoke myth and Sieyes's identification of the third estate and the nation, we find ideological principles favoring greater social and political equality doing two important things. First, they push the latent egalitarianism of most forms of nationalism to the point of revolution. Second, they draw the line between who is a member of the nation and who is not.

Twentieth-century nationalist movements, especially those with a Marxist or communist orientation, run into the same problem of delimiting membership in the nation. We can see this in 1939 when Mao Tsetung distinguished between those groups that were "motive forces" of the Chinese Revolution and those that were its "targets." Clearly, this is his version of the who-is-in and who-is-out dichotomy. Though the workers, peasants, and other groups were in as "motive forces," others like the "landlord class" and the "big bourgeois" were out as "targets."[15] Later, Mao included other groups on his list of targets, though it should be noted that individuals from enemy classes could repent and perhaps eventually be welcomed back among the "people."

NATIONALISM AND NATIVISM

A social phenomenon difficult to distinguish from genuine modern nationalism is *nativism*. Indeed, a certain element of nativism is present in many nationalist movements. Nonetheless, there are critical differences. A classic definition of a nativistic movement sees it as any "conscious, organized attempt . . . to revive or perpetuate selected aspects of [a] culture."[16] Such a movement is a response to contact between two or more distinct cultures.

Typical examples occurred under the impact of western imperialism and colonialism. Imperial rulers or colonial settlers moved into vast areas of Asia, Africa, and Oceania. Through superior military force they were able to seize native lands as outright colonies or to dominate them as "spheres of influence." The white ruler introduces his ways and culture, which sharply contrast with native ways and culture. Little by little the alien ways infiltrate into the daily lives of the subject native population. The alien rulers scarcely attempt to mask their disdain and disgust for the "inferior" native culture. The natives are insulted and injured, even when no slight has been intended.

We can sense the resentment of the natives easily enough. One response is thus the nativistic movement that rejects the aliens, their ways and their culture, lock, stock, and barrel. These movements or their leaders envisage a sort of "golden age" that existed before the onslaught of the alien corruption. Nativism wishes to purge the home culture of all outside influences and to restore things to their pristine state. This involves destruction or expulsion of the corrupt and oppressive alien. He must pay for the evil he has brought and wrought.

Given the paramount importance of religion in traditional societies and cultures, nativistic movements generally take on a strong religious coloration. A veritable plethora of these movements have featured some charismatic leader or messiah claiming to be God's emissary or more. An excellent Islamic instance was the movement of the Sudanese Mahdi (Mahdi = the rightly guided one), Mohammed Ahmed (c.1844–85). At this time "Mahdist expectations were current in the Sudan . . . due in part to social and political discontent with Egyptian rule and in part to a genuine religious revulsion from the low morality of the Egyptian administrators, when judged by the standards of primitive Islam."[17]

In 1881 Mohammed Ahmed declared himself the Mahdi of all Islam. A movement quickly grew around him, aiming to chastize the alien British, Egyptian, and Turkish influences that sullied the true Islamic culture of the Sudan. The movement became a revolt and won a string of victories against the British-led Egyptians. The Mahdist oath said in part that "we have sworn allegiance to you in renouncing this world and abandoning it, and being content with what is with God, desiring what is with God and the world to come, and we will not flee from the *jihad* [i.e., the "holy war" of Islam]."[18] This language reflects the millenary vision of a "new heaven and a new earth" common to many nativistic groups.

Through the bungling of his adversaries and the fanaticism of his followers, the Mahdi came to control much of the Sudan. His greatest success was the capture of Khartoum in January 1885. Six months later he was dead, apparently by natural causes, and though his movement survived for a time it was never quite the same.

For the present century Rupert Emerson has posed the problem of the relationship between nativism and nationalism in modern Africa by noting that "the bulk of the local, more traditionally oriented disaffections and risings which all African colonial regimes have put down . . . did not have the potentiality of turning into modern nationalist movements without substantial changes in the societies from which they arose."[19] Emerson and others contend that the typical nativistic movement is reactionary in the literal sense: Its bank of ideals lies in the real or imaginary past. No modern nationalist movement can rely so wholly on what was. It must be more future-oriented and look more to reform or revolution.

There is another, perhaps more serious, difference between nativism and modern nationalism. The nativist wishes to restore or preserve the cultural integrity of a discernable group. But this sort of "ethnocentrism" usually disdains and disparages all outside or alien cultures. There is a good-versus-evil contrast between insiders and outsiders. The insiders identify with their own group unreservedly and cannot appreciate other cultures. Confronted with the alien ways, their reaction borders on the hysterical.

While many nationalist movements have their own narrow-mindedness as with Fichte's idolization of things German, usually some thought and reflection is involved. In contrast to the nativist's blind group identification, the nationalist is more complex and subtle. To identify with an entity so large and remote as a nation, one has to step back a bit from one's immersion in other narrow groups. Then one can more consciously and deliberately plunge back into identification with the broader entity, the nation.

Both the member of a modern nation and the militant of a nationalist movement admit that other nations exist and have a right to do so. While they naturally prefer their own culture, they generally do not share the nativist's revulsion in the face of other cultures. In fact, the nationalist may do something the extreme nativist never could: that is, he may be quite willing to learn or borrow things from other nations and cultures. The nationalist's very nationalism causes him to look where the nativist shuts his eyes.

THE STAGES OF NATIONALISM

A generation ago the historian E. H. Carr suggested three historical stages in the growth of modern nationalism. Until the late eighteenth century the idea of the nation was embodied in the person of the monarch.[20] The rise of national monarchies resulted from the downfall of medieval "internationalism." In the Middle Ages there had reigned a sort of "republica christiana" because the Catholic Church in practice and the Holy Roman Empire in theory united the European world.

The Reformation of the early 1500s disrupted what was left of the old medieval unity. After the end of the Thirty Years War in 1648, the principle that the monarch could determine the official religion of his state was established. With the decline of religion as the major bone of international contention, territorial disputes both at home and in colonies preoccupied the national monarchs. In economics, "mercantilism" promoted greater awareness of national differences. This doctrine held that a country's economic strength depended on the accumulation of hard currency in the royal treasury and preached protection for home industries.

Despite the economic and colonial conflicts that followed, wars in this period were generally quite limited in aims and intensity. Because religious strife had become less explosive, and modern ideologies were yet to surface as causes of international conflict, the antagonism of states was limited. As Carr points out, "A sovereign waging war no more desired to inflict injury or loss on the subjects of his enemy than a citizen going to law desires to inflict them on the servants of his adversary."[21]

By the late eighteenth century—as anticipated by the writings of Rousseau—a new phase of nationalism, "the democratization of the nation," was under way. The emergence of this democratized nationalism coincided with the rise of the middle class to political and economic predominance. Wherever the old order tried to stem this tide, nationalism obviously presented a revolutionary face. In addition, this broadened base of nationalism "imparted to it a new and disturbing emotional flavor."[22]

The nineteenth century or perhaps better, the century from Waterloo to World War I, was the golden age of democratized nationalism. Even here international conflict was muted, largely through the actual economic dominance of Great Britain. Liberalism, with its stress on individual rights and representative government, reigned in the political realm, while laissez-faire and free trade—sometimes called economic liberalism—held sway in economic affairs.

This second phase was superceded by the third, the "socialization of nationalism." Carr sees three main causes for the change. First, previously disenfranchised groups in the population were brought into full membership in the nation, as the movement toward universal suffrage expanded steadily. Second, the "visible reunion of economic with political power" involved the decline of laissez-faire and the rise of the modern welfare state. The third cause was simply the multiplication of nations and states.

In the third phase of nationalism "the socialization of the nation for the first time brings the economic claims of the masses into the forefront of the picture. . . . The socialization of the nation has as its natural corollary the nationalization of socialism."[23] By this last phrase Carr refers to the growing nationalism of socialist movements as they progressed from the last to the present century. Old-time socialism was internationalist, as reflected in Karl Marx's opening to the *Communist Manifesto:* "Workers of the world unite; you have nothing to lose but your chains!" To the old socialists it seemed evident that workers in one country were the brothers of workers in other countries. Class differences prevented their solidarity with the middle class in their respective countries.

It is clear that the view just stated underestimated the force of national sentiment and nationalistic appeals for the workers of the socialist movement. Add to this the enfranchisement of ever more workers and the beginnings of modern social policies in the generation before World War I, and the response of European socialist parties to the war becomes understandable. What most of them did was to "rally 'round the flag" and support their country's war effort. This horrified those left-wing socialists like Lenin, who considered the war an essentially "bourgeois" affair. National sentiment and nationalism had at long last penetrated to the lowest levels of the social pyramid.

The stage was now set to export nationalism to Third World countries. This led not only to a massive expansion of the phenomenon of nationalism but to a rise in its intensity. "Beyond Europe it spread to countries where every Christian or European tradition was alien, and where the illogical inhibitions which had for so long helped to restrain European nationalism were unknown."[24]

CONCLUSION

This chapter deals with an interpretation of the phenomenon of modern nationalism that many will find controversial. However, if certain key distinctions are borne in mind, its usefulness will be enhanced. First is the vital contrast between nations as groups of people and states as forms of political organization. This contrast runs counter to much daily discourse in the press and academia, where "nations" allegedly do this or that, whereas the real subject is the behavior of states, or, more accurately, of government leaders.

Our nation-versus-state dichotomy suggests situations where there may be nations-without-states (e.g., the Palestinians) or states-without-nations (e.g., Zaire). Other possibilities include genuine nation-states (e.g., France) or multinational states (e.g., the USSR). All of this reflects not only the logical problems of defining terms properly but the political problems raised by nationalism itself.

We have pointed out the difficulty of coming up with a foolproof list of sociological factors (language, religion, ethnicity, etc.) that explains nationhood. The permeation of a distinct group of people with a sense of common identity or national sentiment is an essentially historical phenomenon. However, there is an element of reflectiveness and sophistication that separates both national sentiment and nationalism from the blinder, almost instinctual xenophobia of nativism.

A group's possession of nationhood is what determines the nature and force of nationalism among its members. If the critical mass of the group lacks a strong national consciousness and is still fragmented by ethnic, religious, or other cleavages, the nationalist movement is essentially a *nation-building* movement. If, on the other hand, some people sense a weakening of national sentiment and thus a threat to the nation's integrity, the nationalist movement will be a *nation-restoring* movement seeking to revitalize national sentiment. Although this distinction might imply a contrast between backward and forward-looking movements, most movements have elements of both orientations.

The variety of historical conditions supports the crucial point that nationalism involves an ideal that can join itself to a variety of ideological standpoints. As E. H. Carr's historical survey shows, nationalism arose as a highly restrictive movement in the seventeenth and early eighteenth centuries, broadened to a middle-class phenomenon (democratization of nationalism) in the late eighteenth and early nineteenth centuries, and culminated in the last century or so by reaching the lower social strata (socialization of the nation). Evidently, nationalism takes on a different ideological coloration as we move from the first through the second, to the third phase of its evolution. In the third phase with the mobilization of the masses, the ideal of nationalism naturally blends with ever more radical ideologies.

One confirmation of the relevance of time and place is to compare nationalist movements in the 1920s and 1930s with those in the last three decades. In the former period fascism was "in the air" with Mussolini's coming to power in Italy (1922) and Hitler in Germany in 1933. These countries, particularly Germany, wished to overturn the international status quo, which was still largely dominated by countries possessing large overseas empires like France and Great Britain. Thus, the nationalism of the "national liberation" movements of the 1920s and 1930s took on a veneer of fascism because these movements also wanted to overturn the traditional European "imperialism."

Fascism, however, was apparently defeated in World War II, so that the nationalism of postwar national liberation movements tended to vent its radicalism in other directions. Whereas the USSR was active in the struggle for national liberation even before the Fascists and the Nazis, the rise of communism as the ideological companion of Third World nationalist movements came mainly after 1945. In one sense the fascist flavor of the interwar period was replaced by the communist flavor of the postwar period. At any rate, nationalism does indeed seem to wed itself to a variety of ideological positions.

NOTES

1. A nation-state would be a state where the preponderant majority really considered themselves members of one and the same nation. Such a situation is less prevalent than commonly thought.
2. Clearly the pronouncements of Third World leaders often show little recognition of the problems of ethnic complexity in their own countries. They publicly proclaim the myth that a single encompassing nation already exists or is well on the road to achievement. If minorities cause disturbances it is usually written off as the subversive work of "outside agents."
3. J. G. Fichte, *Addresses to the German Nation* (New York: Harper & Row, 1968), p. 59.
4. Hans Kohn, *The Idea of Nationalism* (New York: Macmillan, 1961), p. 15.
5. Ibid., p. 14.
6. Ibid., p. 15.
7. This follows Anthony D. Smith, *Theories of Nationalism* (New York: Harper & Row, 1972).

8. See Reinhard Bendix, *Kings or People: Power and the Mandate to Rule* (Berkeley: University of California Press, 1978).
9. See Walker Connor, "Nation Building or Nation Destroying," *World Politics* 24 (1972), pp. 319–54.
10. Ibid., p. 336.
11. Smith, *Theories*, p. 87.
12. Kohn, *Idea*, p. 166.
13. Christopher Hill, *Puritanism and Revolution* (New York: Schocken Books, 1970), p. 72.
14. Emmanuel Joseph Sieyes, *What is the Third Estate?* (New York: Praeger, 1964), pp. 56–57.
15. Mao Tse-tung, "The Chinese Revolution and the Chinese Communist Party," in *Selected Works*, Vol. III (New York: International Publishers, 1954), pp. 72–101.
16. Ralph Linton, "Nativistic Movements," in *Reader in Comparative Religion*, ed. W. A. Lessa and E. Z. Vogt Evanston, Ill.: Row, Peterson, 1958), p. 467.
17. Gunther Lewy, *Religion and Revolution* (New York: Oxford University Press, 1972), p. 178.
18. Ibid., p. 182.
19. Rupert Emerson, *From Empire to Nation* (Boston: Beacon Press, 1963), pp. 46–47.
20. On this issue see again, Bendix, *Kings or People*.
21. E. H. Carr, *Nationalism and After* (London: Macmillan, 1945), p. 4.
22. Ibid., p. 8.
23. Ibid., p. 19.
24. Ibid., p. 32.

SUGGESTIONS FOR FURTHER READING

Carr, E. H. *Nationalism and After*. London: Macmillan, 1945.
Connor, Walker. *The National Question in Marxist-Leninist Theory and Strategy*. Princeton: Princeton University Press. 1984.
Kohn, Hans. *The Idea of Nationalism*. New York: Macmillan, 1961.
Minogue, K. R. *Nationalism*. Baltimore: Penguin Books, 1970.
Shafer, Boyd C. *Nationalism: Myth and Reality*. New York: Harcourt, Brace, World, 1955.
Smith, Anthony D. *Theories of Nationalism*. New York: Harper & Row, 1972.

6

UTOPIA AND REVOLUTION

This chapter discusses two distinct, yet interrelated, ideals: utopia and revolution. The connection between the two is almost easier to establish than the thesis that both are ideals in the sense of this text. Many students of revolution have shown how revolutionary ideologies justify violent breakthrough as the necessary first step towards a society unblemished by the social evils of the past—a utopia. Why endure the enormous stress and strain of revolution unless the ultimate pay-off is a society worthy of the label "perfect?" Not all revolutions have been based on a utopian ideology, but most have some tendencies in that direction.

On the other side, we find that some utopians are revolutionists, whereas others are not. Some utopians thus advocate a violent path towards a goal; others reject this strategy either on nonviolent ethical grounds, or because violence complicates the process of change. At any rate, the utopian ideal is broad enough to cover both approaches.

This however, does not tell us how revolution itself can sometimes become an ideal. We can, of course, approach "revolution" in a variety of ways. First, we have seen that it is a strategy to attain political power in order to reach certain ideological objectives. Second, a revolution can be understood as a historical movement animated by an ideology, which, if successful, will set up a genuinely revolutionary regime. Third, "revolution" can become an ideal, if over time the very notion of revolution has acquired a symbolic significance valued in and of itself. In other words, the actual experience of revolution must be cherished to the degree that we can speak of a sort of "revolutionary mystique."

As we will see in the next section, this revolutionary mystique involves a sense of the morally purifying value of revolutionary violence. That is, the violence is not just a "necessary evil," wherein the ends justify the means. It is rather an ennobling form of human experience as such. Moreover, for some, the experience of revolution acquires a "sacred" character that marks it off from the more "profane" realm of ordinary human activities. This gives the notion of revolution certain mythic elements, which would seem to place it among those things we call ideals.

UTOPIA

Utopia literally means "nowhere" and was the title of a renowned work of the early sixteenth century humanist and statesman Sir Thomas More (1468–1535). Today the term is applied to literary works published both before and after More, so long as they contain a vision of an ideal society free of the ills and defects of actual historical societies. The utopian vision disposes itself into *explicit* utopias and *implicit* utopias. In the former the writer fictionalizes or phantasizes life in a perfect or nearperfect society. The more ambitious utopists present us with a detailed blueprint, which serves both to dramatize how rotten things are now and how beautiful they could and should be.

Implicit utopias lack the detailed blueprint of explicit utopias. They project instead a view of man and history that makes the arrival of utopia either a distinct possibility or a foregone conclusion. They parry our thrust for more information with the disclaimer that it would be idle or arrogant to legislate for the future. Indeed, it was the tendency of some early socialists to spell out their (explicit) utopias in considerable detail that prompted Karl Marx to coin the critical term "utopian socialism." Nonetheless, Marx's own vision of the classless society of communism is clearly an implicit utopia.

The Millenium

Before the nineteenth century much if not all utopian speculation had a strong religious, even Christian, inspiration. Sir Thomas More's martyrdom and recent canonization were both due to his staunch Roman Catholicism. A latent religiosity still pervades many twentieth-century utopian visions. The type of religious thought that comes closest to the utopian vision is millenarism. Based upon biblical prophecies as in the Old Testament Book of Daniel and the New Testament Book of Revelations, the millenary mentality has been fascinated with the notion of a thousand-year (millenium = 1000 years) reign. According to millenary prophets and self-proclaimed messiahs, the world we now inhabit is permeated through and through with sin. Whereas orthodox Christianity preaches of Paradise in the heavenly afterlife, millenarism more impatiently promises a "new heaven and a new earth" in our time.

For the millenary enthusiast the existing society is plunged so far into sin and moral depravity that catastrophe and cataclysm are necessary to burn away the accumulated evil. Moreover, millenary doctrines make a rigid contrast between the elect and the damned. This means that most people will perish with the world as we know it. In most, but not all, millenary visions the community of the elect will be led to the New Jerusalem by a charismatic leader or messiah.

Since the community of saints will enter into a "land without evil," certain forms of individualism may give way before "primitive communism." Private property, for example, is out for the saints, and the traditional family, and sexual taboos related to the family structure may also be shelved. On account of these extreme views millenary movements tend to run afoul of existing authorities in church and state. The more flamboyant movements usually end up in armed revolt.

The bizarreness of some millenary movements was tragically illustrated by the mass murder–suicide of the followers of the messianic Rev. James Jones at Jonestown, Guyana in November 1978. Jones had shaped a following of the "insulted and the injured" of Northern California and fed them an unbalanced diet of Christian millenary themes and pseudo-Marxism. As with many predecessors, the messiah decided that American society was too corrupt to harbor his movement.

The move to South America, however, proved only a temporary respite and Jones became more and more obsessed with his evil enemies and persecutors. A visit by a California Congressman was apparently the last straw. Jones then ordered a "revolutionary suicide" for all his followers, and, although some coercion was used, many, some people cheerfully and others stoically drank a concoction of Kool-Aid and cyanide.

Although revolutionary suicide was the final expression of disgust with this world for Jones and his cult, this is certainly not the fate of all millenary movements. They often evolve into less alienated and aggressive communities, which compromise with the surrounding world and can even become virtual pillars of the surrounding community. The coming of the millenium is not openly repudiated, but is quietly and gradually deemphasized.

Utopianism

While there are certain family resemblances between millenarism and utopianism, we should not overestimate these resemblances. There is a serenity to most utopian pictures that is foreign to the frenetic ministrations of the typical millenary prophet or messiah. Utopian thought hits several key themes despite the dizzying variety of the actual models. Three main ones are: (1) eradication of social evils, (2) institutionalization of social harmony, and (3) replacement of politics by administration.

Eradication of Social Evils

The utopian mentality displays extreme sensitivity to the ills and problems of the contemporary society. Poverty, ignorance, superstition, crime, aggressiveness, repressive sexual taboos, inequality, political oppression, unhappiness—these and other social blights are at the center of utopian criticism. Naturally, different utopian thinkers will select some social evils as more hateful than others and advocate their removal from the face of utopian society more strongly.

All utopians, however, express "optimism" about human nature and society. That is, they deny that social evils are rooted in human nature. Poverty, aggression, and the rest do not reflect man's unchangeable psychological or biological constitution. Instead, they are the altogether avoidable by-products of a defective social or economic constitution. Some utopians propose to change human nature completely, while others deny that this is really necessary. This second school of thought maintains that man's antisocial tendencies can be contained by the social organization of utopia. Society, not man is the problem!

Look at poverty, for example. The utopian sees poverty either as the result of maldistribution or underproduction (or both). Through the maldistribution of wealth, the division into rich and poor condemns the masses of the people to a life of squalor and indigence. The utopia will somehow equalize distribution, stamping out poverty once and for all. Many utopians hope to parcel out the produce of society according to true human needs. But we find some disagreement about what those needs are and how they are to be met in utopian society.

Utopias of frugality, such as Plato's *Republic* or More's own *Utopia,* teach that the present poverty of the masses stems mostly from the luxurious and frivolous wants of the rich and powerful. Thorstein Veblen's "conspicuous consumption" and "ostentatious wealth" of the "leisure class," mentioned in Chapter 4, gobbles up social wealth in uproarious extravagance.[1] The utopian solution limits needs to those grounded in human nature. No leisure class will be allowed to set false standards. In the utopia of frugality all satisfy their basic physical needs and, undistracted by fraudulent needs, can fully enjoy religious contemplation, philosophical inquiry, or warm and sincere human relationships.

In contrast, *utopias of abundance* such as Marx's future communist society, deny that any limit can or should be set on the expression and evolution of human needs. Instead of taking current consumption patterns as the fixed standard, utopias of abundance place their faith in the fruits of technological progress. These utopias are supposed to liberate technology in a manner closed off to contemporary society. Even presently unforeseeable needs or wants will be easily satisfied. These utopias are based on the boundless potential of automation and human inventiveness.

Both sorts of utopia relate crime to poverty. When poverty goes, so too will crime, at least as a social problem. When the utopia of frugality virtually defines poverty out of existence by legislating social equality and by paring down needs to the minimum, it also banishes the most potent motives for crime. Crime is very much due to wanting something possessed by others. However, in the utopia of frugality no one can flout those things that excite the envy and violence of others. Crime simply makes no sense any more.

The utopia of abundance eliminates crime in a somewhat different way. Here the burgeoning plenty can supply whatever needs sane people might feel. Why use force and fraud to obtain what can be had for the mere asking?

Social Harmony

All utopias institutionalize social harmony. Without exception utopian theorists have an aesthetic and moral revulsion to conflict in human society. Conflict is wasteful and destructive; it pits the members of society against each other. It poisons human relations and brings out the worst in us. Conflict between individuals, groups, and classes is the chief symptom of the sickness of the present order. In possibly the greatest of all utopias, Plato in the *Republic* denies that existing states (poleis) really are states at all "for each of them is not one state, but many: two at least, which are at war with one another, one of the rich, the other of the poor, and each is divided into many more. To treat them all as a single state is a complete mistake."[2]

Banishing conflict and replacing it with utopian harmony has its price. One critic maintains that "utopias are perfect—be it perfectly agreeable or disagreeable—and consequently there is nothing to quarrel about. Strikes and revolutions are as conspicuously absent from utopian societies as are parliaments in which organized groups advance their competing claims for power."[3] Many utopians equate conflict with change and harmony with stability. For this reason there is a static quality to many utopias that ill accords with our modern preoccupation with change.

Yet we should note that if utopia somehow means a "perfect" society, fundamental change could only signify going backward to the less-than-perfect. It is also true that more modern utopias produced under the influence of rapid technological change, tend to be more fluid and avoid the institutional deep-freeze of most pre-nineteenth-century utopias.

Politics or Administration

The classic utopian dream to replace politics by administration involves a peculiar view of both. In the utopian perspective ordinary politics is a shoddy competition for special advantages, privileges, and pay-offs. The politician is seen as a cynical and corrupt egotist ready to steal all he can from the public. Competitive politics is thus an unprincipled, irrational way to run a society. It survives because there is as yet no consensus about the proper ends of society and the appropriate means to achieve them.

A utopia, however, has decided these issues. Because all agree on a certain way of life embodied in certain institutions, political conflict becomes superfluous. The only problem remaining is that of the means and methods required to achieve utopian goals. This is not a political problem, but an administrative problem. Clarity and consensus about goals makes it easy to apply reason and knowledge to implementation. Public policies will find the right answer and will take shape with serenity and scientific detachment.

Because of the sublimation of politics into administration, utopias generally envision rule by an elite of experts. Because administration is a science—at least for most utopians—training and talent available only to a few will characterize a utopia's rulers. We can sense this notion in George Santayana's idea of "rational government," which is based on "a scientific criterion and scientific method."[4] Excluded from the elite would be "prophets, reformers, agitators, politicians, . . . demagogues, . . . persons elected by majority votes."[5] To suit modern conditions the new elite would instead include "anthropologists, medical men, and scientific psychologists . . . ." By maintaining that rational government would be "autocratic but not totalitarian"[6] Santayana represents the antidemocratic character of most utopias.

REVOLUTION

Revolution has become something of a fashionable word in the twentieth century. Not only have communists used the word unceasingly, but a host of movements and regimes both on the right and on the left have intoned "revolution" to describe what they have done or hope to do. Not content with applying the label to 1776, American historians sometimes speak of the Jeffersonian, Jacksonian, and New Deal "revolutions." Often this is mere rhetorical excess, but the ideal or myth of revolution does reverberate mightily through the political spectrum.

In all such uses and abuses of the term "revolution" there remains a sense of dramatic breakthrough, of a pace of change well beyond the normal, of a historical point of no return. There is irony in this because long ago, before the politicization of the term, "revolution" mostly designated circular astronomical movements that return to their starting point.[7] Indeed, the modern idea of revolution presupposes other ideas that are not found before 1600.[8] It requires, for example, a break with the "cyclical" conception that sees history repeating a predetermined sequence of phases. In this view there is no true novelty in the world, only a recurrence of the same events.

Revolt and Revolution

The modern idea of revolution requires some idea of *progress*, the sense that things are not only to be novel, but better as well. Progress means that over time there is growth in the achievement of some value or set of values. The values can be such things as freedom, justice, democracy, peace, equality, enlightenment, prosperity, internationalism, and so on. Progress obviously means that sooner or later a decisive change is possible. If it is to be sooner, the argument may be made that revolution is essential to progress.

This is why revolution should be sharply distinguished from mere *revolt*. Revolt often gets confused with revolution since both involve violence. But the aim of revolt is definitely not to break through to a wholly new society or polity. It aims instead to restore the rights, privileges, economic well-being, or way of life of some group. The sentiment of revolt that sometimes moves declining aristocracies, tax-ridden peasants, starving urban "mobs," or oppressed native peoples is often conservative or even reactionary.

This means that people in revolt do not seriously question the traditional institutions and social relationships. They seek to restore these to their pristine vigor and often protest their loyalty to symbols of traditional authority such as the king. This is well illustrated by medieval baronial rebellions in England, for

> whenever the barons were taking action which might lead to or allow for the fragmentation of the state, they embraced a form of ritual protest in which they affirmed their desire to hold it together. Their charge, that rebellion was against the King's wicked advisers and not against the King himself, served this purpose.[9]

Revolution, on the contrary, aims to go beyond the existing order, not to restore it or reform it. An ideology becomes revolutionary when it attacks the status quo by showing what is wrong and why, and projects some image—perhaps a utopian one—of the postrevolutionary order. Modern revolutionary ideologies, in addition, involve some notion of strategy or how to make the revolution. These strategies single out the main revolutionary forces and the weak points of the old regime.

Violence and Revolution

A common thread of revolutionary strategies is violence. Many revolutionists view violence as a tragic necessity, unavoidable because the ruling classes will not go down without a fight. Karl Marx sometimes saw hope that violence could be avoided in certain countries. But some revolutionary theorists, a minority to be sure, actually envisage a morally purifying role for revolutionary violence. Not only does violence sterilize the postrevolutionary society against the lingering contamination of the past, it even ennobles its practitioners.

Such a vindication of violence comes from Georges Sorel, a French theorist of revolutionary anarcho-syndicalism. At the turn of the century, Sorel was appalled by the "decomposition of Marxism," the loss of revolutionary nerve. Marxist and socialist movements were succumbing to the tranquillizers of parliamentary democracy and social reformism. Their rhetoric was radical, their behavior was conservative. Violence, Sorel claimed, could change all this because violence by the proletariat "not only makes the future revolution certain, but it seems also to be the only means by which European nations—at present stupified by humanitarianism—can recover their former energy. This kind of violence . . . tends to restore to [capitalism] the warlike qualities which it formerly possessed."[10] Then, the militant capitalists will confront the militant workers in class war.

In the Sorelian perspective, proletarian violence appears as a "very fine and heroic thing; it is at the service of the immemorial interests of civilization."[11] Sorel was disgusted by the mediocrity and conformity of modern society and hoped to unleash man's more heroic sentiments. Sometimes he seemed to say that who wins the struggle—the proletariat or the bourgeoisie—is less important than the sublimity of violence itself. The revolution thus becomes less important as the transition point between the old and the new societies and more important as the arena for a liberating and ennobling violence.

Half a century later, the apostleship of violence was taken up by the black writer and psychologist Frantz Fanon (1925–61). Fanon was born in the West Indies but spent most of his adult life in France and North Africa. He was concerned with anticolonialist revolution, especially in Africa. He bitterly resented the inferior status accorded to native black populations by the white settlers and other imperialist overlords. Such sentiments are widely held and natural, but the vehemence with which

Fanon extolled the violent vengeance of the "wretched of the earth" went beyond the ordinary.

The white settlers and imperialist overlords have robbed the native colonial masses of their humanity. They have debauched and degraded them for generations. But Fanon does not see passive acceptance of fate in the native, but rather a smouldering resentment. "The look that the native turns on the settler's town is a look of lust, a look of envy; it expresses his dreams of possession: to sit at the settler's table, to sit in the settler's bed, with his wife if possible. The colonized man is an envious man."[12] The outlet for these pent-up emotions is violence against the settlers and the imperialists.

In Fanon's view, this violence has value at both the collective and individual levels. In the first case violence binds the natives together, "since each individual forms a violent link in the great chain, a part of the great organism of violence which has surged upward in reaction to the settler's violence in the beginning. The groups recognize each other and the future nation is indivisible."[13] Violence is the crucible of the nation-in-formation.

For the individual himself, "violence is a cleansing force. It frees the native from his inferiority complex and from his despair and inaction; it makes him fearless and restores his self-respect."[14] Whether it is Sorel's moralistic approach or Fanon's psychological approach, we certainly appreciate how revolutionary theorists can endow violence with a meaning beyond the "necessary evil." As we will see in chapter 15, it is possibly this taste for violence that makes fascists so enamored of the term "revolution." Clearly it is the case that for some the revolutionary mystique has less to do with a coherent program of social change than it does with the exhilaration of those who practice violence.

The Revolutionary Myth

For many movements and regimes, *their* revolution takes on the aspect of a true and proper myth.[15] The complex reality of actual revolutions is dramatically simplified. The revolution involved is freed of the moral blemishes, the petty cruelties, the doubts and defects, the betrayals and hesitations of actual revolutions. As Mircea Eliade suggests, actual history is replaced by a sacred history narrating the "origins" of movement or regime. Although "supernatural beings" are not literally present at the foundation, revolutionary heroes appear in larger-than-life perspective.

A powerful modern revolutionary myth is that of the French Revolution of 1789. For elements of the French left and center, the Revolution loses the complexity and moral ambiguity of such a massive event. Like the Hollywood movies of old the Revolution is depicted as a "bloc" where the good characters are clearly set off from the bad ones. Arrayed on the side of revolution are progress, enlightenment, equality, fraternity, democracy, and other worthy things; arrayed on the other side are reaction, superstitution, privilege, bondage, repression, and aristocracy.

As a critical historian puts it, one version of the myth runs as follows:

> there was once a social order called feudalism. This was a terrible ogre and lived in a castle; but for centuries a bourgeois Jack the Giant-Killer climbed the beanstock of economic progress, until finally in the French Revolution he liquidated the old order and put in its place something called alternatively bourgeois society or capitalism.[16]

This mythical account of the Revolution short-circuits the full explanation of the real historical event.

The myth of the French Revolution responds to a kind of national nostalgia. A French sociologist once found that his countrymen "have a weakness for the word revolution because they cherish the illusion of being associated with past glories."[17] The myth is especially attractive to intellectuals: "To the intellectual who turns to politics for the sake of diversion, or for a cause to believe in or a theme for speculation, reform is boring and revolution is exciting. The one is prosaic, the other poetic."[18] In modern French politics the myth of the Revolution is always there, just waiting for some symbolic issue to make it surface. For example, discussion over aid to parochial schools often employs the idioms of 1789.

A somewhat similar revolutionary myth has become prevalent in modern Mexico. There a revolution broke out in 1910 and for a decade afterward bloody chaotic factional wars dominated the country. Some semblance of order returned in the 1920s, and in the next decade a stable pattern of government was established. Since then Mexico has been ruled by a single party called the Party of the Institutionalized Revolution (PRI). Under the PRI Mexico has pursued cautious reform, occasionally punctuated by more vigorous attacks on social problems.

The myth of the Mexican Revolution is replete with heroic figures such as peasant leader Emiliano Zapata and the cowboy guerrilla Francisco (Pancho) Villa. The myth contributes much to legitimize the protracted rule of the PRI. As a former president of Mexico put it in 1961:

> The party to which we belong maintains the philosophy of the Mexican Revolution, desires the fulfillment of the constitutional principles which epitomize the ideal and postulates of said revolution, and considers that the measure of our progress is to be found in the improvement of all levels of our society.[19]

It is one of history's many ironies that regimes that are moderate or even counterrevolutionary try to wrap themselves in the mantle of the revolutionary myth. Contemporary Mexico is as good an example of this as any.

CONCLUSION

In this chapter, we have examined utopia, which seems a likely candidate to serve as an ideal, and revolution, which some might argue does not. Utopia is a perennial concern of the urbanized civilizations, because the utopian ideal presents the picture of a social system that has solved social problems once and for all. The utopian vision splits into those elaborate blueprints often found in fiction and those enticing hints scattered through formal social or philosophical treatises. The first we called explicit utopias and the second implicit utopias.

Both types of utopia assume that immediately, or after some transitional period that alters his nature, man can be a worthy inhabitant of the perfect society. For some the movement towards utopia requires a strong revolutionary push; for others, utopia will come, but only after the lengthy accumulation of bit-by-bit improvements that completely transform man and society. Ironically then, the utopian vision sometimes justifies a go-slow approach to social change. Evolution, not revolution, is the preferred pattern.

While utopian literature has grown voluminously through the centuries, our own era has seen the emergence of its opposite—anti-utopian literature. Novels like Eugene Zamiatin's *We* in the 1920s, Aldous Huxley's *Brave New World* in the 1930s, and George Orwell's *1984* in the 1940s described the nightmare societies that could result when attempts were made to harness modern technology to achieve the classic utopian goals of complete social harmony and solution of social problems. However different, these and other anti-utopian novels depict the degeneration of the utopian dream into the totalitarian nightmare.

The utopian disaster occurs when a society seriously tries to fit the square human pegs into the round holes demanded by the regimented social order of the would-be utopia. Human freedom is annihilated as the "new societies" of Zamiatin, Huxley, and Orwell show how privacy is tantamount to treason. Moreover, a ruthless elite of thought-controllers and brainwashers employ the latest techniques to enslave and befuddle the masses, not to liberate them as classic utopias promise.

Though we linked some utopians with a revolutionary approach to change, our own treatment of revolution as an ideal in its own right goes somewhat beyond this. The core of our argument is that since the great

French Revolution of 1789 the exhilaration and violence of revolution have attained a sort of mystique that fully entitles us to agree with a study that sets out to show that "revolution is an ideal as much as it is a process, or a call to action, or a way of life."[20]

NOTES

1. Thorstein Veblen, *The Theory of the Leisure Class* (New York: Funk & Wagnall's, N.D.). Veblen himself produced something of an implicit utopia in his book *The Engineers and the Price System*.
2. Plato, *The Republic*, trans. F. M. Cornford (New York: Oxford University Press, 1960), p. 113.
3. Ralf Dahrendorf, *Essays in the Theory of Society* (Stanford: Stanford University Press, 1968), p. 109.
4. George Santayana, *Dominations and Powers* (New York: Charles Scribner's Sons, 1951), p. 434.
5. Ibid.
6. Ibid., p. 435.
7. See Arthur Hatto, " 'Revolution': An Enquiry into the Usefulness of a Historical Term, " *Mind* 58 (1949), pp. 495–517. Also helpful is Peter Calvert, *Revolution* (New York: Praeger, 1970).
8. Hannah Arendt, *On Revolution* (New York: Viking Press, 1964).
9. Joel T. Rosenthal, "The King's Wicked Advisors and Medieval Baronial Rebellions," *Political Science Quarterly* 87 (1967), p. 609.
10. Georges Sorel, *Reflections on Violence* (Glencoe, Ill.: The Free Press, 1950), p. 106.
11. Ibid., p. 113.
12. Frantz Fanon, *The Wretched of the Earth* (New York: Grove Press, 1968), p. 39.
13. Ibid., p. 93.
14. Ibid., p. 94.
15. The great student of myth, Mircea Eliade points out that "myth narrates a sacred history; it relates an event that took place in primordial time, the fabled time of the 'beginnings.' In other words myth tells how, through the deeds of Supernatural Beings, a reality came into existence, be it the whole of reality, the Cosmos, or only a fragment of reality—an island, a species of plant, a particular kind of human behavior, an institution." *Myth and Reality* (New York: Harper & Row, 1968), pp. 5–6.
16. Alfred Cobban, *Aspects of the French Revolution* (New York: W. W. Norton, 1970), p. 95.
17. Raymond Aron, *The Opium of the Intellectuals* (New York: W. W. Norton, 1962), p. 42.
18. Ibid., p. 43.
19. Adolf Lopez Mateos, "Philosophy and Progress of the Revolutionary Program," in *Is the Mexican Revolution Dead?* ed. S. R. Ross (New York: Alfred A. Knopf, 1967), pp. 169–70.

20. Robert Blackey and Clifford T. Paynton, *Revolution and the Revolutionary Ideal* (Cambridge, Mass.: Schenkman, 1976), p. 4.

SUGGESTIONS FOR FURTHER READING

Carr, E. H. *Studies in Revolution.* New York: Grosset & Dunlop, 1964.
Howe, Irving, ed. *1984 Revisited: Totalitarianism in our Century.* New York: Harper & Row, 1983.
Kateb, George. *Utopia and its Enemies.* New York: Schocken Books, 1972.
Manual, Frank, ed. *Utopias and Utopian Thought.* Boston: Beacon Press, 1967.
Manual, Frank and Manual, Fritzie, eds. *Utopian Thought in the Modern World.* Cambridge, Mass.: Harvard University Press, 1979.
Mumford, Lewis. *The Story of Utopias.* New York: Viking Press, 1971.

7

NEO-INDIVIDUALISM

This chapter deals with three variants of individualism that we call "neo-individualism": libertarianism, radical feminism, and environmentalism. While individualism of one sort or other characterizes much social and political thought over the ages, our three versions of neo-individualism respond to concerns surfacing in a particularly acute way in recent times.

LIBERTARIANISM

While the libertarian ideal of individualism has certain family resemblances with the neoclassical defense of capitalism (Chapter 4), anarcho-individualism (Chapter 8), and classic liberalism (Chapter 12), it is reducable to none of these. Libertarianism can only be fully understood against the backdrop of the emergence of totalitarianism and the modern welfare state since the 1930s.

Libertarianism represents the most radical form of individualism, short of outright anarchism. However, while the leading schools of anarchism have generally rejected capitalism in favor of some sort of "socialism," libertarianism exalts the pure capitalist economy as the surest expression and defense of individuality. Nevertheless, the near anarchism of some libertarian doctrines has prompted the expression "anarcho-capitalism." However, the libertarian defense of capitalism would legitimize a degree of economic inequality that true anarchists could not abide.

The highly personalized work of Ayn Rand is a leading expression of the libertarian ideal of individualism, even if it sometimes takes an extreme and occasionally unrepresentative form. A brilliant novelist, she developed the libertarian ideal both in fictional works and polemical essays. Originally from Russia, Rand's bitter hatred for communism carries over into anything that smacked of "collectivism," whether in economics, politics, or morality.

More than a true political philosophy, Rand's teaching constitutes a moral credo that raises individuality to the highest level. Utterly rejecting any theological notions or ideas that rank the community over the individual, she held that the individual is the basic unit of society, the prime focus of moral concern, and the sole source of human creativity.

The root cause of our modern troubles is the philosophy of *altruism*, a moral position that effectively destroys the supreme value of individuality. Altruism, the notion that man should place the welfare of others above his own, is the root of all evil, not money. Indeed, money is cherished by Rand as a just reward and fair estimation of the individual's inherent excellence. For this reason the mouthpiece character John Galt, in her novel *Atlas Shrugged*, further maintains that "the moral symbol of respect for human beings, is *the trader*. We, who live by values, not by loot, are traders, both in matter and in spirit. A trader is a man who earns what he gets and does not give or take the undeserved."[1]

Rand's uncompromising attack on all forms of altruism went so far that she entitled a book of essays *The Virtue of Selfishness*. And indeed in her philosophy altruism is a vice and selfishness a virtue. Such a reversal of what some consider the central tenet of the Judeo-Christian ethic is no accident. For Rand altruism is degrading and demoralizing both for the self and the other (alter in Latin means other). On the other hand, selfishness for Rand does not mean a petty, sniveling self-indulgence, but rather accepting full personal responsibility for one's life and fate. Clearly, if everyone were selfish in this sense, the purported need for altruism—taking care of others—would in most cases disappear.

Altruism is the villain of the piece because it plays upon the morbid guilt feelings of the donor and keeps the recipient in a state of childish subservience. Neither party can develope a mature, confident outlook on life, which, of course, should culminate in a fair and equitable and truly voluntary exchange of goods and services. The ethics of altruism is always gratuitous: it preaches that someone has a prescriptive right to a free ride on someone else's back.

The extreme form of this is seen in any doctrine that holds that self-sacrifice is the highest good. For Rand the notion that one person should sacrifice himself for the sake of another is radically evil. It is an affront to human dignity and an open invitation to prefer death over life. It is thus clear that many elements of Christian moral teaching—self-sacrifice, the duty of charity, renunciation, even "turning the other cheek"—run afoul of Rand's notion of individuality.

From this standpoint modern socialism and welfare-state theories simply politicize the notion that man, indeed, is his "brother's keeper." Such noxious notions are so deeply engrained in our culture that a genuine individualism plays virtually against a stacked deck. This results in a misplaced sense of duty that makes the truly excellent individual feel remorse even in his own achievement, which necessarily places him far above the ordinary run of men.

Ethical altruism and its political correlates, socialism and welfarism, thus allow second-rate human types to transform their sense of envy and inferiority into a supposedly valid moral position. Rand uses harsh language like "moochers" and "looters" to describe the behavior of those who would either play upon the guilt feelings of the creative minority or employ the unabashed force of the state to fleece the creators of wealth of their well-gotten gains.

Rand is openly elitist and if she fails to use the "superman" rhetoric of Friedrich Nietzsche, it is clear that the chosen few are the ultimate concern of her work. The heroes and heroines of her novels are uncompromising nonconformists with an almost obsessive love for their chosen line of work. Howard Roark of *The Fountainhead* is an avant-garde architect whose break with traditional styles runs into the simple-minded prejudice of the mediocrities that surround him. He is almost persecuted for his genius and is recognized by only a few choice spirits who operate on the same elevated plane as he.

Dagny Taggart of *Atlas Shrugged* is an aloof super-manager of a railroad line, who struggles valiantly against the incompetence and superciliousness of her brother and a swarm of public policies that penalize excellence in the name of a morbid egalitarianism. The "looters" that ultimately destroy the American and world economy in *Atlas Shrugged* are a bizarre coalition of misguided "altruistic" idealists and cynical opportunists who live parasitically upon the talent of a shrinking remnant of creative industrialists. The total economic collapse that ensues is the inevitable result of tying the hands of the natural aristocracy of creative economic leaders.

Rand's rendition of libertarianism thus involves an elitism that differs somewhat from the traditional defenses of aristocracy and of capitalism. In the first case, traditional aristocratic doctrines defend the privileged position of the select minority because it rules for the sake of the whole community. In the second, we can recall Adam Smith's idea that capitalism benefits the whole community by creating the maximum of social wealth, part of which trickles down to the lower orders of society.

While such notions are not totally absent from Rand's philosophy, it is clear that, for her, defending institutions on "public" or "community" grounds is fraught with danger. Thus, the life and work of the Howard Roarks and Dagny Taggarts and the rest have an intrinsic value. Society is almost irrelevant or positively threatening to their achievement. We can see this when she reverses the usual notion that morals would be irrelevant to a Robinson Crusoe alone on his island, and maintains instead that without morals the stranded Englishman would soon come to grief. This is so because, for Rand, morality is really a system of rules necessary to maintain human existence, not simply a set of social principles.

Rand called her philosophy "objectivism." Calling herself a modern disciple of Aristotle, she maintained that objective truth could be reached through the faculty of rationality, which is lodged only in the minds of discrete individuals. "Mysticism" in all forms was the enemy of clear thinking and right action. Indeed, she dubbed "mystics of the spirit" all those who sought to degrade man beneath a nonexistent divinity and "mystics of muscle" all those who sought to degrade him by force below some nonexistent higher "social" good. "No matter how loudly they posture in the roles of irreconcilable antagonists, their moral codes are alike, and so are their aims: in matter—the enslavement of man's body, in spirit—the destruction of his mind."[2]

Because of this ultrasensitivity to the rights and privileges of human personality, the libertarianism of Rand and others hates anything smacking of coercion. Particularly vulnerable here are the policies of the welfare state because they involve a redistribution of wealth through the monies, goods, and services dispensed by government. Should those whose wealth is taken by taxes and other forms of government revenue demur, the force of the state is there to make them fork it over.

Far superior to this coercive exchange of goods and services is one that is purely voluntary. This would mean dismanteling much of the apparatus of modern government or "privatizing" the public sector. Voluntary exchanges would replace public policies and thus coerciveness would disappear. Now many "conservatives" would like to cut government down, but often their argument focuses on alleged inefficiency. The distinctly libertarian argument is that government beyond the very barest minimum is in itself an unwarranted abridgement of human freedom.

RADICAL FEMINISM

What we call radical feminism must be distinguished from certain kindred movements and ideologies, before we can really appreciate how it represents a true variant of neo-individualism. In the last century many reformist and radical movements took up the cause of women's rights. It must be recalled that in the Victorian era, in addition to a whole range of legal disabilities, custom and tradition had marked out a certain "place" for women in the social order that was completely different from that occupied by men. Women, of course, could not vote or hold office; in most cases they were excluded from the professions; and at home, they were under the strict tutelage of fathers, husbands, or other male "protectors."

Moreover, there was a clear "double standard" in sexual mores insofar as men could indulge themselves in forms of behavior that were absolutely ruinous for women. Having children out of wedlock was a cause of immediate social and even familial ostracism. A woman was "fallen," while a man was merely "sowing his wild oats." In the light of the extreme disparities between the rights and privileges of the two sexes, Victorian reformers like the liberal John Stuart Mill made progress in the women's question part of their social and reform agendas. More radical thinkers like the Marxist August Bebel maintained that only with the coming of socialism would their be a quantum leap in the position of women in society.

At the very close of the nineteenth century, Thorstein Veblen's *The Theory of the Leisure Class* (1899) argued almost satirically that the showy but nonproductive position of upper class women resulted from the male-dominated leisure class's need to display them as virtual trophies. According to Veblen the leisure class sought ways to show that its way of life had nothing whatever to do with productive activity. These ignoble pursuits were assigned to the lower classes. Even earlier, however, women were victimized in a different way because the warrior elite that is the forerunner of the present-day leisure class could only emerge by foisting upon women the everyday drudgery of menial tasks necessary to keep the primitive community going.

In Veblen's day the women's movement was dominated by the suffragettes, who demanded the vote for women. It is sometimes forgotten that the suffragettes, especially in the United States and Great Britain, were driven to violence, though rather mild, in order to demonstrate their point. When women's suffrage came to most countries just after World War I, women's activists went after the formidiable array of legal and cultural barriers to greater equality between the sexes.

In the 1960s and 1970s "women's liberation" became rather more militant because in the opinion of many women the gains obtained from the 1920s to the 1950s, though real, were too little and mostly too late. In the United States the "equal rights amendment" (ERA), as yet unenacted, became the rallying symbol for a divergent coalition of those unhappy with lingering inequalities for women.

What we call "radical feminism" is not synonymous with the trend toward greater equality for women, support for ERA, or even "women's lib" in general. These things are supported by women who are often moderate or even conservative in their political views. Radical feminism is *radical* and radical means going to the roots of anything. This means that attacking lingering abuses one by one or "raising the consciousness" of women is by no means sufficient to effect the degree of change contemplated or implied in radical feminism. Many ardent women's rights activists want substantial change but they do not envisage the complete rethinking of the concepts of man and woman, male and female, masculine and feminine that radical feminism entails.

Radical feminism is indeed a form of individualism and it maintains that the present structure of society along with the beliefs that support it are still highly repressive of a genuine individuality. While not denying the severity of repression along the lines of class or race—the kind that ordinary radicalism protests against and wishes to remedy, radical feminism sees the repression of women as far more significant and really the key to eliminating all forms of repression. In fact, some radicals, even if successful in their hopes for change, would unwittingly perpetuate the repression of women and thus fail in their ultimate goal of a free society.

This can happen, radical feminists argue, because they are willingly or unwillingly subject to the ideas and institutions of *patriarchy*. Patriarchy is a broad term that suggests that the basic unit of society is the family and that the father is the "natural" head of the family. By extension patriarchy means that older men have power and authority in all social institutions whether civil, ecclesiastical, or political. Extreme examples abound as with the Roman paterfamilias, who virtually had the right of life and death over wife, children, and other dependents.

Despite changes over the centuries, "our society, like all other historical civilizations, is a patriarchy. The fact is evident at once if one recalls that the military, industry, technology, universities, science, political office, and finance—in fact, every avenue of power . . . is entirely in male hands."[3] The circumscribed role and status of women as well as their lack of opportunity is deeply engrained in the institutions and underlying beliefs of modern civilization. The male preponderance in positions of power, prestige, and wealth is accepted as "natural," "just," inevitable,"—in short, as legitimate. This is so because members of both sexes are indoctrinated with a value system and general view of the world that assumes and sanctifies patriarchy.

Thus, even today when certain past extremes of patriarchy have been subdued in "advanced countries," beliefs and behavior confirm that women are fit to do certain things and not others and that men are fit to do certain things and not others. That women's roles are almost always inferior, subordinate, and demeaning follows naturally from the patriarchical "ideology" that both sexes subscribe to. Since ideological beliefs govern behavior, women act in a way that reinforces the stereotypes that both sexes share about women. There is no apparent way to break out of this vicious cycle.

The basic premise of the patriarchical ideology is that the division of labor, functions, roles, and status between men and women is *natural*. That is, the institutional forms and cultural attitudes reflect biological differences between the two sexes. "Machismo," the stereotype of the aggressive, domineering male as opposed to the timid, submissive female is thereby grounded in the unalterable constitution of reality.

But for radical feminists this is the fatally weak link in the chain of argument essential to the patriarchical ideology. This is so because though there may be some natural sexual differences, these in no way support the masculine-feminine dichotomy that undergirds patriarchical society. Thus, attitudes towards what is properly masculine and what is properly feminine are *products of culture, not nature*. We have simply been socialized into accepting the invidious contrast of male-female stereotypes as iron-clad laws of nature.

These delusions have been perpetuated so long because as the dominant group, men have a vested interest in legitimizing their position. As Kate Millet puts it:

> Important new research not only suggests that the possibilities of innate temperamental differences seem more remote than ever, but even raises questions as to the validity and permanence of psycho-sexual identity. In doing so it gives fairly concrete positive evidence of the overwhelmingly cultural *character* of gender, i.e. personality in terms of sexual identity.[4]

This means that practically everything about the roles and status of contemporary men and women is based on myth.

If half the members of contemporary society are deformed and stunted by such an arbitrary system, there can be no genuine individuality and individualism. A true individualism would have to sweep away the repressive relics of patriarchy and the baseless stereotypes of gender and see what new forms of individuality and personality would develop when we start from scratch. Radical feminism is a very militant radicalism because it must consider every institution and every social custom as indelibly tainted by patriarchical ideas.

ENVIRONMENTALISM

Concern with the environment is largely a twentieth-century development. Only by then have the negative results of the Industrial Revolution reached a critical level. But is such a concern an "ism" and an ism that qualifies as an ideal. The answer naturally depends on what precisely one means by environmentalism. A British statesman at the turn of the century once said, "We are all socialists now," and it might be said in our time that "we are all environmentalists now." The British statesman meant that virtually all agreed on using government to help the poor and the needy. Similarly, today everyone wants to "protect the environment." However, neither a turn of the century socialist or a contemporary environmentalist would be satisfied with such vague accounts of their special "ism."

At the risk of some oversimplification, we will present a view of environmentalism that does have the substance and coherence of an ideal, if not of an ideology. It is an ideal that involves a "world-view" clashing sharply with certain assumptions of other ideals and ideologies found in this book. The world-view involved strikes its most telling blows against the optimistic notion of progress that we find in communism, liberalism, and utopias of abundance.

One version of the progress doctrine highlights material and technological progress. In this view, the development of scientific knowledge will bring technological applications, which will alleviate and someday eliminate human misery. A day will come with a more abundant life for all on a global scale. Karl Marx argued that the coming of communism would so liberate technology that man would be truly free—this is still the guiding assumption of the communist East. Herbert Spencer argued that only capitalism would speed us towards peace, progress, and prosperity—in many ways this is still the guiding assumption of the capitalist West.

An implicit assumption of these progress theories is that the energy needed to run the technology is virtually boundless. Though technology uses energy, the optimistic view maintains that technology itself will find new and alternative sources of energy to keep the engine of progress running. The conservatives and other dissenters who pointed to the social and environmental costs involved in indiscriminate growth could be dismissed as hysterical Cassandras born too late or quaint aesthetes with little knowledge and less liking of the common man. The evidence was all in favor of the optimists.

However, after World War II and especially after 1960, events began to take a hand. Air and water traditionally considered limitless gifts of nature looked more and more like scarce resources. The pollution problem, always present, rose higher on the agenda of industrialized countries. Economists began to emphasize "externalities," the harmful side-effects of industrial production, as an ever more serious concern. But perhaps the grand blow was administered by the Arab oil embargo of 1973–74. The shortages and rapid and steep price hikes that resulted made the point painfully clear that energy resources could be depleted and substitutes highly costly or nonexistent. There was a rather glaring contradiction to undiluted optimism.

For Jeremy Rifkin these events spelled the death of progressivist optimism and the birth of a new "world-view." The new approach would be based on a more valid understanding of science and the recognition that a technological impasse had been reached. Though not the first to do so, he based his "agonizing reappraisal" of reigning theories and practices upon the notion of "entropy" in physics.[5] Here we can only hope to get a nontechnical idea of this application of Newton's second law of thermodynamics. The general meaning of the entropy principle is that whenever any process using energy in the physical universe occurs, some of that energy is irretrievably lost. Though energy cannot be created or destroyed in the absolute sense, expenditures of energy deplete the bank of usable energy. In the classic example, there can be no "perpetual motion machine" that runs forever. Sooner or later it will run down.

When entropy increases (i.e., when needed energy is lessening in a system) the system becomes disorganized and malfunctions. A trivial example would be the erratic course and ultimate fall of a smoothly running top, after the kinetic energy imparted to it with our initial snapping movement runs out. More broadly,

> The Entropy Law says that evolution dissipates the overall energy for life on this planet. Our concept of evolution is the exact opposite. We believe that evolution somehow magically creates greater overall value and order on earth. Now that the environment we live in is becoming so dissipated and disordered that it is apparent to the naked eye, we are for the first time beginning to have second thoughts about our views on evolution, progress, and the creation of things of material value.[6]

Of course, the ultimate implication of the entropy principle is the running down of the cosmos, but before that happens we have plenty to worry about.

Under the twin illusions of virtually boundless progress and of technology's ability to solve the problems that it itself has created, mankind has launched on a ruthless race to manufacture as much as it can for immediate consumption. The symptoms of this ruthlessless, of course, are the environmental, economic, energy, and population crises. Rather than an unlucky convergence of independent negative trends, these crises, with their social and political ramifications, are ultimately traceable to the "entropy crisis." We have gambled on nature's boundless generosity and the game is now going against us. Since energy is not limitless, we have had too many systems operating at more than full energy capacity, and now those systems display the signs of "system overload" and shutdown.

Most disheartening is the conclusion that higher technology in a broader entropic perspective is by no means more efficient than lower technology. More sophisticated technologies are simply different, not necessarily better, ways of doing things. The problem is that high technology generally involves greater utilization of energy resources, many of which are nonrenewable. Indeed, "the faster we streamline our technology, the faster we speed up the transforming process, the faster available energy is dissipated, the more the disorder mounts."[7] Quite simply, without a radical change in perspective, we are on a collision course with disaster. Whether we call it an "eco-crisis" (ecology crisis) or even more broadly an "entropy crisis" radical environmentalists see doom ahead.

The only alternative, they say, is a dramatic change in world-view. Conservation efforts help, but they do not really attack the heart of the problem. A world-view based on entropy means a radical reconstruction of our ideal of human existence and the good life. This involves a new attitude towards ourselves and nature, which will lead to a dramatically new set of social priorities as well as a new set of expectations in the life-style of individual citizens. "In a low-entropy culture the individual is expected to live a more frugal or Spartan life style . . . . In the new age, the less production and consumption necessary to maintain a healthy, decent life, the better."[8]

In Jeremy Rifkin's view, this changeover from an affluent or "high-entropy" society to a low entropy society bears the aspect of a religious reformation. Indeed, "all of the great teachers of wisdom have embraced the values inherent in low entropy life. Buddha, Jesus, Muhammed, and the prophets of Israel, the mahatmas of India all led exemplary lives of simplicity, voluntary poverty, and communal sharing."[9]

All of these saints and prophets, of course, also claimed that the more ascetic life style would actually liberate the individual from the rat-race of competition and the self-defeating quest for material aggrandizement. Simplicity meant freedom. Although not all environmentalists would go so far, they generally recommend a de-emphasis on those material goods whose production requires so much energy as to worsen the "crisis," however precisely it is characterized. This is why environmentalist movements, like the "Greens" in West Germany who were able to win representation in parliament, are sometimes criticized as middle class. As they change life styles so as to put less emphasise on consumer goods and creature comforts, they are possibly threatening the present jobs and satisfactions of lower class people. These latter have at long last reached a certain standard of living that eluded their fathers and grandfathers, and now they are asked to cut back on their consumption patterns because of environmentalist concerns.

CONCLUSION

We have surveyed three highly distinctive versions of what we called neo-individualism. While the animating themes of each naturally have roots in the past, each has taken new meaning in the 1960s and 1970s. Each is a "radical" doctrine because it challenges so fundamentally the reigning assumptions of western countries, if not the whole world. Each preaches a form of individualism that either seeks to protect individuality from certain clear and present dangers or to change dramatically those patterns of thought and behavior that obstruct the emergence of a truly free human individual.

Libertarianism finds individuality so threatened by the modern welfare state that it hopes to dismantle government and distribute its functions to voluntary agencies that work for a profit. The present system not only foils our freedom by a maze of laws, rules, and regulations, it forces us to pay for services we neither want nor need in the form of taxes. This amounts to the forcible confiscation of the wealth that the individual has produced.

The "looters" and "moochers" who thrive on this iniquitous system prey upon the bogus guilt feelings that altruistic doctrines of all sorts arouse in the productive and creative members of society. Only by returning to the principle of fair and voluntary exchange for all goods and services with the market as ultimate arbiter can liberty and individuality be rescued.

Radical feminism is discontented, but for other reasons. Despite token and superficial changes, all existing societies are patriarchies that institutionalize a false and debasing inequality between the sexes. Based on the erroneous principle that contemporary roles of men and women somehow reflect innate personality differences between the sexes, patriarchy prevents half the population of all societies from developing their truly human (not male, not female) potential. Only a dramatic change of thinking will make women's liberation a reality, not just a slogan.

Environmentalism, at least in the version we have described, also demands a radical rexamination of the basic principles underlying our society. Our faith in technological progress, which began in the seventeenth century has led us to the brink of disaster. We have raped the environment and now the victim is striking back. We have ignored the clear implications of the well established entropy principle that energy is limited, not boundless. Warning signals of the future disaster, such as the various energy crises, should bring it home to modern man that he has pursued the strange gods of massive wealth and superabundant technology far too long. A return to a simpler life will not only alleviate the entropy crisis, it will bring us together as individuals, and bring us closer to nature. There, as many have taught through the ages, is where true freedom lies.

NOTES

1. Ayn Rand, *Atlas Shrugged* (New York: New American Library, 1957), p. 948.
2. Ibid., p. 953.
3. Kate Millet, *Sexual Politics* (New York: Ballantine Books, 1983), pp. 33–34.
4. Ibid., p. 39.
5. See Henry Adams, *The Degradation of the Democratic Dogma* (New York: Capricorn Books, 1958).
6. Jeremy Rifkin, *Entropy: A New World View* (New York: Viking Press, 1980), p. 55.
7. Ibid., p. 79.
8. Ibid., p. 208.

SUGGESTIONS FOR FURTHER READING

Ellul, Jacques. *The Technological Society*. New York: Vintage Books, 1969.
Millett, Kate. *Sexual Politics*. New York: Ballantine Books, 1978.
Rand, Ayn. *Atlas Shrugged*. New York: New American Library, 1957.
———. *The Virtue of Selfishness: A New Concept of Egoism*. New York: New American Library, 1964.
Rifkin, Jeremy. *Entropy: A New World View*. Viking Press, 1980.

PART 2

IDEOLOGIES

We are about to take a journey across the left–right ideological spectrum. But what do the terms left, right, and center really mean? Historically they refer to something rather trivial: the sitting arrangement in French parliaments in the years following the French Revolution of 1789. It so transpired that advocates of more political, social, and economic equality sat together on the left side of the semicircular legislative chamber, while their bitterest enemies, who disdained egalitarianism in favor of traditional political, social, and economic hierarchies, congregated on the right side. The moderate elements had little choice but to occupy the rows of seats in the center.

As time went on the term "left," "right," and "center" were applied to what the French called "spiritual families." The leftist spiritual family responded to such symbols as revolution, equality, socialism; the one in the center favored liberty, constitutionalism, property, and equality of opportunity; the one on the right looked to tradition, order, religion, monarchy, and aristocracy. Because much the same trio of spiritual families was found in most countries of nineteenth-century Europe, it was but a short step to apply "left," "right," and "center" everywhere in the West.

While in general we can say that the whole spectrum moved to the left in the one-hundred odd years from the fall of Napoleon I to the outbreak of World War I, the three labels covered more or less coherent groupings. The problem in the classification arose after World War I when communism and fascism emerged as so-called totalitarian movements. Whereas communism was supposedly on the far left and fascism on the far right, the political style of these movements, and the highly repressive regimes instituted in their name, caused some observers to claim that these were kindred phenomena. Indeed, Friedrich and Brzezinski's classic *Totalitarian Dictatorship and Autocracy* (1956) argued that, from that standpoint of political regimes, fascism and communism were "basically alike."

If such basic similarities were more important than apparent differences, then conceiving far left and far right as opposites on a spectrum would make little sense. This conclusion, however, was based on the policies and performance of Stalin's Russia (1929–53), Nazi Germany (1933–45), and Fascist Italy (1922–43), not on a convergence of ideological principles. Indeed, the communists contrived to distinguish themselves as much as possible from the fascists, while the latter considered themselves the staunch defenders of a western civilization threatened by the "Bolshevik" peril.

Our conclusion can only be that at least on the plane of ideology, the emergence of "totalitarianism" has not cancelled out important differences of principle between the opposed ends of the spectrum. This is the rationale for the precise sequence of chapters that follows.

8

ANARCHISM

Anarchism both as an ideology and a political movement seemed an endangered species after World War I. The last two decades have seen a comeback, however. Works that had been out of print for nearly half a century were reissued in cheap editions and anarchist slogans sounded on the streets and on the campus. There were many reasons for this resurgence. The "affluent society," while it doubtless mitigated poverty, alienated and antagonized groups of young people and intellectuals. They found contemporary society ugly, unjust, repressive, and crass. The business-dominated society of the West was hardly distinguishable from the bureaucracy-dominated society of the East. These discontented people saw in anarchism a revolutionary doctrine and style that cast a plague on the houses of both capitalism and communism.

Anarchism literally means no-rule or no-government. For centuries anarchism was an undercurrent found mostly among poets and religious/philosophical sectarians. It was hardly a political theory, let alone an ideology. Only in the decades before and after 1800 did anarchism become a doctrine with a message for the twentieth century. In this chapter we will first consider two types of pure anarchism, classic anarchism and anarcho-syndicalism; then we will cover individualistic anarchism or "anarcho-individualism."

CLASSIC ANARCHISM

Two Russian thinkers bring classic anarchism from the middle of the last century to the first part of the present one. They are the aristocratic revolutionaries Michael Bakunin (1814–76) and Peter Kropotkin (1842–1921). Their myriad writings cover the keynotes of classic anarchist doctrine: (1) the negation of the state; (2) the abolition of private property; (3) revolution; (4) the attack on religion; and (5) the new cooperative order.

The Negation of the State

"Anarchy" in one connotation suggests chaos or violent disorder. Though some anarchists advocate this sort of "anarchy" as a step toward a new society, the ultimate anarchy they seek would be peaceful, orderly, and cooperative. But it would be an order without the state as we know it. Whether it would be without rules or governance of any sort is a more problematic issue. At any rate, classical anarchists like Bakunin or Kropotkin attack the modern centralized bureaucratic state as the negation of human freedom.

The state is the enemy; every moment longer it lasts is a standing affront to human dignity and freedom. The state has arisen from violence and conquest. Though it may on rare occasions play a positive role, it bears the earmarks of its origins. It is ever the tool of a clique of exploiters against the rest of society. Bakunin denies that the state is "a natural human society which supports and reinforces the life of everyone by the life of all—quite the contrary, it is the immolation of every individual as well as of local associations . . . it is the limitation, or rather the complete negation, of the life and of the rights of all the parts [of the whole society]."[1] The state is a bloodsucker drawing its vitality from the society of victims.

Of course, many nonanarchists have expressed fear of the state. And yet, they generally felt that with democracy or socialism the state would cease to be the tool of the rapacious few and serve the whole people instead. Bakunin dismissed such thinking as a cruel hoax. Reforms in the state, no matter how radical, signify at best a change in masters, not an end to domination. A "democratic" state is a change in form alone from the absolutism of the most tyrannical autocrat.

Indeed, a so-called democratic state may be worse than others, since it covers up its oppressiveness with the fake trappings of "majority rule" and the "will of the people." Democratic paraphernalia cannot, however, disguise the hierarchic and minoritarian character of the state. There will always be a dominant clique, which is the true and sole beneficiary of the state. Even the election of "workers' representatives" to "bourgeois" parliaments changes nothing, for when these people move into a "purely bourgeois environment and into an atmosphere of purely bourgeois political ideas," they will "become middle class in their outlook, perhaps even more than the bourgeois themselves."[2] This is the chief reason why universal suffrage is "the surest means of making the masses cooperate in the building of their own prison."[3]

If a change in the political order avails nothing, perhaps changing the economic bases of society to socialism will be strong enough medicine. Though Bakunin wanted pure socialism badly, he completely rejected the idea that it could do much to moralize and humanize the state. This issue was involved in his long and bitter dispute with Karl Marx. Marx had always maintained that the state would *temporarily* survive the overthrow of capitalism and the beginnings of socialism. In his counterblast at Marx, Bakunin foreshadowed much that occurred after the Russian Revolution of 1917. While a socialist or "people's" state might kick out the old privileged classes, he warned that it too involved a government, which along with the usual political administration

> will also administer the masses economically, concentrating in the hands of the State the production and division of wealth, the cultivation of land, the establishment and development of factories. . . . All that will demand an immense knowledge and many heads 'overflowing with brains' in this government. It will be the reign of *scientific intelligence*, the most aristocratic, despotic, arrogant, and elitist of all regimes.[4]

In this we sense the "anti-intellectualism" that prevails in certain anarchist circles. Such a viewpoint takes the dual form of disdain for intellectuals and a preference for philosophies that play down the role of reason or intellect in human affairs. We will see this again with Sorel's anarcho-syndicalism.

The Abolition of Private Property

Bakunin thought of himself as a "socialist" and his successor as chief theoretician of anarchism, Peter Kropotkin, often used the expression "anarchist communism." Kropotkin put this position simply and clearly:

> In common to all socialists, the anarchists hold that the private ownership of land, capital, and machinery has had its time; that it is condemned to disappear; and that all the requisites for production must, and will become the common property of society, and be managed in common by the producers of wealth.[5]

He and his mentor agreed that private property inevitably produces classes, which leads in turn to the state.

Because private property is the precondition of capitalism, it is no surprise that it possesses a virtually divine sanction for the bourgeoisie. According to Bakunin, "property is a god," which has "its theology" and its "morality."[6] Private property allows the accumulation of capital, which means that some people can live "without working" on the backs and labor of others. "Morality, as the bourgeois understands it, consists in exploiting someone else's labor."[7]

Once the system of private property is abolished and replaced by common ownership, man will become truly free. His only constraints will be the laws of nature, not the laws of the state. But freedom under socialism will be real and secure only if the state accompanies private property into the museum of historical antiquities.

Revolution

Classical anarchism is revolutionary. Neither the advance of humanity nor true freedom can coexist with capitalism and the state. Both Bakunin and Kropotkin as well as their present-day disciples became revolutionary activists. The two Russians even spent time in prison for their exertions. They believed that the sole escape from the modern state's tyranny was to destroy it root and branch. Violence is necessary as the ruling classes will resist their displacement. Bakunin's customary pithiness is represented in his statement that "revolutions are not a children's game nor an academic debate where only vanities kill each other, nor yet a literary joust where only ink is spilt. Revolution is war, and whoever says war says destruction of men and things."[8]

Several points distinguish the classical anarchist. One is repudiation of political parties as the organization weapon for the revolution. Anarchists see political parties as organizations that by violence or guile seek political power in the state. Parties, thus, are part of the problem, not part of the solution. They are forever implicated with the state and a party aiming to abolish the state is a contradiction in terms. Understandably, anarchists never call their political organizations parties and never or almost never participate in elections or governments.[9] They refer to their often loosely organized groups as "alliances," "federations," "confederations," "unions," and the like.

Our second point concerns the love–hate relationship between classic anarchists and revolutionary socialists of the Marxist persuasion. Orthodox Marxists look to the "proletariat" or urban industrial working class as the revolutionary class par excellence. Following Marx, they ridicule the revolutionary pretensions of other classes. Bakunin and other anarchists, on the contrary, denied that the organized industrial workers were the true "flower of the proletariat." More worthy of this tribute was "that great *rabble of the people* . . . ordinarily designated by Marx and Engels in the picturesque and contemptuous phrase *Lumpenproletariat*, I have in mind that 'riff-raff,' that 'rabble' almost unpolluted by bourgeois civilization."[10] This outcast group bore within itself "all the seeds of the socialism of the future" and was alone "powerful enough" to pull off the "social revolution."[11]

Bakunin also turned the tables on Marx with respect to other groups. For example, Marx considered peasants a reactionary group too divided and narrow-minded to join the revolution. Bakunin felt that even though peasants might heed the revolutionary call more slowly than workers, they were still ready for it. Three things predisposed the peasants to revolution: first, the "barbarous" civilization of the peasants kept them uncorrupted and preserved their "simple, robust temperament and . . . energy." Next, hard manual labor produced "an instinctive hatred for all the privileged parasites of the state, and for all exploiters of labor." Finally, despite certain prejudices peasants are in fact joined to the workers by their "common interests" as "toilers."[12]

Despite such professions of faith in the masses, Bakunin sometimes favored closed conspiracies. This led him at one point to an alliance with a particularly unscrupulous revolutionist by the name of Sergei Nechaev. Nechaev was the main author of the so-called "Revolutionist's Catechism." This document represents the harsher side of anarchism as a movement that sometimes advocated "propaganda by deed" (i.e., terrorism). Two passages will give the flavor of this "catechism," which is an extreme and minority statement:

> The revolutionist is a doomed man. He has no personal interests, no affairs, sentiments, attachments, property, not even a name of his own. Everything in him is absorbed by one exclusive interest, one thought, one passion—the revolution.
>
> The whole ignoble social system must be divided into several categories. In the first category are those who are condemned to death without delay. The association should draw up a list of persons thus condemned in the order of their relative harmfulness to the cause so that the preceding numbers may be removed before the subsequent ones.[13]

While Nechaev's ruthlessness was atypical, it must be recalled that terrorism and assassination have sometimes been the stock in trade of certain professed anarchists.

The Attack on Religion

Of all modern ideologies classic anarchism launched perhaps the most vigorous attack on religion. Whereas Marx dismissed religion as an "opiate of the people," the anarchists expended more time denouncing religion. One reason for this was philosophical. Religion is a form of idealism or spiritualism that contradicted the materialistic view of modern science. Religion had no basis in reality; it was superstition through and through. As Bakunin saw it, whoever needs religious or theological mysteries must "renounce his reason and return, if he can, to naive, blind, stupid faith. . . ."[14]

But it is clearly more than the falsehood of religion that prompted Bakunin to say that "if God really existed, it would be necessary to abolish him."[15] What enflamed many anarchists was the social and political role of religion. Both Bakunin and Kropotkin saw religion as a buttress of the hated state. Priests and rulers had for centuries engaged in a vicious conspiracy to defraud the people of their liberties. Organized religion thus served to keep the masses in bondage to the powers that be.

Particularly offensive was the Christian doctrine of "original sin," according to which all mankind was justly punished for the primordial rebellion of Adam and Eve against God. It depicted man as a fallen, weak creature fit only for the tutelage of priests and governments. Thus theology gave a religious justification to the state's authority. The anarchist answer was to expose the fraud. As Bakunin asked rhetorically, "Is it necessary to point out to what extent and in what manner religions debase and corrupt the people? They destroy their reason, the principal instrument of human emancipation, and reduce them to imbecility, the essential condition of their slavery."[16]

The New Cooperative Order

We have established that anarchists preach the destruction of the modern state and its apparatus. But does this necessarily involve abolition of all authority and organization? The answer is clearly negative. While rejecting all supernatural claims of authority, Bakunin accepted, as do most anarchists, a kind of common-sense approach to authority: "I receive and I give—such is human life. Each directs and is directed in turn. Therefore there is no fixed and constant authority, but a continual exchange of mutual, temporary, and, above all, voluntary authority and subordination."[17] Thus in an anarchist society leadership is voluntary, provisional, and without special privileges or prestige. There will be no chance for it to solidify into a rigid hierarchy.

If voluntarism is one pillar of anarchist society, the other must be decentralization. The evil of the modern state is its centralized absorption of regional and local energies and diversity. The cure is to reverse the historical process and thus leave the state functionless and powerless. Anarchist society develops from the bottom up. It begins at the local or communal level, moves through the regional and national levels, and culminates in a kind of world federation of peoples. Federation is the mechanism that will blend the principle of decentralization with the coordination required by modern economic society.

Because the local unit or commune is the basic nucleus of the future society, Kropotkin in particular showed great interest in the medieval commune in Europe. Finding examples in the past allows some radical thinkers to claim that their most ambitious projects are not hopelessly fantastic or visionary. The precedent is that the medieval town flourished *without the modern state*. As Kropotkin enthusiastically pointed out: "Self-jurisdiction was the essential part, and self-jurisdiction meant self-administration. But the commune was not simply an 'autonomous' part of the state—such ambiguous words had not yet been invented . . . —it was a state in itself."[18]

These and similar ideas in later anarchists suggest that we ought not to take their term anarchy too literally. No doubt they all wish to obliterate the modern state, but this does not necessarily mean no rule or governance whatsoever. Instead, and this is the point of so many glowing references to the medieval commune, the classic anarchists want a radical and irreversible decentralization of political power. Their vision thus resembles a vast mosiac of "mini-states" more than it does a world of solitary individuals.

ANARCHO-SYNDICALISM

Anarcho-syndicalism is a variety of anarchism that envisages the modern trade union as both the weapon to overthrow capitalism and the nucleus of the new society to come.[19] Its most prominent spokesman is Georges Sorel. As an anarchist, Sorel naturally rejects parties and parliaments because they are related to the state. These formations were not only nonrevolutionary; they were repressive by their very nature. Like other anarchists he scorned the idea that democratic reforms could alter the parasitical nature of the state. Past experience here was decisive and hopeless, for "almost always the expectations of the reformers have been disappointed; all the attempts to constitute an administration independent of the interests of political parties have been useless. In France, administrations became more corrupt as politics became more democratic."[20]

Having ruled out parties and parliaments as agents of change, Sorel and anarcho-syndicalists hail the trade union as the savior of modern society. Since unions are essentially economic units not wedded to the state, they are the appropriate vehicles to make revolution. Sorel's strategy is for the unions to call a "general strike" that will polarize society into two warring camps. The workers want revolution and the bourgeoisie does not.

Workers will hurl themselves into the struggle because they are animated by the "myth of the general strike." Sorel's "myth," as we have seen in earlier chapters, is neither an ideology nor a utopia. For him these latter are rational constructs and as such are impotent to mobilize a revolutionary mass movement. Instead, the myth is a vague presentiment of the future, which appeals to passion rather than reason.

Since Sorel mistrusts intellect, he mistrusts intellectuals as well. Intellectuals hope to take over the spontaneous workers' movement and to superimpose their owns views upon it. This will surely short-circuit the revolution for "the true vocation of the intellectuals is the exploitation of politics." For Sorel the politician's role closely resembles that of "the courtier and does not require any industrial aptitude . . . . Intellectuals want to persuade the workers that their interest is to bring them . . . to power and accepting the hierarchy of ability, which subordinates the workers to politicians."[21]

Sorel wished to limit the trade unions to collective bargaining and other economic activities—at least until the climactic moment of the general strike. Cooperative and mutual aid societies were a kind of training ground for the proletariat's future role. "It is in the bosom of capitalist society that not only the new productive forces, but also the relations of a new social order—what can be called the moral forces of the future—should develop."[22]

Naturally, with Sorel's contempt for ideologies and utopias we would not expect a detailed plan of the future society. We are not left completely in the dark, however. Anarcho-syndicalism, after all, involves a sort of "self-managed socialism," somewhat reminiscent of the "guild socialism" of Chapter 4. Both doctrines demand the public ownership of the basic means of production and exchange. Both stress the trade union as the strategic group in modern society and assign it control over the future industrial order. The main difference besides guild socialism's consumerism is its central Commune, which smacks too much of the state to satisfy anarcho-syndicalists.

In the postrevolutionary society the unions will become managers and will directly operate all factories and other enterprises. Coordination will be accomplished once more by the federal principle, though this "federalism" will be functional rather than territorial as we find with classic anarchism. Beyond this Sorel and anarcho-syndicalists in general have little to say about the future.

ANARCHO-INDIVIDUALISM

The classic anarchism of Bakunin and Kropotkin and the anarcho-syndicalism of Sorel and others have one essential point in common: their fundamental concern is with *collectivities*, whether the whole society or lesser groupings like the commune and trade union. It is not that these types of anarchism deny the importance of individual freedom; it is rather that these doctrines situate that freedom in a larger collective context. The individual will be free, once the state is annihilated and the vacuum is filled by lesser geographical or functional collectivities.

However, there has also been a secondary current of anarchism that is more emphatically concerned with the individual. This tradition is yet more fearful of organization as such—so much so that even revolutionary organizations aimed against the state can appear a threat to individual freedom. The type of resistance to the state favored by what we call anarcho-individualism is *civil disobedience*. In this context civil disobedience means that the individual refuses to obey laws on the grounds of a personal ethical decision.

He bases this refusal either on a general rejection of the state's authority or on his moral dismay over a particular law or policy. As all anarchists view the state as unmitigated violence, the anarcho-individualist protest can take the form of radical pacifism. This means that this sort of anarchism will generally abjure revolutionary violence directed against the state. This is quite different from classic anarchism and anarcho-syndicalism.

Anarcho-individualism seems to exert a special attraction for poets, philosophers, and religious thinkers. In all these categories falls Henry David Thoreau (1817–62), an American author of the early nineteenth century. Thoreau's individualism was so strong that from time to time he seemed compelled to return to the country-side to live in virtual solitude away from civilization and close to nature.

Thoreau's hope for "no-government" was a gradualist one. He was thus no revolutionist. Nevertheless, he did preach civil disobedience because of the preeminent status of individual moral responsibility. Civil disobedience is a necessity because

> the only obligation which I have a right to assume is to do at any time what I think is right. It is truly enough said, that a corporation has no conscience; but a corporation of conscientious men is a corporation *with* a conscience. Law never made men a whit more just; and, by means of their respect for it, even the well-disposed are daily made the agents of injustice.[23]

Thoreau was an abolitionist and we can see how the slavery issue figures in his attitudes toward the contemporary state. "How does it become a man to behave toward this American government today?" he asked. His answer was that "he cannot without disgrace be associated with it. I cannot for an instant recognize that political organization as *my* government, which is the *slave's* government also."[24]

As the slavery issue divided American society before the Civil War, the Vietnam war did in the late 1960s and early 1970s. It seems hardly an accident that several restatements of theories of civil disobedience and, more radically, anarcho-individualism parallelled the US involvement in Indo-China. One of these comes from the philosopher Robert Paul Wolff, who pessimistically concluded that it was virtually impossible to reconcile the authority of the state with the "autonomy" of the individual.

Wolff particularly attacked Rousseau's doctrine of the General Will, which we discussed in some detail in Chapter 2. Recall that Rousseau had argued that only in a truly unified society could the good of the individual and the community merge so completely that any law favored by the majority would in a sense be the individual's own law. Freedom was thus obedience to such a law—"autonomy" literally means one's own law.

As an anarcho-individualist Wolff is forced to dismiss Rousseau's argument as an ingenious play on words. The problem is that true autonomy cannot be reconciled with any sort of collective (state) coercion of the sort Rousseau suggests when he maintains that inducing subjection to the General Will is really "forcing" people to be "free." Influenced by Immanuel Kant, the late eighteenth-century German philosopher, Wolff defines freedom or autonomy as obedience to a law that we not only prescribe to ourselves but are also willing to convert into a general rule binding on all others in the same ethical context. From this standpoint it is almost accidental whether any given law supported by the state's authority corresponds to the moral choice of the free individual.

If by chance such law does correspond, then the individual's voluntary obedience does not jeopardize his autonomy and he remains free. This is the only sort of obedience that can be called a matter of right. Sometimes there are reasons to obey, prudential ones that occur to us when we obey to avoid some damage or harm. Staying out of jail does make prudential sense; we are merely bowing to superior force. These are not matters of right. Wolff thus boils the problem down to a simple dilemma:

> Either we must embrace philosophical anarchism and treat *all* governments as nonlegitimate bodies whose commands must be judged and evaluated in each instance before they are obeyed; or else, we must give up as quixotic the pursuit of autonomy in the political realm and submit ourselves (by an implicit promise) to whatever form of government appears most just and beneficient at the moment.[25]

With Wolff's acceptance of the second alternative, we do not necessarily submit to a *democratic* state. This is so because a democratic state is inherently no more or no less legitimate than any other form of state.

CONCLUSION

In this chapter we have examined three major currents of modern anarchist ideology: the classic anarchism of Bakunin and Kropotkin, Sorel's anarcho-syndicalism, and the anarcho-individualism of Thoreau and Wolff. For classic anarchism the enemy is the state, which represents the negation of all human freedom. The cure is a radical revolutionary assault on the state, followed by a reconstruction of society on a voluntary, federalist, decentralized basis. Society should be organized from the bottom up, not from the top down. Anarcho-syndicalism shares these ideas, but looks to the trade union both as the revolutionary force and as the building-block of the post-revolutionary "socialist" system.

With anarcho-individualism the focus is displaced from collective units to the supreme value and importance of the individual and his freedom or autonomy. There is far less stress on revolutionary strategy which certainly preoccupied both Bakunin and Sorel. Indeed, non-violence and pacifism really prevents anarcho-individualists from launching a violent collective attack against the state. Resistance thus takes the form of civil disobedience, wherein the individual asserts his superior moral right as against any laws or policies of the state.

Ideas associated with both classic anarchism and anarcho-individualism had their strongest recent influence in the 1960s. The movement known as the "New Left" in Europe and America had a strong influence on college students and youth in general. While the New Left cannot be considered precisely anarchist, observers sometimes used the expression "anarchoid" to suggest a restlessness and rebelliousness that distinguished the New Left from the "old left" of communists and social democrats.

NOTES

1. Michael Bakunin, *The Political Philosophy of Bakunin*, ed. G. P. Maximoff (New York: The Free Press, 1964), p. 206.
2. Ibid., p. 216.
3. Ibid., p. 277.
4. Michael Bakunin, *Bakunin on Anarchy*, ed. S. Dolgoff (New York: Vintage Books, 1972), p. 319.
5. Peter Kropotkin, *Kropotkin's Revolutionary Pamphlets* (New York: Dover Publications, 1970), p. 46.
6. Bakunin, *Philosophy*, p. 179.
7. Ibid., p. 180.
9. There are some partial exceptions to this rule. Sometimes anarchists destroy or deface voting ballots in order to express their disdain for elections and all that goes with them. Also, during the Spanish Civil War of 1936–39, certain

anarchists overcame their revulsion towards participating in governments and joined the Loyalist forces in their struggle against the Nationalists led by General Francisco Franco.

10. Bakunin, *Anarchy*, p. 294. *Lump* in German means tramp or bum.
11. Ibid.
12. Bakunin, *Philosophy*, p. 204.
13. Max Nomad, *Apostles of Revolution* (New York: Collier Books, 1961), pp. 232–33.
14. Michael Bakunin, *God and the State* (New York: Dover Publications, 1970), p. 15.
15. This, of course, inverts Voltaire's famous saying, "If God did not exist, we would have to invent him."
16. Bakunin, *The State*, p. 25.
17. Ibid., p. 33.
18. Peter Kropotkin, *The Essential Kropotkin*, ed. E. Capouya and K. Tomkins (New York: Liveright, 1975), p. 184.
19. The French word for trade union is *syndicat*, the Italian is *sindacato*.
20. Georges Sorel, *From Georges Sorel*, ed. J. L. Stanley (New York: Oxford University Press, 1976), p. 75.
21. Ibid., p. 79.
22. Ibid., p. 85.
23. Henry David Thoreau, "Civil Disobedience," in *The Anarchists,* ed. I. L. Horowitz (New York: Dell, 1964), p. 314.
24. Ibid., p. 315.
25. Robert Paul Wolff, *In Defense of Anarchism* (New York: Harper & Row, 1970), p. 71.

SUGGESTIONS FOR FURTHER READING

Apter, David and Joll, James, eds. *Anarchism Today.* Garden City, N.Y.: Anchor Books, 1972.

Horowitz, Irving L., ed. *The Anarchists.* New York: Dell, 1964.

Joll, James. *The Anarchists.* Boston: Little, Brown, 1964.

Pennock, J. Roland, and Chapman, John W., eds. *Anarchism.* New York: New York University Press, 1978.

Sargent, Lyman T. *New Left Thought: An Introduction.* Homewood, Ill.: Dorsey Press, 1972.

Woodcock, George. *Anarchism.* New York: Meridian Books, 1962.

9

COMMUNISM

MARXISM

The works of Karl Marx (1818–83) and Friedrich Engels (1820–95) are the foundation of modern communist ideology. Marx and Engels formed one of the closest and longest-lived intellectual partnerships in history. Although recent students point out differences of emphasis between the two, we will, for the purposes of this text, consider Engels the alter ego of Marx.

Despite his originality, Marx, like Newton, would have admitted that he stood on the shoulders of giants. Various influences flow into the body of thought we call Marxism. The three chief ones generally singled out are: (1) British political economy, (2) French utopian socialism, and (3) German philosophy, especially that of Hegel.

We have had an inkling of British political economy in chapter 4, the chapter on capitalism. Marx admired "bourgeois" economists such as Adam Smith, David Ricardo, James and John Stuart Mill, and others. They had at least tried to study economics "scientifically" and had thereby revealed *some* of the workings of the capitalist economy. Their common weakness was that they considered capitalism to reflect "eternal laws" of human nature—a fatal mistake.

French utopian socialism maintained that true equality and the elimination of poverty could not be achieved under capitalism. Private ownership of the means of production was an historically obsolete institution. Henri de Saint-Simon (1760–1825), for one, preached that production should be organized scientifically under the guidance of industrial experts. He complained that the "scientists, artists, and artisans, the only men whose work is of positive utility to society, and cost it practically nothing, are kept down by the princes and other rulers who are simply more or less incapable bureaucrats."[1] In some ways he was an early prophet of the "managerial revolution" discussed in Chapter 4. Charles Fourier (1772–1837) developed an elaborate scheme of productive and social organizations called "phalantaseries." These groupings, which promised sexual as well as socioeconomic liberation, were the framework of a radically new society. For Marx these and other speculations were interesting but incurably "utopian" and naive. Left out in such schemes was not only the need for revolution, but also the recognition that revolutionary change itself could not be reduced to neat little utopian blue-prints.

Possibly the greatest influence of all on Marx was the great philosopher G.W.F. Hegel (1770–1831). Hegel's "dialectical" way of thinking deeply affected Marx's ideas. Hegel, however, was an *idealist*, who believed that mind or spirit was the essence of reality. For Hegel world history was ultimately the history of the world-spirit working itself out through time.

Despite this untenable idealism, two key points of Hegel's view of history appealed to Marx. First, history is a unity, a single process; second, it is also a progress, an advance toward a goal of higher ethical value (freedom for Hegel, communism for Marx). Progress, however, develops "dialectically" for both Hegel and Marx. Such dialectical progress differs from "evolutionary" progress because it involves conflict and leaps forward rather than moving slowly and steadily.

We must now get a better grasp of that most elusive idea, the dialectic. To do this we can employ the trio of thesis, antithesis, and synthesis. The thesis is the original state or condition of something. Since dialectical thinking sees the world as dynamic rather than static, every thesis gives rise to its opposite or antithesis. There is thus a *contradiction*—a crucial Marxist notion—between thesis and antithesis. Then the contradiction is resolved by a movement to a third stage or synthesis. Dynamism comes into play again and even this synthesis acts as a new thesis and the process is repeated once more although at a higher stage of development. These contradictions move history and ensure the necessity of further progress.

More specifically, the synthesis or third stage of the process both "preserves" and "annuls" the two previous stages of thesis and antithesis. In other words the new contains elements of the old and the old contains elements of the new. A common sense example would be to mix two glasses of fluid, one sweet and one bitter, after tasting each separately. If we taste the mixture we recognize traces of both sweetness and bitterness: they have been *preserved*. On the other hand, pure sweetness and pure bitterness are gone: they have been *annulled*. The resulting "bitter-sweet" taste (synthesis) is qualitatively different from what preceded it and represents something new in the world.

A Marxist example of the old containing the new occurs whenever a new economic system (mode of production) develops within an old social system (relations of production). Capitalism, for instance, was a long while developing within the bosom of its historical predecessor, feudalism. Marx felt that no social system would be replaced before it had advanced technology to the fullest extent it could. An example of the new containing the old will occur right after the revolution, when traces of capitalist ideology and organization will linger for a time.

How does the synthesis or new higher stage emerge? For Marx, this emergence is not smooth and even, but drastic and dramatic. What happens is that under an apparently tranquil surface, contradictions become intensified and aggravated. At a certain point, the situation breaks down and there occurs a cataclysmic change. A classic example from nature of this "nodal point" of change is water freezing at exactly 0°C. and boiling at 100°C. This nodal point idea is also the basis for giving a "revolutionary" interpretation to Marxism, for is not revolution a sudden, drastic, and dramatic breakthrough to something new and different?

Two Marxes?

Marx was a complex thinker whose writings responded to changing political situations spanning four decades. There should be little surprise then if controversy rages over what Marx "really said" or "really meant." Further fuel was added to the fires of controversy in the 1930s with the publication of the so-called Paris Manuscripts or "early writings" of 1844. There are two widely divergent schools of thought about the significance of these documents. One school minimizes it and considers them more or less juvenile exercises. They are mere foreshadowings of the mature Marx's more adequate teachings after 1848.

The opposed school finds the early manuscripts far more exciting. They see revealed a more "humanistic" Marx relatively unburdened by the later technical, economic, and philosophical complexities. If this group does not exactly see "two Marxes," they at least warn that his later works must be read in the light of the earlier ones.[2] Though a middle position between the schools seems advisable for this text, a brief look at the early writings might help us better understand Marx's developed system.

Probably the leading idea of the Paris Manuscripts is *alienation*. By this notion Marx highlighted the capitalist's separation of the worker from the results of his labor. Marx reads an enormity of ethical meaning into this simple point. It is unjust in the context of Marx's "labor theory of value." According to that doctrine, goods or commodities have a value (exchange-value) only because they represent human labor time added to raw materials.

To produce commodities requires labor. Because the capitalist does not pay the worker 100 percent of the value the worker produces, a relationship of *exploitation* exists between the two. Even this injustice does not capture the full damage of the "alienation of labor." For the worker alienation means "not only that his labor becomes an object, an *external* existence, but that it exists *outside him*, independently, as something alien, and that it becomes a power on its own confronting him."[3]

In more concrete and moral terms, alienation means that, on the job, the worker "does not affirm himself but denies himself, does not feel content, but unhappy, does not develop freely his physical and mental energy, but mortifies his body and ruins his mind. The worker therefore feels himself outside his work, and in his work feels outside himself."[4] Capitalism deforms and denatures man; his need to create and to project himself in and through productive activity is frustrated by the very foundations of this economic system. Man can only realize himself, be truly free and truly human, by going beyond capitalism.

Mature Marxism

For many people the expressions "dialectical materialism" and "historical materialism" are synonomous with Marxism.[5] Materialism, the common theme here, is an ancient philosophy. The classic version holds that the world is made up of matter, motion, and the void (i.e., empty space). All that happens in the world results from the changing relations of matter and motion. There are no supernatural spirits, there is no immaterial God or gods, and the human mind is a by-product of the behavior of matter. Marx's wrote his doctoral dissertation on the classic Greek materialists.

Marx, however, thought that classical materialism was static and unhistorical. It reduced everything to raw crude matter. Marx's materialism, on the contrary, featured the emergence of novel properties such as human life and mind that reflected the historical dynamism of the dialectical approach. For Marx and Engels this revamped materialism translates into the importance of the economic factor to the movement of history and society. Engels's famous summation of the "materialistic conception of history" sets out from the notion that

the production of the means to support human life and, next to production, the exchange of things produced, is the basis of all social structure; that in every society . . . the manner in which wealth is distributed and society is divided into classes or orders is dependent upon what is produced and how the products are exchanged. From this point of view the final causes of all social changes and political revolutions are to be sought, not in man's brains . . . , but in changes of the modes of production and exchange. They are to be sought not in the *philosophy*, but in the *economics* of each particular epoch.[6]

This general approach is called *economic determinism* and suggests that politics and culture are basically developed and conditioned by the economic organization of society.

In the Marxist version the "substructure" is the economic base of society, the mode of production and exchange. Examining this substructure reveals how things are produced (the technology), and how things are distributed (ownership and classes). Society's "superstructure" comprises the state and "ideology." Marx viewed the state as the tool of the ruling class and once asserted that "the executive of the modern state is but a committee for managing the common affairs of the whole bourgeoisie." Thus, in normal circumstances, the state's job is to protect the ruling class from any possible threat from the exploited majority. For certain brief periods, however, when there is a balance between contending classes, the state temporarily assumes a sort independent arbiter role.

Marx means by 'ideology" what most today would call "culture."[7] Religion, law, morals, philosophy, art, and literature are *ideological forms that defend and disguise the rule of the ruling class*. Along with political domination, the ruling class exerts a virtual domination of culture. In this sense, ideological forms are a "false consciousness" whereby the exploited masses see the world in a way that confirms the power of the ruling class. Until this false consciousness is replaced by genuine "class consciousness," the ruling class cannot be overthrown.

The dominant position of the ruling class depends upon its ownership and control of the means of production and exchange. In other words its political and cultural preeminence stems from its economic might. The accuracy of the "economic-determinist" label for mature Marxism was confirmed by Engels. In several writings after Marx's death, he admitted that he and Marx had exaggerated the prevalence of substructure over superstructure to make the point more emphatic.

They wanted to counter the one-sidedness of bourgeois thinkers who virtually ignored economic factors. But even with this reservation Engels leaves no doubt about how he views the basic relationship. Though he concedes that different aspects of the superstructure, especially political ideas, movements, and institutions "also exercise their influence upon the course of the historical struggles and in many cases preponderate in determining their form," the "economic movement finally asserts itself as necessary."[8]

At one level, the dynamic factor in the economic movement of history is the class struggle. All previous social systems have been overthrown because a new class has ousted and replaced an old class. A class is "new" insofar as it embodies a new mode of production and old insofar as it embodies an obsolete mode of production. At a second level, the driving force of history is the advance of technology. Marx argued that in the long run technology will always go forward. Thus, a ruling class that once represented an advancing technology will eventually become a drag on further progress. This seals its doom.

Such a "technological determinism" allows Marx to propose a scheme of stages (or epochs) of history. In the beginning there was "primitive communal society," which knew neither private property nor classes. The existence of this epoch shows Marx that neither of these institutions is really essential to human society. At one time they did not exist, and they will not exist in the future. Primitive communism was replaced by slave-owning society, in which slave-owners were the ruling class and slave labor was the main means of production. In the Middle Ages slavery was replaced by feudalism. The feudal epoch had the aristocracy as the ruling class and land (with peasant serfs tied to it) as the chief means of production.

As did its predecessors, feudalism created those groups and forces that ultimately destroyed it. Specifically, it was the growth of the urban economy and its "bourgeoisie" that made up the forces that advanced capitalism.[9] As the capitalist economy based on money and wage labor grew to maturity, the class struggle between the bourgeoisie and the feudal nobility intensified. In the end, the conflict took an increasingly political form and culminated in revolution. Such a revolution firmly entrenched capitalism and the new bourgeoisie ruling class, and occurred historically in England in the 1640s and France in the 1790s.

Capitalism is founded upon the exploitation of wage labor. The factory worker or proletarian, in contrast to slaves and serfs, is legally free, but Marx derides this freedom as more or less the freedom to starve. In technical terms, the capitalist takes away much of the value produced by the worker as "surplus-value," most of which goes to profit.

With capitalism too, technology moves beyond the framework of its "relations of production." Marx pointed to numerous symptoms of the impending crisis of the system. Chief among these is a *fall in the rate of profit*, since the capitalists are forced to invest more and more in the vain attempt to keep abreast with the rapid advance in technology. Because smaller capitalists cannot keep up in this race, they fall back into the working class and become "proletarianized." Eventually, this will produce a society polarized into a small group of big capitalists confronting a vast mass of proletarians.

Another crisis symptom of capitalism is the impoverishment (or "immiseration") of the proletariat. Since the threatened capitalists need more profits to survive, they must squeeze the workers harder (i.e., increase exploitation). They can get away with this temporarily because there exists an "industrial reserve army" of the unemployed who will work for the lowest of wages. This selfsame polarization and impoverishment, however, pushes the proletariat to full class consciousness. Once this happens, it is but a short step to a workers' political party and a revolutionary onslaught against capitalism.

Marx argued that this overall process would be *spontaneous,* as the proletariat would engineer its own liberation. Beyond this, however, there are several cloudy areas. One concerns the necessity for violent revolution. Sometimes Marx seemed to think that violent revolution alone could get rid of capitalism. At other times he suggested the possibility that socialism could arrive with more tranquillity. In a speech of 1872, for example, he acknowledged the importance of the "institutions, customs, and traditions of different countries" and declared further that "we do not deny that there are countries like America, England, (and, if I knew your institutions better, I would add Holland), where the workers can achieve their aims by peaceful means."[10]

Troublesome too is what precisely Marx had in mind with his rather rare expression "the dictatorship of the proletariat." Was this transitional phase between the end of capitalism and the coming of full communism a lawless regime to repress the old ruling capitalists or was it a mass democracy with a proletarian majority?

Whatever the nature of the transition, the classless society of communism would ultimately come. The revolution would abolish private property in the means of production and exchange. This would destroy the very basis of social classes. Classlessness involves eventual statelessness, since the state is the product of the division into classes. However, Marx and especially Engels rejected the anarchist idea that the state would be instantly destroyed by the very act of revolution. As Engels put it:

> the first act by virtue of which the state really constitutes itself the representative of the whole society—this is, at the same time, its last independent act as a state. State interference in social relations becomes, in one domain after another, superfluous, and then dies out itself; the government of persons is replaced by the administration of things, and by the conduct of processes of production. The state is not 'abolished.' *It dies out.*[11]

"Propertyless," "classless," "stateless,"—these are all negative terms. There are some more positive traits to future communism, even if Marx gives more of a sketch than a full portrait. The guiding rule of produc-

tion and distribution is: "From each according to his ability, to each according to his needs." The first part of this rule raises the issue of the general motivation to work and of how production will be organized under communism. Why should people work at all, if they are to be provided with their needs? For Marx this is no problem at all, because productive activity in a truly free society becomes a real human need in itself. Human nature impels us to express ourselves in production. People avoid work only in the alienated and exploitative class societies.

As to the organization of production, the problem is more complex. Marx argued that a fixed division of labor was one of the stigmas of a class-bound society. And yet, future communism was to be a super-productive and well-coordinated society. How could freedom of choice be reconciled with the need for organized diversity of production? This problem too Marx felt would solve itself, since natural differences would lead different people into different branches of activity. Thus, the old rigid mandatory division of labor would be superceded by a system where people can change their work easily and often.

Marx chose the phrase "to each according to his needs" quite deliberately. While he believed in a sort of moral equality of individuals, he did not think them carbon copies of each other. Absolutely equal distribution would mean that some people would get too much of some things and too little of others. Marx left it to individual discretion to determine each person's needs—and this is part of the reason that the communist society would mark "the leap from the realm of necessity into the realm of freedom."

LENINISM

Without a doubt the second great figure in the development of communist ideology is the great Russian revolutionary leader V.I. Lenin (1870–1924). Debate has raged throughout this century between those who argue that Lenin simply "creatively developed" the Marxism of Marx and those who see him deforming and perverting it. Final judgment on this controversy is difficult, but a few points of clarification might help. Earlier in this text we suggested that revolutionary ideologies have three main aspects: the first, critique, involves the moral and political indictment of the status quo; the second, affirmation, depicts the future or possible society that should replace the present; the third, strategy, tells us how to make the revolution.

In terms of critique and affirmation, little in Lenin goes beyond or sharply diverges from Marx. The evils of capitalism and the blessings of future communism were axiomatic to him. It is thus on revolutionary strategy that reconciling Marx and Lenin becomes a problem. Two points should be kept in mind here. First, Lenin was born more than a half-century after Marx. Around 1848 Marx thought that the proletarian revolution was imminent. However, by his death thirty-five years later, only the short-lived Paris Commune of 1871 had come to pass. Lenin thus had to explain the nonoccurence of the revolution, and, of course, to prescribe remedial action. The second point is that Lenin was a revolutionary in an underdeveloped, predominantly peasant country, whereas Marx saw advanced western Europe with its large proletariat as the epicenter of revolution.

Possibly the most important document in the history of modern communism is Lenin's pamphlet *What Is To Be Done?* (1902). Lenin was one of the leaders of the revolutionary Marxist party known as the Russian Social Democratic Labor Party. After 1900 the party was split between pro-Lenin advocates of an elitist party and anti-Lenin advocates of a mass party open to all workers. Because Lenin's faction won a majority vote at a Party Congress, they became known as the Bolsheviks (majority-ites). The losing group of minority votes got the label Mensheviks (minority-ites). Shortly before World War I the two groups split into distinct political parties.

In this dispute over organization Lenin raised some vitally important issues. Recall that Marx saw the revolution as the "spontaneous" action of the proletariat itself. Lenin, without openly contradicting Marx, denied that spontaneity thesis in the strongest terms. "The history of all countries," he wrote, "shows that the working class, exclusively by its own effort, is able to develop only trade-union consciousness, i.e., it may itself realize the necessity for combining in unions, to fight against the employers and to strike to compel the government to pass labor legislation, etc."[12] Trade-union consciousness is thus very far removed from revolutionary political consciousness. The latter could reach the proletariat only from "without," largely from "bourgeois intellectuals" like Lenin himself.

Lenin's revolutionary strategy was thus based on an elite party of professional revolutionaries. Membership in this new type of party was highly selective: most ordinary workers could not make the grade. To be a professional revolutionary means that one places the revolution over all other considerations and develops a grasp of revolutionary theory beyond the reach of the masses. Students and intellectuals in general would weigh more heavily than true workers in the scales of the party.

Russian revolutionists were neither the first nor last to debate the elite versus mass party format. In the nineteenth century "Blanquism"—associated with the colorful French revolutionist Auguste Blanqui (1805–81)—declared the need for a highly conspiratorial clique to make the revolution on behalf of the ignorant and impotent masses.[13] Lenin vigorously denied that his "vanguard" party smacked of Blanquism. He once compared the party to the mythical hero Antaeus, whose massive strength was lost when he lost contact with the Earth, his mother. The party was the hero and the masses the true source of strength. True, the party was a vanguard, but how strong is an advance group of seasoned shock troops without the rest of the army to back it up?

Organization was Lenin's strongest concern. His formula, "demo-cratic centralism," tries to combine two distinct goals. On the one hand, Lenin stressed the need for "iron discipline" in the revolutionary struggle. On the other hand, he and his party were heirs to the radical democratic tradition of European socialism. Democratic centralism thus has democratic and centralist aspects in leadership and party discipline.

On the national level, following Lenin, all communist parties have three levels of leadership.[14] The lowest level is the Party Congress, which meets once every several years and represents the grass roots membership in the country. The middle level is a smaller group called the Central Committee. The top level finds several smaller groups, generally called the Secretariat and the Politburo—short for Political Bureau of the Central Committee. As democratic centralism requires that lower party organs elect the higher ones, the Party Congress elects the Central Committee, which in turn chooses the Secretariat, Politiburo, and other top groups. On the centralist side, authority flows downward as decisions of higher groups are binding on lower ones. Centralism is also seen when members are prohibited from publicly criticizing the current party line (policy). On the other hand, democracy reemerges in the periodic party conferences, where free and open debate is followed by a majority vote.

The chief functions of this vanguard party are political leadership and ideological propaganda. In the first instance, the party will organize the mass of workers into an effective political force. This can involve both legal and illegal activity, taking part in elections or boycotting them, adopting violence or compromise as a strategy. Contrary to some views Lenin did not rule out terrorism. This strategy comes out in his ideas of "armed struggle" and "partisan warfare." Armed struggle is carried out "by individuals and by small groups. Some belong to revolutionary organizations, while others (the *majority* in certain parts of Russia) do not belong to any revolutionary organization."[15]

Lenin sharply divided the two aims of armed struggle: (1) it "aims at assassinating individuals, chiefs and subordinates in the army and the police"; and (2) it aims at "the confiscation of monetary funds both from the government and from private persons."[16] These funds would partly go to the party treasury and partly to preparing revolution and supporting armed struggle. Partisan warfare carries things a bit further: it comes into play "when the mass movement has actually reached the point of insurrection and when fairly large intervals occur between the 'big engagements' in the civil war."[17]

On the other hand, in certain conditions Lenin supported participation in "bourgeois" parliaments. After the Russian Revolution of 1917 he was critical of the "infantile disorder" of those "left-wing" communists abroad who demanded instant revolution regardless of the political situation.

> It is just because the backward masses of the workers and, to a still greater degree, of the small peasants are in Western Europe much more imbued with bourgeois-democratic and parliamentary prejudices than they were in Russia that it is only from *within* such institutions . . . that Communists can (and must) wage a long and persistent struggle . . . to expose, dissipate and overcome these prejudices.[18]

Thus, it is up to the party leadership to determine whether armed struggle, partisan warfare, full-scale insurrection, or the Trojan Horse of parliamentarism is the "correct" party line at the moment.

The propaganda role of the party, whether exposing "bourgeois prejudices" or spreading Marxist ideas, has two sides to it. First, there is *agitation*, which involves face-to-face encounter with small groups. Propaganda proper involves broader-scale techniques such as print media and speeches before big crowds. In time, the two approaches were fused in "agitprop."

The revolutionary role of peasants is another point where Lenin departed from Marx. Marx had little use for peasants: they were not truly a "class" and represented "barbarism within civilization." These defects precluded concerted political, let alone revolutionary, activity. Clearly Lenin had to revise this outlook or face some unpleasant consequences. If, as orthodox Marxists were saying, a truly socialist revolution requires a critical mass of industrial workers, then Russia would have to wait generations. Rural peasants would have to become urban proletarians by the millions—an unacceptable prospect to Lenin.

His solution was to reappraise the revolutionary potential of the peasants. He divided them into the three categories of rich, middle, and poor. The rich peasants were clearly aligned with the bourgeoisie and were thus completely antirevolutionary. The middle peasants were "waverers" and could go either way. The poor peasants, however, were "semi-proletarians" and could be won over to the side of the revolution.

The particulars are a bit more complex than this. In 1905 and 1906 Russia experienced a genuinely revolutionary situation, aggravated by defeats at the hands of Japan in the Far East. Russian Marxists debated the character of the near-revolution and the strategy appropriate to it. Lenin could not call the anticipated revolution purely and simply a proletarian one. Its immediate aspect would be "bourgeois-democratic," involving the overthrow of the Czarist autocracy and the establishment of a bourgeois republic. According to Lenin, since the bourgeoisie was afraid to go all the way with their own revolution, the political formula would have to be "the revolutionary-democratic dictatorship of the proletariat and the peasantry."

This meant that the time-span that the orthodox Marxists saw between the bourgeois and proletarian revolutions was greatly narrowed. Once the democratic revolution was secured, socialist revolution becomes the top item on the agenda.

> The proletariat must carry out to the end the democratic revolution, and in this unite to itself the mass of the peasantry in order to crush by force the resistance of the autocracy and to paralyze the instability of the bourgeoisie. The proletariat must accomplish the socialist revolution and in this unite to itself the mass of the semi-proletarian elements . . . in order to crush by force the resistance of the bourgeoisie and paralyze the instability of the peasantry and petty bourgeoisie.[19]

In all this Lenin never renounced the leadership role of the proletariat and, of course, its party.

Still another explanation for the tardiness of the world revolution is offered in Lenin's theory of "imperialism." He called imperialism the "highest stage of capitalism," the way it operates in the era of monopolies. Imperialism allows capitalism to postpone its overthrow by buying off domestic labor with profits snatched from underdeveloped countries. This results in a mad scramble for colonies and "spheres of influence" so as to squeeze profits from them.

The coveted profits come in several ways. First, the dominated peoples of Asia and Africa become captive markets compelled to buy up the inevitable surpluses of the imperialist countries. Also these countries are a source of cheap raw materials and cheap labor, which helps to cut costs and boost profits. These arrangements are like fingers in the leaking dike of capitalism.

But, according to Lenin's theory, the very structure of imperialism that shores up capitalism in the short run will bring it down in the long run. Imperialism has so unified the world economy that Lenin compared it to a single chain. But a chain is no stronger than its weakest link, and the weak link of imperialism is the underdeveloped countries. Conflicts between rival western imperialist powers will result in "imperialist war," which weakens the capitalist countries. Just as important, "imperialism is leading to annexation, to increased national oppression, and, consequently, also to increasing resistance."[20] Such resistance will eventually destroy the last prop of the moribund capitalist system.

Imperialism was written before the Russian Revolution of 1917. Thereafter Lenin could use the new Soviet state as the fulcrum of world revolution. He thus formed the Communist International or Comintern as a union of all Communist parties of the world. The importance of nationalism and anticolonialism to Soviet strategy is seen in Lenin's draft theses for the second Comintern Congress. There Lenin advocated a "policy that will achieve the closest alliance of all national and colonial liberation movements with Soviet Russia."[21]

Though Lenin let the exact shape of the alliance be dictated by the specific situation, he did not wish the Communist Party to be swallowed up. The Comintern "must enter into a temporary alliance with bourgeois democracy in colonial and backward countries but must not merge with it and must under all circumstances uphold the independence of the proletarian movement even if it is in its earliest embryonic form."[22] Thus Lenin laid the basis for Soviet strategy that has sometimes baffled both friends and enemies of communism. The "temporary alliance" with bourgeois democracy sometimes meant support even for anticommunist movements and regimes.

TROTSKYISM AND STALINISM

By the time of Lenin's death in 1924, a power struggle to assume his mantle as leader of both the Soviet state and international communism was under way. The two main protagonists were Joseph Stalin (1879–1953) and Leon Trotsky (1879–1940). With Trotsky's expulsion from the Soviet Communist Party and his exile in 1928, Stalin was well on the way towards the leadership role he would occupy in world communism for the next generation. While Stalin's position made him the leading ideologist of communism, Trotsky led a heretical oppositionist movement until he was assassinated by a Stalinist agent in 1940. Thus, Stalinism and Trotskyism form competing ideological strands in modern communist ideology.

Trotskyism

Trotsky was the first of the two to make a significant ideological impact with his theory of "permanent revolution" in 1905 and 1906. Recall that Marxists were debating the meaning of the abortive Russian Revolution of 1905. For some it was a purely bourgeois affair ushering a long period of capitalist development. Lenin, we saw, reduced the gap between the bourgeois and socialist revolutions. Trotsky was more radical still for he saw virtually no gap at all. His major difference with Lenin was his lingering mistrust of the peasants.

Trotsky's theory of permanent revolution, which resurfaced in the 1920s and 1930s, was actually a theory of *continuous* or *uninterrupted* revolution. Its overall view of the process of revolution requires that

> for an indefinitely long time and in constant internal struggle, all social relations undergo transformation. Society keeps on changing its skin. Each stage of transformation stems directly from the preceding. This process necessarily retains a political character. . . . Outbreaks of civil war and foreign wars alternate with periods of "peaceful" reform. Revolutions in economy, technique, science, the family, morals and everyday life develop in complex reciprocal action. . . .[23]

Regarding the 1905 revolution, Trotsky maintained that the "bourgeois-democratic" phase of the revolution would be brief. The proletariat would be forced to drive the revolution forward until it became truly socialist. This continuous revolution would spark revolutions in the West.

Tackling orthodox Marxists head on, Trotsky maintained that "it is possible for the workers to come to power in an economically backward country sooner than in an advanced country."[24] The orthodox doctrine that "the dictatorship of the proletariat is in some way automatically dependent on the technical development and resources of a country" he attacked as a "prejudice of 'economic' materialism simplified to absurdity."[25] Such notions were not overly remote from Lenin's outlook, but they kept Trotsky out of the Bolshevik Party until 1917.

The second round of the fight over permanent revolution occurred in the 1920s during Trotsky's struggle with Stalin. After final victory in the Russian Civil War in 1921 the Bolshevik government headed by Lenin proclaimed the New Economic Policy (NEP). This made certain concessions to capitalism in agriculture and small business. But this lull in the tempo of revolution ran counter to the acceleration of "permanent revolution." Thus, in 1923 Trotsky warned that "the fairly great bureaucratization of the party apparatus is inevitably accompanied by the development of conservative traditionalism with all its effects."[26] In other words, Trotsky wanted to "rev up" the revolution because slowing it down would allow counterrevolutionary elements to make a comeback. Stepping up change at home and exporting revolution abroad was his prescription for the hardening of the revolutionary arteries.

By the 1930s the now exiled Trotsky thought that his direst prophecies had been realized. Holding back the revolution had led to a "bureaucratic degeneration" in the Soviet state. Stalin and his henchmen had "betrayed" the revolution. More broadly, there had occurred a "revolutionary Thermidor" because a revolution "is a mighty devourer of human energy, both individual and collective. The nerves give way.

Consciousness is shaken and characters are worn out."[28] There was a tremendous let-down with a "long period of weariness, decline and sheer disappointment in the results of the revolution. The ebb of the 'plebeian pride' made room for a flood of pusillanimity [cowardliness] and careerism. The new commanding caste rose to its place upon the wave."[29]

In Trotsky's estimation, the lackluster Stalin was the creature rather than the creator of the new system. While it was not full or true socialism, neither was it a full return to capitalism. For Trotsky, the Soviet Union was a "contradictory society half-way between capitalism and socialism."[30] The potential for both advance and retreat was there. With such ideas as these, Trotskyism has been a fringe communist group for half a century.

Stalinism

Stalin always presented himself as the most orthodox ideological disciple of the great Lenin. His major works in the 1920s all had "Leninism" in their titles. His ideological contributions, which are sometimes underestimated, mainly regard nationalism and the theory of the state. For the rest he largely parroted Lenin's ideas, even if he often ignored them in practice.

Stalin's initial treatment of nationalism came early. Lenin was taken with the young revolutionary, whose non-Russian (i.e., Georgian) ethnic background seemed to qualify him as a Bolshevik expert on nationalities. The result was a book on *Marxism and the National Question* (1913). It is a rather competent survey that defines a nation as a "historically constituted, stable community of people, formed on the basis of a common language, territory, economic life, and psychological make-up manifested in a common culture."[31]

The policy position that Stalin (and, of course, Lenin) developed was the "right of nations to self-determination." In concrete terms this meant that a nation "may arrange its life in the way it wishes. It has the right to arrange its life on the basis of autonomy. It has the right to enter into federal relations with other nations. It has the right to complete secession. Nations are sovereign, and all nations have equal rights."[32]

This liberal-sounding rhetoric was often observed more in the breach than in reality after the Russian Revolution. But it showed greater sensitivity to nationalism than was found with some Marxists, and on occasion with Marx himself. There were nationalistic overtones in Stalin's "socialism in one country," his counter-slogan to Trotsky's "permanent revolution." Stalin charged that Trotsky's demand for immediate world revolution would provoke imperialist intervention in the Soviet Union. Instead, socialism should be allowed to develop in the

USSR, which would eventually possess a magnetic appeal to the peoples of the world. To refute the charge of abandoning world revolution, Stalin argued that the "final victory" of socialism was tied to world revolution. "In the country where it is victorious the revolution must not regard itself as a self-sufficient quantity, but as a support, as a means for hastening the victory of the proletariat of all countries. It constitutes at the same time the beginning and the premise of the world revolution."[33]

By the 1930s certain developments pushed Stalin further down the road of nationalism. He began to favor the Great Russians above the other peoples in the Soviet Union. Works of literature that were condemned as "bourgeois ideology" in the 1920s were now hailed as monuments of Russian culture. Even some of the old czars like Ivan the Terrible were newly heralded as builders of the Russian state.

In Stalin's eyes there was no real contradiction between this Soviet patriotism and the *Communist Manifesto*'s assertion that the "workingmen have no country." Stalin thus pointed out in 1931 that in "the past we had no fatherland, nor could we have one. But now that we have overthrown capitalism and power is in the hands of the working class, we have a fatherland, and we will defend its independence."[34]

As Stalin beefed up the bureaucratic, military, and police aspects of the state after 1930, a certain ideological problem came up. The state was not withering way as classical Marxism had predicted. By 1938 Stalin felt confident enough to meet this point by a frontal attack. He argued that Engels's famous "withering-away" doctrine related to conditions wholly different from the present ones. The Soviet Union was a "socialist" state and thus was only in the first phase of postrevolutionary society. Full communism would come later. Moreover, the Soviet Union faced a "capitalist encirclement" of implacably hostile powers.

Stalin thus criticized those who simply quoted texts and he openly proclaimed the irrelevance of the withering-away doctrine. Its correctness depended on two points: (1) looking only at the internal development of the socialist state; and (2) the victory of socialism world-wide or in a majority of countries. Capitalist encirclement made the two points moot so that the Soviet Union had to have "a well-trained army, well-organized penal organs, and a strong intelligence service," and "consequently, must have its own state, strong enough to defend the conquests of socialism from foreign attack."[35]

However, the really important ideological innovation came when Stalin asked and answered a vital question: "Will our State remain in the period of communism also? Yes, it will, if the capitalist encirclement is not liquidated, and if the danger of military attack is not eliminated . . . ."[36] Though he also stipulated that the state would indeed wither away should there come a "socialist encirclement," Stalin had clearly burnt an important ideological bridge behind him.

Years later a similar point was made when Stalin in a philosophical discussion of language pointed out that

the superstructure is a product of the [economic] base; but this does not mean that it merely reflects the base, that it is passive, neutral. . . . On the contrary, no sooner does it arise than it becomes an exceedingly active force, actively assisting its base to take shape and consolidate itself, and doing everything it can to help the new system finish off and eliminate the old base and the old classes.[37]

Here again is not only a theoretical justification of a strong state but also grounds for using culture to further the goals of the regime. For a time in the early 1960s the Soviets returned again to speculations about the state's demise. But practice was apparently so far removed from theory at this time that the discussion itself withered away.

MAOISM

No account of twentieth-century communist ideology would be complete without the ideas of the great leader of China, Mao Tse-tung (1893–1976). The Chinese call Maoist ideology "the thought of Mao Tse-tung." It has the virtue of combining the "universal truths of Marxism-Leninism" and the "unique experience of the Chinese Revolution." Mao's genius, in the Chinese view, lay in synthesizing these two elements of ideology. However, we must here limit the discussion to several key themes: voluntarism, the peasantry, populism, and nationalism.

Voluntarism

"Voluntarism" signifies the force and effectiveness of the human will, at either the collective or the individual level. It is usually contrasted with "determinism," which suggests that physical or material forces of some sort govern human behavior. We have already seen that Marxism tends to an economic determinism. Marx's description of the downfall of capitalism and the inevitability of communism falls into line with this.

Lenin, Trotsky, and Stalin in their different ways pushed voluntarism and played down determinism. And yet, Mao probably outdid them on this score. We see this in the Maoist preoccupation with the mental aspect of reality. While purges and terror were not wholly foreign to the history of Chinese Communism, Mao always felt that "thought reform" could change a person's attitudes and behavior. This notion was applied to two different targets.

First, it was applied to former "class enemies" of landlord or big bourgeois background. Mao felt that many with this background could be rehabilitated. "To exercise dictatorship over the reactionary classes does not mean that we should totally eliminate all reactionary elements, but rather that we should eliminate the classes to which they belong. We should use appropriate methods to remould them and transform them into new men."[38] If they were pressed to confess their misdeeds against the "people" and exercized self-criticism in an open public forum, they might redeem themselves in the eyes of the revolution.

Thought reform was also applied to members of the Communist Party, who strayed from the path of the Maoist doctrine. While such "deviationism" could mean death in Stalin's USSR, Mao preferred milder measures. Various "rectification" campaigns were conducted, whenever Mao felt the need to bring ideological thinking into line. Discussion would be fostered at all party levels. Here as well self-criticism was intended to get the "cadres" back on the Maoist track.

Another example of Mao's faith in will and collective attitudes is the so-called Great Leap Forward of 1958–59. This was an attempt to industrialize China rapidly without developing all the elaborate technology usually considered necessary. Mao felt that he could harness the collective enthusiasm of the masses and simply overwhelm technical problems. Mao inspired if he did not actually write words suggesting that

> we cannot follow the old patterns of technical development of every other country in the world, and crawl step by step behind the others. We must smash conventions, do our utmost to adopt advanced techniques, and within not too long a period of history. . . . When we talk of a Great Leap Forward we mean just this. Is this really impossible? Are we boasting or shooting off our mouths? Certainly not. It can be done.[39]

That the actual shortcomings of the Great Leap failed to dampen Mao's faith in human collective will is seen in his launching of the Cultural Revolution of 1966–69. Here Mao unleased youth and other hyperactive elements to shake up the ossified bureaucratic structure of the Chinese Communist Party. Enthusiasm took precedence over structure.

The Peasantry and Populism

Mao's emphasis on the role of the peasantry both before and after the Communist victory in 1949 is doubtless related to his own rural background. In the 1920s he had already termed the peasants the "driving force" of the Chinese Revolution. This separated him from the more orthodox Communists who clung to the idea of an urban-centered proletarian revolution. Mao's whole revolutionary strategy was premised on retreating from the cities to the countryside and the peasants. The rural "base areas" would implement land-reform and other policies designed to attract peasants to the Communist banner. Over time these areas would multiply and expand, and in the end "the countryside will surround the cities."

Yet it is not just political strategy that endeared the Chinese peasantry to Mao. His "populism" also drew him towards them. Populism, in the loose sense we use it in this chapter, suggests that the common people have a sort of folk wisdom and rustic simplicity that compares most favorably to the airs and pretensions of academics, intellectuals, and other elite elements. Recall that for centuries the Confucian culture of the old Chinese Empire had involved the privileged status of the learned elite. As Mao was born a subject of the empire which fell in 1911, his populism is partly a reaction to the lingering elitist tradition.

It is one of the ironies of modern history that intellectuals often manifest the harshest anti-intellectualism and Mao himself is a case in point. Intellectuals and bureaucrats, he held, have become isolated and insulated from the tough realities of everyday life. They become puffed up with pride and treat ordinary folk as lower forms of life. These groups can form a virtual caste cut off from the rest of the people. Mao unceasingly fulminated against such a perversion of revolutionary goals. In 1958, for example, he complained of professors that

> we have been afraid of them ever since we came into the towns. We did not despise them, we were terrified of them. When confronted by people with piles of learning we felt we were good for nothing. For Marxists to fear bourgeois intellectuals, to fear professors while not fearing imperialism is strange indeed. I believe this attitude is a survival of the slave mentality.[40]

Mao thought the book-learning of professors and intellectuals inferior in important respects to the life-learning of ordinary peasants. Accordingly, he suggested that the elite groups should get a good taste of the "real" world. In 1964 he proposed that students and professors in the humanities be "sent down" to the countryside or the factories for a stay of five months. In these places, they "will acquire some perceptual knowledge. Horses, cows, sheep, chickens, dogs, pigs, rice, sorghum, beans, wheat, varieties of millet—they can have a look at all these things. . . . To get some experience of the class struggle—that's what I call a university."[41]

In the Maoist perspective a humble peasant could possess more genuine wisdom and contribute more to society than some scholar basking in international renown. Though well-educated himself, Mao took pleasure in claiming that he was a graduate of the "university of the greenwoods." Mao's populism also affected his views on art and artists. "Experts," he once wrote, "should be respected: they are very valuable to our cause. But we should also remind them that no revolutionary writer or artist can produce any work of significance unless he has contact with the masses, gives expression to their thoughts and feelings, and becomes their loyal spokesman."[42]

Nationalism

If Marx disdained nationalism, Lenin manipulated it, and Stalin succumbed to it, Mao in a sense outdid them all. Unlike other communist leaders, he rarely left China and never visited the West. This lack of cosmopolitanism was associated with an intense feeling of national pride. Mao's espousal of communist revolution resulted partially from resentment of the harm caused by western imperialism in China. This great land, which for centuries thought of outsiders as "barbarians," was chopped into western spheres of influence, though it was never directly colonized. Injured national feeling has often supplied fuel for extremist movements. Even before he became a communist, as part of the patriotic May Fourth Movement of 1919, Mao had written that

> our Chinese people possesses great inherent capacities! The more profound the oppression, the greater the resistance; that which has accumulated for a long time will surely burst forth quickly. . . . One day the reform of the Chinese people will be more profound than that of any other people, and the society of the Chinese people will be more profound than that of any other people.[43]

Though always proclaiming the "universal" truth of Marxism-Leninism, Mao also stressed the importance of specific Chinese conditions. This, after all, was the reason for the shift from an urban to a rural strategy. It is clear that Mao saw no conflict between his working for national revolution on nationalistic grounds and working for social revolution on the grounds of Marxist-Leninist world revolution. As he remarked in 1937: "This patriotism and internationalism are by no means in conflict, for only China's independence and liberation will make it possible to participate in the World Communist Movement."[44]

This linking of the national and social revolutions also stems from Mao's analysis of social classes. Certain of these, e.g., the big bourgeoisie and "evil gentry," actually support and profit from the imperialist penetration of China. Their economic interests lie more with their foreign masters than with the sound body of the Chinese people. True national liberation, therefore, presupposes a social revolution directed against these selfsame reactionary classes.

One side of Mao's nationalism was his attack on "wholesale wester-nization." This latter process downgraded things Chinese in favor of importing and aping things western, regardless of their relevance. Mao hoped to learn from the West, especially technologically, in order to overcome Chinese backwardness. But this in no way necessitated aban-doning the entire Chinese cultural tradition. Certain of the native ways and lore can be adapted to speed the advance of the new China.

Perhaps a still more important sign of nationalism came with the outbreak of the Sino-Soviet dispute in the early 1960s. National pride was a strong motive on the Maoist side. While Mao had for years praised the Soviet Union and Stalin, there were limits to how much he would subordinate China to the great northern neighbor. As the dispute heat-ed, Mao seemed to maintain that the Soviet "revisionists" were scarcely better than the American "imperialists." Both superpowers aimed at "hegemony" at the expense of smaller and weaker powers. Mao implied that the Chinese had not fought for two decades to overcome one form of imperialism just to fall into the lap of another.

CONCLUSION

Space limitations have forced high selectivity in this chapter's treatment of the evolution of communist ideology. The selectivity is evident in dealing with just five central figures: Marx, Lenin, Trotsky, Stalin, and Mao. Certainly, Castroism, though its ideological development came after Fidel Castro's seizure of power in Cuba in early 1959, has animated certain revolutionary movements in Latin America. In Chapter 2 our discussion of Yugoslav "self-management" covered part of that coun-try's claim that "Titoism" represents the truest rendition of modern communist ideology.

All of these versions of communist ideology agree, however, in the virtual necessity for violent revolution succeeded by a single-party dic-tatorship. With this in mind, in the 1970s many people were excited by the emergence of so-called "Eurocommunism." Eurocommunism was particularly related to the theory and practice of the Italian, Spanish, and French Communist Parties. These parties seemed to renounce revolu-tionary strategy and dictatorial ambitions. While they pledged to work for "socialism," they claimed to do so within the rules of the game of constitutional democracy. This fundamental change would thus entail a total repudiation of the "Stalinist" past, when Communist Parties ruthlessly subverted constitutionalism.

Whatever the ultimate significance of Eurocommunism, we have seen several important transformations in communist ideology in the hundred-odd years from Marx's *Communist Manifesto* to the death of Mao in 1976. The first such transformation is from Marx's determinism to Mao's voluntarism. Though this is a degree difference rather than a complete turnaround, Marx's concern with the economic-technological substructure and the spontaneous workers' movement is strongly qualified by Mao's voluntarism and preoccupation with the mental and cultural aspects of reality. We can view Lenin's ideas on organization, Trotsky's permanent revolution, and Stalin's notions of state and super-structure as early stages in the transformation.

A second transformation involves change from Marx's extreme urban emphasis to the rural peasant strategy of Mao. Marx's classic proletarians were urban industrial wage-earners in advanced western countries, who would spearhead world revolution. Lenin's redefinition of the revolutionary role of the peasants gives rise to a different focus of communist strategy, though he still retains a strong urban and proletarian orientation. It was left to Mao, spurred by actual political conditions in China, to declare that an urban proletarian strategy in China was foredoomed to failure. Instead, the peasantry was elevated to a "driving force" of the revolution, which led to the strategy of "encircling the cities" and the Maoist exaltation of the peasant.

The final transformation is the move from the pure internationalism of Marx to the qualified internationalism of Mao. Marx, though born a German, was definitely a cosmopolitan figure, at home in a number of European countries. He sincerely felt that existing national differences would be phased out in the future. Lenin and Stalin, operating in a multinational empire where ethnic nationalism was rising and not declining, sought to capture nationalism for the cause of revolution. They eventually came up with the slogan "national in form, socialist in content" to cater to nationalism and national sentiment. With Mao, opting for nationalism seems as much a product of personal feeling as of conscious strategic policy. His attacks on blind westernization and attitudes toward the Sino-Soviet dispute illustrate this. What Marx would think of these transformations is one of those intriguing questions that no one can answer with certainty.

NOTES

1. Henri Comte de Saint-Simon, *Selected Writings,* ed. F. M. H. Markham (Oxford: Basil Blackwell, 1952), p. 74.
2. If these writers prefer the "young" Marx to the "mature" Marx, they generally blame Engels for diverting him from the earlier paths and giving a more rigid cast to the development of Marxist doctrine.
3. Karl Marx, *Economic and Philosophical Manuscripts of 1844* (Moscow: Foreign Languages Publishing House, 1961), p. 70.
4. Ibid., p. 72.

5. Marx seemed to prefer "scientific socialism" to characterize his doctrines. Engels produced his *Socialism: Utopian and Scientific* to contrast the two modes of socialist thought. After the death of Marx he sometimes used the expression "the materialist conception of history."

6. Friedrich Engels, *Socialism: Utopian and Scientific*, in Marx and Engels, *Selected Works*, vol. II (Moscow: Foreign Languages Publishing House, 1958), p. 136.

7. We will return to this subject in our concluding chapter.

8. Engels, in *Marx & Engels: Basic Writings on Politics and Philosophy*, ed. L. S. Feuer (Garden City, N.Y.: Anchor Books, 1959), p. 398.

9. Indeed, the word "bourgeois" in various western languages is related to our suffix "burg" in city names.

10. Karl Marx, "Later Political Writings 1864–82," in *Karl Marx: Selected Writings*, ed. D. McLellan (New York: Oxford University Press, 1977), p. 594. Marx warned, however, that in most continental countries "it is force that will be the lever of our revolutions." p. 595.

11. Friedrich Engels, in *The Marx-Engels Reader*, ed. R. C. Tucker (New York: W. W. Norton, 1972), p. 635.

12. V. I. Lenin, *What Is To Be Done?* (New York: International Publishers, 1929), pp. 32–33.

13. Blanqui advocated a conspiratorial elitist strategy of revolution instead of a mass explosive onslaught, which he felt could be easily quelled by the public authorities.

14. Lenin's Bolsheviks only adopted the name Russian Communist Party in 1918 and in 1924 became the Communist Party of the Soviet Union (B)—the "B" was retained until 1952 and referred to the old Bolshevik name.

15. Lenin, *Marx Engels Marxism* (Moscow: Foreign Languages Publishing House, n.d.), p. 197.

16. Ibid.

17. Ibid., p. 201.

18. V. I. Lenin, *'Left-Wing' Communism: An Infantile Disorder* (New York: International Publishers, 1940), p. 48.

19. V. I. Lenin, *Two Tactics of Social-Democracy in the Democratic Revolution* (New York: International Publishers, 1963), p. 85.

20. V. I. Lenin, *Imperialism: The Highest Stage of Capitalism* (New York: International Publishers, 1939), p. 121.

21. V. I. Lenin, *On Politics and Revolution*, ed. J. E. Connor (New York: Pegasus Books, 1968), p. 316.

22. Ibid., p. 319.

23. L. D. Trotsky, *Permanent Revolution* (New York: Pioneer Publishers, 1965), p. 8.

24. Ibid., p. 195.

25. Ibid.

26. L. D. Trotsky, *The New Course* (Ann Arbor, Mich.: University of Michigan Press, 1965), p. 51.

27. "Thermidor" refers to the month of the new French Revolutionary calendar (1789), in which the radical faction headed by Robespierre was purged and replaced by more moderate figures. More broadly, Thermidor suggests that all revolutions lose their dynamic force sooner or later, and that some traditional ideas and institutions return.

28. L. D. Trotsky, *The Revolution Betrayed* (New York: Merit Publishers, 1965), p. 88.
29. Ibid., p. 89.
30. Ibid., p. 255.
31. Joseph Stalin, "Marxism and the National Question," in *The Essential Stalin,* ed. B. Franklin (Garden City, N.Y.: Anchor Books, 1972), p. 60.
32. Ibid., p. 71.
33. Joseph Stalin, *Leninism,* vol. I, ed. J. Fineberg (New York: *International Publishers,* n.d.), p. 134.
34. Joseph Stalin, *Problems of Leninism* (Peking: Foreign Languages Press, 1976), p. 528.
35. Ibid., p. 931.
36. Ibid., p. 935.
37. Stalin, in *Essential Stalin,* p. 408.
38. Mao Tse-tung, *Chairman Mao Talks to the People,* ed. S. Schram (New York: Pantheon Books, 1974), p. 169.
39. Ibid., p. 231.
40. Ibid., p. 116.
41. Ibid., p. 213.
42. Mao Tse-tung, "Talks at the Yenan Forum on Art and Literature," in *Mao Tse-tung: An Anthology of His Writings,* ed. A. Freemantle (New York: New American Library, 1963), p. 257.
43. Mao Tse-tung quoted in Frederick Wakeman, Jr., "The Patriot," in *Mao Tse-tung in the Scales of History,* ed. D. Wilson (New York: Cambridge University Press, 1977), p. 237.
44. Ibid., p. 244.

SUGGESTIONS FOR FURTHER READING

Hunt, R. N. C. *The Theory and Practice of Communism.* Baltimore: Penguin Books, 1964.
Hsiung, James C. *Ideology and Practice: The Evolution of Chinese Communism.* New York: Praeger, 1970.
Lichtheim, George. *Marxism: An Historical and Critical Study.* New York: Praeger, 1965.
Marcuse, Herbert. *Soviet Marxism.* New York: Vintage Books, 1961.
Meyer, Alfred G. *Communism.* 5th ed. New York: Random House, 1984.
————. *Leninism.* New York: Praeger, 1962.

10

SOCIAL DEMOCRACY

Like communism, social democracy traces certain of its roots back to Karl Marx. Some contemporary social democrats would even describe themselves as "Marxists." But if they do, they have a certain reading and interpretation of Marx in mind. It is less the Marx of 1848 proclaiming the specter of revolutionary "communism" haunting Europe than the Marx of 1872 speaking to Dutch workers about a possibly peaceful transition to socialism.

Classical social democracy in the late nineteenth century grew out of the conviction that revolution was a poor way to bring socialism about. Revolution itself was an open admission that democratic methods had not been tried in earnest. Since these methods might take longer to work, the abolition of capitalism might be accomplished over a protracted period rather than at one fell swoop. This is why the slogan "evolutionary socialism" came to characterize the political strategy of social democracy in the last decades of the nineteenth century. Another apt slogan was that socialism should be instituted by "ballots rather than bullets."

The debate between revolutionary and evolutionary socialists was finally crystallized by Lenin's famous "twenty-one conditions" for membership in the Communist or Third International in 1919.[1] This led to the clear split of revolutionary and evolutionary socialists into communist (or workers) parties and social democratic (or socialist) parties on the other. Lenin's own revolutionary party, the Bolsheviks, we must recall, had assumed the label Russian Communist Party only in 1918. Before the Russian Revolution of 1917 the lines were blurred with the same party often harboring warring factions of the two schools of socialists. Before World War I in Italy, for example, the more radical figures were known as the "maximalists," since they wanted maximum or immediate socialism at any cost. Their moderate opponents were called "minimalists," since they were content with smaller reformist steps toward the socialist ideal.

There is one keynote heard throughout the century of social democratic thought: *the indispensability of democracy.* In the 1880s and 1890s social democrats refused to abandon the path of democracy in favor of any shortcut to socialism. It was axiomatic to them that you cannot fully and truly have socialism without democracy. Democracy is both a means to an end (a socialist economy) and an end in itself (a just political order).

For all social democrats before World War I, and for many afterwards, true democracy would inevitably bring socialism along in its tow. This confident expectation was based on two assumptions: first, that the working class would soon constitute an electoral majority; and, second, that workers would be drawn to socialism like bees to honey. The sheer weight of numbers would guarantee eventual socialism. The indispensability of democracy is also the basis of the social democratic critique of modern communism. This conviction also joins together social democrats on the two sides of the post-World War II debate over nationalization and planning.

REVISIONISM AND FABIANISM

The evolutionary current of social democratic thought is represented by the "revisionism" of the German social democratic leader Eduard Bernstein (1850–1932) and the parallel thinking of the British Fabian socialists. *Fabian Essays in Socialism* edited by the great British dramatist George Bernard Shaw was published in 1889. The difference between those socialists who advocated a violent overthrow of the hated capitalist order and the evolutionary revisionists and Fabians was more than a matter of temperament or simple attitude toward violence. Many revolutionists sincerely believed that capitalism could not be dislodged without a violent revolutionary shake-up.

It was this last doctrine that Eduard Bernstein revised, thus giving birth to "revisionism."[2] Bernstein antagonized his fellow socialists not just because he rejected the violent road to socialism, but also because he called several doctrines of Marx himself into serious question. This was too much for the more orthodox social democrats like Karl Kautsky (1845–1938), though in other respects Kautsky was close to Bernstein and came even closer (as we shall see) in later years.

First, we must bear in mind that Marx generally taught that as capitalism approaches its demise the condition of the working class worsens. Capitalists in their doomed attempt to keep current with bur-geoning technology squeeze more "surplus-value" out of the workers by cutting their real wages. However, this deterioration or "immisera-tion" also galvanizes the working class into a striking force that will destroy capitalism. Socialism was thus contingent on a violent upheaval triggered by abject proletarian misery.

Bernstein called this doctrine the "catastrophic theory" and resoun-dingly rejected it. There was a cruel irony here as it clearly maintained that "progress depends on the deterioration of social conditions." Bern-stein spotted two flaws in this topsy-turvy formula for working-class liberation. First, it dismissed a whole series of political reforms and economic improvements that would benefit workers in immediate and tangible ways.

From the standpoint of the catastrophists, battles for universal suf-frage, better working conditions, government programs for the sick and weak were highly doubtful. They were at best political warm-up matches for the revolutionary main event, and at worst attempts to deflect the working class from its true revolutionary mission. (This latter view was later formalized in Lenin's scathing denunciation of trade-union consciousness in 1903.)

Bernstein's answer to this critique was that the political and eco-nomic reforms so disdained by revolutionaries were, in fact, the precon-dition of both socialism and the working class's emancipation. This is the case because when the workers "do not possess very strong eco-nomic organizations of their own, and have not attained, by means of education in self-governing bodies, a high degree of mental indepen-dence, the dictatorship of the proletariat means the dictatorship of the club orators and the writers."[4] In other words, those who despise the piecemeal improvements of the workingman's political and economic condition condemn him to the political tutelage of the "intelligentsia."

For Bernstein improvements are not only valuable in themselves; they help pave the way to socialism by creating a stronger and more sophisticated working class. And yet, Bernstein pointed to a still worse defect in the theory of catastrophe: it was false. In the strict Marxist scenario, for example, a "polarization of wealth" would occur with a tiny super-rich minority confronting the swollen mass of poverty-strick-en workers. One side of this process would be the concentration of industry and ownership, wiping out the small businessmen or "petty bourgeoisie." Against this, Bernstein pointed out that "far from society being simplified as to its divisions compared with earlier times, it has been graduated and differentiated both in respect of incomes and of business activities."[5]

The middle-level social groups have not been proletarianized and society thus confutes the nice dialectical contrast assumed by cata-strophists. Nor has the "immiseration" thesis been validated. Workers' conditions are improving, not getting worse. These improvements have been gained by hard work; they have not been handed to the workers on a platter. Socialism will come, but it will not come from a degraded, atomized mass of wage-slaves. Its coming presupposes a sophisticated, educated, well-organized, and confident working class—not social catastrophe.

It is thus clear to Bernstein that those who truly want socialism will work for the piecemeal reforms that will raise the material, moral, and mental level of the workers to a point where socialism is the logical conclusion of a vast historical movement. "Revolution" becomes super-fluous and "the dictatorship" of any class wholly out of date. Romantic impatience with the historical process will bring about the "dictatorship of club orators and writers," not the true liberation of the working class. To social democrats, Bernstein's fears in this respect were amply con-firmed in Russia after 1917.

Even before Bernstein, members of the British Fabian Society had developed a similar rationale for a gradual reformist road to socialism. Led by famous intellectuals like Bernard Shaw and the science fiction writer and historian H. G. Wells, the Fabians had named their society after Fabius Maximus, a Roman general famous for avoiding battles against the great Carthaginian leader Hannibal. Fabius was no coward, but his strategy was to be patient and wear the enemy down before finally defeating him once and for all. This symbolized for the Fabians their own rejection of a revolutionary cataclysm ushering in socialism. Bernard Shaw, for example, pointed out that

the experienced Social Democrat converts his too ardent followers by first admitting that if change [to socialism] could be made catastrophically it would be well worth making, and then proceeding to point out that as it would involve a readjustment of productive industry to meet the demand created by an entirely new distribution of purchasing power, it would also involve, in the application of labor and industrial machinery, alternatives which no afternoon's work could effect.6

Shaw and the Fabians, like Bernstein and the revisionists, denied any "quick-fix" approach to socialism.

Nonetheless, the movement toward socialism was unstoppable. More political democracy was the antechamber to socialism or economic democracy. Western societies were becoming more democratic politi-cally. The *Fabian Essays* themselves were published shortly after the Third Reform Act, which had given most Englishmen the right to vote. The need for gradualism and the need for democracy were closely linked in the political approach of the Fabians.

Indeed, for Sidney Webber, one of the more eminent Fabians, all serious students of society, whether or not they were socialists, recognized that

important organic changes can only be (1) democratic, and thus acceptable to the majority of the people, and prepared for in the minds of all; (2) gradual, and thus causing no dislocation, however rapid may be the rate of progress; (3) not regarded as immoral by the mass of the people, and thus not subjectively demoralizing to them; and (4) in this country at any rate, constitutional and peaceful.[7]

Fabian gradualism stemmed from two factors. One was a peculiar British disdain for untested innovations and abstract theories. This "muddling-through" approach to getting things done was prevalent among British liberals and conservatives.

The second factor was the confidence that they were winning—that the victory of socialism was the unintended consequence of the ideas and policies of even the most antisocialist leaders. As Webb put it, "The Socialist philosophy of today is but the conscious and explicit assertion of principles of social organization which have been already in great part unconsciously adopted. The economic history of the century is an almost continuous record of the progress of Socialism."[8]

Thus, both the Fabian and revisionist transition to socialism was most optimistic. Democracy, valuable in and of itself, would hasten socialism's coming. The birth of the new society from the womb of the old would be as painless as successful natural childbird.

SOCIAL DEMOCRACY AND SOVIET COMMUNISM

A second stage and major theme in the evolution of modern social democracy was its highly critical view towards the Russian Revolution of 1917 and the Soviet state it established. The basic thrust of the social democratic critique of communism could almost be deduced from the notions of Bernstein and the Fabians. Both sources had argued that any premature forcing of socialism would bring disaster. Ironically, it was Bernstein's old adversary Karl Kautsky who provided one of the earliest (1918) and most incisive social-democratic indictments of Soviet communism.

Kautsky's book *The Dictatorship of the Proletariat* applies the social-democratic maxim that socialism without democracy is a monstrosity. The title suggests the first major issue involved, for Marx, we have seen, used the expression "dictatorship of the proletariat" rarely and imprecisely. After the Bolshevik takeover in late 1917, Lenin used the term to justify repressive measures instituted by his new government. In January 1918, for example, he dissolved the Constituent Assembly, which contained a leftist majority, but a Bolshevik minority. Lenin's design for a single-party state seemed clear to many.

Kautsky completely rejected Lenin's reading of Marx. For Lenin the dictatorship of the proletariat meant a hard-line repressive regime that worked to crush the bourgeoisie. Kautsky objected, however, that once the term "dictatorship" was taken to mean a government, the hopes for democracy were dashed. From his perspective, any dictatorship means government exercised *against* the majority of the people. Historically, such dictatorships took two basic forms. The first, "jesuitism," involved the rule of a paternalistic elite, which governs the masses supposedly for their own good. The other, "Bonapartism," meant a military dictatorship based on force of arms. Neither had anything to do with true democracy.

Countering Lenin, Kautsky denied that Marx had anything like jesuitism or Bonapartism in mind with his "dictatorship of the proletariat." Rather, Marx had envisaged a broad social condition, in which the proletariat made up the majority of the populace. At that point, socialism could be voted in democratically. This is important, since for Kautsky, "we understand by modern socialism not merely social organization of production, but democratic organization of society as well."[9]

Kautsky naturally repudiated Lenin's claim that the suppression of political parties and civil liberties somehow proved that "proletarian democracy is a million times more democratic" than "bourgeois" democracy. Lenin further held that the Bolshevik party was the true representative of the proletariat and thus should govern alone in the name of that class. This was democratic because the single party was the party of the majority social class.

In Kautsky's eyes Lenin's rationalization of single-party rule was the sheerest deception. The crucial distinction is that parties *govern*, while social classes *rule*. Here governing means conducting day-to-day policy and administration. Ruling is a much broader and vaguer position of social predominance. Thus, even if the proletariat, as a class, "rules," this is no warrant for the political monopoly of a single party. As Kautsky pointed out:

> Parties and classes are therefore not necessarily coterminous. A class can split up into various parties, and a party may consist of members of various classes. A class may remain the rulers, while changes occur in the governing party, if the majority of the ruling class considers the methods of the existing governing party unsuitable, and that of its opponents more appropriate.[10]

Thus, the Bolshevik claim to be the one and only party of the proletariat is a fraud. Democracy requires a number of political parties. There may be democracy in the absence of socialism; there can be no true socialism in the absence of democracy.

The errors and repression of communism come from a fatal misreading of history. Kautsky, along with Bernstein and the Fabians, was certain that socialism was the future of human society. But they all believed as well that its coming was premised on a certain level of social and economic development. The broad spectrum of changes that this involved represented for Kautsky the true "social revolution." More explicitly this meant

> a profound transformation of the entire social structure brought about by the establishment of a new method of production. It is a protracted process, which may be spread over decades, and no definite boundaries can be drawn for its conclusion. It will be the more successful, according to the peaceful nature of the forms under which it is consummated. Civil and foreign wars are its deadly foes.[11]

Kautsky warned against confusing this profound and protracted social revolution with either political revolution or civil war.

A political revolution could possibly usher in a period of social revolution, but in itself was a violent, spasmodic affair. Of course, a revolutionary attempt may cause a long spell of violence in a civil war. This is precisely what occurred in the Russian Revolution of 1917. The grand tragedy for Kautsky is that this has aborted the true social revolution.

In Kautsky's estimation, conditions in Russia in 1917 were not truly ripe for the maturing of an authentic social revolution. Here Kautsky is sticking to the orthodox Marxist idea that the change to socialism would come first in the advanced industrial countries of the west. Russia is too backward to be a real pathbreaker in the social revolution. In these unfavorable circumstances, the dictatorship of the proletariat" touted by Lenin and the communists amounts to "nothing but a grandiose attempt to clear by bold leaps and bounds or remove by legal enactments the obstacles offered by the successive phases of normal development."[12] To follow Kautsky's own metaphor: it is as if a woman in the early stages of pregnancy got impatient and tried to induce early delivery. Too early a birth can lead to tragedy.

The coming of socialism requires certain social and economic conditions. These are far more complex than the weakness or even the collapse of this or that "bourgeois" regime. Crucial is the widespread conviction in the minds of the masses that socialism is an idea whose time has indeed come. Modern communism, because of Bolshevik recklessness, has been hopelessly damaged by the attempt to sidestep this important precondition. Social democrats have never ceased to repeat this point first made by Karl Kautsky.

THE DEBATE OVER NATIONALIZATION

The previous two phases of social-democratic ideology assumed that "socialism" meant public ownership of the basic means of production and exchange. While social democrats often counseled delay through scrupulous regard for majority rule, they foresaw a time when basic industry would be public and the whole economy run according to a central plan. Naturally, the workings of the new economic institutions would be supervised by the representatives of the people.

However, before and after World War II certain social democrats began to question these premises. Were public ownership and imperative central planning really essential to the ideals encompassed by the word "socialism"? In fact, by about 1960 most social democratic parties in Europe had internal majority factions that rejected complete nationalization and total central planning. This doctrinal development was and is strenuously opposed by a left-wing minority who cling more strictly to the traditional socialist ideal. This debate over the nature of socialism has sometimes been bitter and always instructive. We will call the position that separates public ownership from the essence of socialism the moderate view, and the traditional idea of their inseparability the leftist view.

The moderate social democratic theory pivots around one positive and one negative point. The former maintains that many of the traditional aims of socialism can be achieved without resorting to full-scale public ownership of industry. Major segments of the economy can remain in private hands, so long as government regulation and the modern welfare state operate effectively. The negative point maintains that the very large-scale organization envisaged by much of classic socialism may constitute a threat to liberty and democracy, even if ownership is public.

C.A.R. Crosland developed a classic statement of the moderate position and first published it in 1956.[13] Crosland's first task is to maintain that "socialism" does not simply mean public ownership. This is so because there is no simple, single "essence" of socialism. Indeed, there have been a "bewildering variety" of doctrines that are somehow "socialist." Moreover, there is no common economic form to these doctrines and movements. Instead, we find "certain moral values and aspirations," shared by the divergent schools of socialist throught.[14]

In Crosland's understanding, this common residue involves five key elements. First, socialism protests against the "material poverty and physical squalor which capitalism produced." Second, there is concern for "social welfare" with special reference to the poorer and weaker members of society. Third, socialism espouses the "classless society" and an egalitarian drive to enhance the rights and status of the working man. Fourth comes a repudiation of the harshness of the old competitive view and a desire for a fraternal and cooperative order. Finally, there is a critique of traditional capitalism directed against its "inefficiencies" and "notably its tendency to mass unemployment."[15]

Because these ideas combine several specific criticisms of old-fashioned capitalism with social aspirations once thought incompatible with it, it was natural for classic socialists to cut the Gordian knot by demanding full public ownership of the means of production and exchange. Understandable in its time, this viewpoint has become obsolete in the post-World War II era. The first reason is the set of changes that have transformed capitalism beyond recognition. The second reason has to do with certain "sociological" findings that considerably lessen the attractiveness of public ownership and management of large industrial organizations.

To Crosland the transformation of capitalism includes three basic trends that began before World War II but matured only afterwards. First of these is the growth in the role and functions of the state. In contrast to the "laissez-faire" of classic capitalism, the modern economy, spurred by the Great Depression and the war, is closely controlled by government. This "sea change" flows against the old idea that public ownership was the only antidote to the runaway irresponsibility of private capitalists and their mastery over the "bourgeois state." In recent times, on the contrary, the state "consciously regulates (or seeks to regulate) the level of employment, the distribution of income, the rate of accumulation, and the balance of payments; and its actions heavily influence the size of industries, the pattern of output, and the direction of investment decisions."[16]

The crucial point is not merely the expanded role of the state, but its orientation. That is, the state is no longer "the executive committee" of the ruling (capitalist) class. As Crosland puts it, "The fact that governments now exercise this pervasive economic power, and that they do so from motives other than a desire to prop up private business, would be sufficient by itself to outmode most prewar, semi-Marxist analyses of class power."[17] Much of the old rationale for nationalization is lost in the face of these changes.

A second major transformation in the structure of capitalism is the altered balance of power between owners and workers. For the old-time socialists the system of private ownership enshrined the permanent domination of capitalists over workers. The major new factor here is the growing strength of the workers. A key aspect of this is the political and economic power of the trade unions, which has finally redressed the old imbalance that favored the businessmen. Another is the stronger bargaining position gained by workers because of the full employment policy of the modern welfare state. In other words, the old Marxist idea of a vast "industrial reserve army" of unemployed who could take the places of rebellious or dissatisfied workers is no longer valid.

Perhaps an even more significant shift has occurred within the leadership of the typical large firm in the modern economy. Crosland makes much of the "divorce between ownership and control" that we discussed in Chapter 4. The basic idea is that the legal owners of modern large enterprise (stockholders, large and small) do not really control the policies and decisions of the management. For Crosland, "this partial change in the character of the decision-making function naturally calls for men with a different outlook and equipment, and therefore different interests and motives from those of the traditional capitalists."[18] This change also means that some of the old class-struggle themes behind the traditional demands for public ownership lose their relevance.

The "managerial revolution" also contributes to the third major transformation. This involves a change in the attitudes of businessmen themselves. In the old days businessmen would parade their individual success in the dog-eat-dog world of competitive capitalism. Those who fell by the wayside in this struggle were considered deserving of their fate because of their personal "unfitness" or incompetence. Such stridency from businessmen, however, has been considerably toned down both by the failures of the old-fashioned capitalism and the new distribution of economic and political power.

There is a new tone insofar as "agressive individualism is giving way to a suave and sophisticated sociability: the defiant cry of 'public be damned' to the well-staffed public relations department: the self-made autocratic tycoon to the arts graduate and the scientist: the invisible hand . . . to the glad hand. Private industry is at last becoming humanized."[19] These changes of attitude and personnel mean that modern businessmen do not feel the fear and loathing for government that their ancestors did. Moreover, they admit that the "profit motive" is not sufficient justification for their firms: the firm and its leaders have come to accept social responsibilities wholly alien to the old-line capitalist establishment.

These three transformations caused Crosland to doubt whether the term "capitalism" could still be applied to the postwar western economies. At any rate, the case for public ownership was seriously weakened. But let us recall that Crosland stressed a more negative point against it. The socialist ideal had assumed that certain dehumanizing features of capitalism would automatically disappear once public ownership was installed. Crosland questions this optimism once again because ownership is not the crucial factor involved. The real problem is "large-scale" organization itself. The unpleasant fact of life is that "a collectivized economy, with no private owners, is no less characterized by the alienation of control than a capitalist economy."[20]

Crosland is suggesting that the employee tends to lose control over his work in huge firms, regardless of who owns them. The Soviet experience is once more chastening to moderate social democrats. Nevertheless, Crosland's rejection of wholesale public ownership as a cure-all does not mean that he is entirely happy with the social and economic status quo. Inequalities still abound and needless suffering and privation are all too prevalent. The agenda of the welfare state is uncompleted and many valuable reforms still await implementation. Programs that aim at the "hardcore" poor, more equality of educational opportunity, environmental and quality-of-life issues, more worker participation at the workplace—these and other areas will keep social democratic reformers busy well into the next century. The objectives, if not precisely the instrumentalites, of the classic socialists will yet give social democrats a sense of direction.

Leftist Social Democracy

Left-wing social democrats, like R. H. S. Crossman who, with Crosland, was a member of the British Labor Party, are rather more dissatisfied with the progress of western societies. They share the same commitment to political democracy and a similar dismay at communist regimes as their moderate adversaries—leftists, however, are somewhat more prone to favor a "neutral" foreign policy in the Cold War than are the pro-American social democratic moderates. The leftists' much more critical stance toward contemporary western societies is both cause and effect of their abiding faith in the anticapitalist core of traditional socialism.

They see the transformations portrayed by the moderates as far less pervasive and far more superficial. They see the inequalities and inefficiencies of contemporary capitalism as more galling and persistent. They are thus far less ready than the moderates to abandon the public ownership solution to these lingering evils. Since the rich get richer, even if the poor do not get poorer in absolute terms, and since poverty and pollution clearly indicate the failure of our present economic system to allocate resources properly, the nationalization of industry or some other form of public management seems eminently attractive.

As Crossman saw it in 1959, the appeal of communism to under-developed countries will determine the future of freedom in the modern world. For the world's hungry majority communism's performance does alleviate certain discontents. But he is alarmed because the "kind of Keynesian managed capitalism which has evolved since the war is intrinsically unable to sustain the competition with the Eastern bloc to which we are now committed."[21] When confronted with the choice between the economic change plus despotism offered by the communist model and the economic stagnation plus political freedom offered by the west, poorer countries may well choose their stomachs before their brains.

Left-wing social democrats like Crossman see just one way to avoid this unpleasant result. Western countries must combine their admirable concern with freedom with rapid and substantial movement towards the goals of equality and mass well-being associated with traditional socialism. This means profound socioeconomic change for,

> whatever our intentions, wishes, or individual capabilities, the nations of the Western world will be unable to strengthen themselves by developing adequate public services until the public sector becomes the dominant sector in our economies. Only in this way shall we make it possible to work out a true national resources budget, which strikes the proper balance between production and consumption goods and ensures that community interests are given their proper priority over individual consumption.[22]

Such an expanded public sector naturally will involve substantial nationalization, although even here Crossman voices fear of the new bureacratic-managerial elite that troubles all modern social democrats.

What distinguishes leftists like Crossman from moderates like Crosland is their belief that truly democratic methods of planning and economic management will be found. Fear of communism and its perversion of socialism must not deter true socialists from going beyond capitalism. Care and caution does not mean paralysis.

CONCLUSION

In this chapter we have traced the major trends of social-democratic ideology. Originating with the German revisionists and the British Fabians, social democracy first became a distinct ideological system by rejecting the revolutionary road to socialism in favor of the slower and surer route of political democracy. The Russian Revolution of 1917 further hardened the positions separating revolutionary socialists (communists) and evolutionary socialists (social democrats). A third phase culminating in the 1950s found many social democrats considering the old socialist ideal of public ownership obsolete. Structural changes had so transformed traditional capitalism that certain of the abuses that outraged earlier social democrats were gone and others seemed remediable.

In addition, the Soviet experience and the operation of nationalized industries has indicated that workers' alienation was not automatically ended by ousting the capitalist owners. Large-scale public organizations could be just as empty and oppressive as private organizations.

Left-wing social democrats, however, are still strong, as their recent victories in the British Labor Party would suggest. They, of course, are far less content with the changes modern capitalism has undergone. While they would not necessarily move immediately to full nationalization of industry, they would significantly expand the public sector at the expense of the private sector. This reflects both their traditional anticapitalism and their conviction that effective and equitable planning of even a so-called "mixed economy" necessitates direct governmental control over strategic segments of the economy.

One interesting result of the evolution of mainstream or moderate social democracy is its convergence with the modern liberal standpoint discussed in Chapter 12. As social democracy has moved away from pure socialism, modern liberalism evolved out of classic liberalism by moving away from pure laissez-faire capitalism. This convergence means that modern social democrats and modern liberals often are in substantial agreement on important issues. Perhaps the main difference is that even today it would be easier for social democrats to advocate government programs to solve social problems than it is for modern liberals. The latter's individualism would make them a bit more cautious about government and bureaucracy.

NOTES

1. The Communist International or Comintern was founded on March 4, 1919, at the initiative of Lenin and the Russian Communists. It was the alternative to the Second International (socialist), which Lenin considered far too conservative to represent the interests of world proletarian revolution. In 1920 Lenin and others had drawn up the famous "Twenty-One Conditions" for membership in the organization. These conditions were designed to exclude nonrevolutionary elements. "While losing for the Comintern a goodly number of sympathizers, the conditions did ensure that each member section of the International possessed a certain standard of Leninist orthodoxy in fundamental principles and aims, as well as in matters of organization, strategy, and tactics." Kermit E. McKenzie, *Comintern and World Revolution 1928–1943* (New York: Columbia University Press, 1964), p. 31. As part of

Stalin's attempt to cement good war-time relations with the West, the Comintern was dissolved in 1943.
2. In the late 1950s and 1960s the term "revisionism" was used in the debates among and within communist countries. First, the term was applied to Yugoslavia, and then, with the outbreak of the Sino-Soviet dispute, the Chinese used it as a term of abuse against the Soviets. The connection between this sort of "revisionism" with that of sixty years earlier and social democracy is quite tenuous. It is best to keep the two quite separate.
3. Eduard Bernstein, *Evolutionary Socialism* (New York: Schocken Books, 1961), p. 213.
4. Ibid, p. 219.
5. Ibid., p. 49.
6. George Bernard Shaw (ed.), *Fabian Essays in Socialism* (Garden City, N. Y.: Dolphin Books, n.d.), pp. 224–25.
7. Sidney Webb, in *Fabian Essays*, p. 51.
8. Ibid., p. 47.
9. Karl Kautsky, *The Dictatorship of the Proletariat* (Ann Arbor: University of Michigan Press, 1964), p. 6.
10. Ibid., p.32.
11. Ibid., p. 55.
12. Ibid, p. 98.
13. C.A.R. Crosland, *The Future of Socialism,* rev. ed. (New York: Schocken Books, 1963).
14. Ibid, p. 65. Here, of course, the tenor of Crosland's argument runs counter to the interpretation of chapter 4 of this text, where "public ownership" and "socialism" are closely linked.
15. Ibid., p.67.
16. Ibid., p. 30.
17. Ibid., p. 10.
18. Ibid., p. 15
19. Ibid., p. 18.
20. Ibid., p. 37.
21 R.H.S. Crossman, *The Politics of Socialism* (New York: Atheneum, 1965), p. 111.
22. Ibid., p. 110.

SUGGESTIONS FOR FURTHER READING

Bernstein, Eduard. *Evolutionary Socialism.* New York: Schocken, 1961.
Crosland, C.A.R. *The Future of Socialism.* rev. ed. New York, Schocken, 1963.
Kautsky, Karl. *The Dictatorship of the Proletariat.* Ann Arbor: University of Michigan Press, 1964.
Labedz, Leopold, ed. *Revisionism: Essays on the History of Marxist Ideas.* New York: Praeger, 1962.
Myrdal, Gunnar. *Beyond the Welfare State.* New York: Bantam Books, 1967.
Titmuss, Richard M. *Essays on the Welfare State.* Boston: Beacon Press, 1969.

11

CHRISTIAN DEMOCRACY

Although some might dispute the consideration of Christian Democracy as a full-fledged ideology, no one would seriously deny that it is one of the most successful political movements in the postwar world. In the 1940s and 1950s Christian Democratic parties were dominant in Italy and Germany and have retained considerable strength since then. Similarly, in France, the Netherlands, Switzerland, Austria, and parts of Latin America, such parties receive a very respectable amount of support.

While Christian Democratic parties are not clones of each other, they all reflect the political importance of Roman Catholicism. There are now two exceptions to this rule: one, in West Germany where the Christian Democratic party has appealed to substantial numbers of Protestants; the other, in the Netherlands, where the 1970s saw the emergence of a Christian Democratic Party that merged two small Protestant parties with the somewhat larger Catholic Peoples Party.

ORIGINS OF CHRISTIAN DEMOCRACY

Although Christian Democratic parties and leaders show a pragmatism and opportunism similar to other parties and leaders, writing off the "Christian" element of their programs and proclamations would be a serious mistake. Modern Christian Democracy is the result of trends in the late nineteenth century aiming to bring Catholicism closer to the social problems and political currents of the times. To sense the importance of these developments, a little historical background is necessary.

It was the French Revolution of 1789 that forced the Roman Catholic Church into an even more active political role than previously. During certain phases of the revolution, the Church in France underwent persecution. Though later phases saw a modus vivendi between the state and the church, shock waves of the initial confrontation spread throughout Europe and lasted well into the next century. The French Revolution became the center of liberal and democratic ideas that sometimes clashed resoundingly with the institutional position, social doctrines, and philosophical teachings of the Church. The first result was the Church's embracing a conservative viewpoint close to the conservatism we will discuss in Chapter 12. This ultraconservative stance lasted nearly a century after the trauma of the French Revolution.

Naturally, over this long span, attempts were made by individual Catholics, lay and clerical, to bring liberal, democratic, and even socialistic currents into the Roman Catholic scheme of things. These were generally rejected by the Popes and the Church hierarchy of the day. The acme of this papal hard-line was the famous *Syllabus of Errors* of Pope Pius IX, which was issued in 1864. The *Syllabus* was a listing of false, pernicious, and heretical ideas that threatened to mislead the unwary faithful.

Pope Pius referred to many "errors" about the nature of religion and the role of the Church. He rejected separation of church and state, questioned toleration of other religions, and affirmed the absolute truth of traditional Catholic doctrine. Perhaps the eightieth error encapsulates all the rest. Here Pope Pius warned against the false notion that the "Roman pontiff can, and ought to, reconcile himself, and come to terms with progress, liberalism, and modern civilization."[1]

However, it was not very long after Pius's death in 1878 that a definite softening of the Church's official attitude occurred. Pope Leo XIII (1878–1903), though preserving part of his predecessor's legacy, sensed that immovability on all issues could throw many people into the hands of the Church's sworn enemies. To forestall this desperate flight to socialism and radicalism, the Church should address the burning social and political issues of modern times. It had to explore the causes of those ideologies and movements it feared and deplored. Just to shout at them would not make them go away. Such is the meaning of Leo's pontificate.

One of the first substantial moves from ideas to action came in Italy nearly two decades after the death of Leo XIII. At the close of World War I a priest, Don Luigi Sturzo, founded and led the Popular Party. Unfortunately, the times were too turbulent for the lasting success of a moderate Catholic party of reform. Outflanked on the left by the Socialists and Communists, and on the right by the Nationalists and newly born Fascists, the Popolari weakened and soon lost the support of the Church hierarchy. Much more successful was the launching of the Italian Christian Democratic party after World War II.

Perhaps the best way to understand the ideology of modern Christian Democracy is to start with the teachings of the medieval philosopher St. Thomas Aquinas (c. 1225–1274). Next we should look at the birth of modern Christian Democracy in terms of the social ideas of Pope Leo XIII. Finally, we can bring Christian Democracy into the postwar period of its maximum influence by examining the social and political philosophy of Jacques Maritain, a French thinker who profoundly influenced it.

ST. THOMAS AQUINAS

Although "Thomism" (i.e., the philosophy of St. Thomas Aquinas) has never been declared the official philosophy of the Roman Catholic Church, to say nothing of Christian Democratic parties, it exercises a formative influence on Christian Democracy. Naturally, St. Thomas advanced a "theocentric" view of the world that makes the world and all in it the creation of God. He thus concerned himself both with complex theological issues and more mundane ethical and political questions. What connected all these topics was his view of the various types of law in the world. The most basic law of all was "eternal law," the law of God's own mind. Eternal law constitutes the overall plan that God has made for his whole creation. Accordingly, mere mortals can only hope to grasp certain aspects of the Divine Providence.

Derived from the eternal law is natural law, the ethical foundation of human society. Natural law involves the commands that God has issued to govern the relations among his creatures. It can be known by all rational creatures, so that even non-Christians can know its essential principles. It prohibits such things as murder, theft, incest, and other vices and crimes.

At a more specific level than natural law, we have human law. While ideally the provisions of human law should follow the precepts of natural law, this sometimes proves difficult. There is a certain unavoidable variability in how closely actual legal systems of communities can live up to natural law. Human law, moreover, emerges in two basic forms. First, the "law of nations" derives more or less directly from natural law. These are rules of equity and comity that are observed in all times and places. On the other hand, St. Thomas points to "those norms which derive from the natural law as particular applications" and which make up civil law which any city determines "according to its particular requirements."[2] Thus, we can say that the "law of nations" embodies the "letter" of natural law, while "civil law" is related more to its "spirit."

As a Christian philosopher St. Thomas could not rest content with human law and natural law with their basis in human reason and human experience. Another kind of law, divine law, is necessary to provide guidance in specifically religious areas. Human and natural law would suffice if man were simply and purely a natural creature, but he has a soul and eternal destiny as well. Divine law, which is made known to us through revelation and the Gospel, relates specifically to human salvation and human duty.

In addition to his Christian inspiration, St. Thomas was an ardent disciple of the ancient Greek philosopher Aristotle. Indeed, his favorite expression for the Greek thinker was simply "the Philosopher." From Aristotle, St. Thomas derived the idea that man is a social and political animal. His nature, as God created it, disposes man to need and seek the society of his fellow creatures. In this sense also the state is intended by God to answer to man's basic nature. The state, therefore, has an ethical purpose: the welfare of the whole community. In St. Thomas's thirteenth-century perspective this unitary goal could best be achieved through the government of one ruler and so he advocated the monarchical form of government.

It is only in this latter conclusion that modern Christian Democrats would decline to follow St. Thomas. That natural and divine law should be the basis of everyday law and morality so far as this is possible is not disputed. Also retained is the idea of the state as a "natural" community that should strive to promote the welfare of all its citizens. The difference, of course, is that "democracy" in some sense is preferable to "monarchy." We see a sort of transition point of these doctrines in the encyclicals (i.e., general letters of church doctrine) of Pope Leo XIII. There the Church abandons its earlier suspicions about democratic government and takes a more neutral stance towards forms of government. This paves the way for the full-scale reconciliation of Catholicism and democracy embodied in modern Christian democracy.

LEO XIII

In certain of his encyclicals Pope Leo XIII took occasion to bemoan the growth of socialism and other forms of antireligious radicalism. His animosity towards these movements sometimes recalled that of Pius IX. However, where the latter hurled anathemas at these hateful groups and their ideas, Leo looked at the causes of their growth as well. The Industrial Revolution had unleashed forces that had degraded broad segments of the working class. Poverty and immorality were rife in urban centers. Simple greed afflicted many capitalists who squeezed ever more out of their workers without real concern for them as members of the human family. Unscrupulous extremist agitators were adept at fishing in such troubled waters.

The social teachings of Leo XIII essentially form the central theme of modern Christian Democracy: *How to reconcile the values and traditions of traditional society with the need to improve social conditions in a social framework.* Certain aspects of traditional society have a more enduring value than others. These are the family, private property, and social diversity. Concern for these things carries over into modern Christian democracy.

Of the utmost importance for Pope Leo was the family. He articulated its basic place in Roman Catholic social doctrine in the following way: "We have the family, the 'society' of a man's house—a society very small, one must admit, but none the less a true society, and one older than any State. Consequently, it has rights and duties peculiar to itself which are quite independent of the State."[3] Leo spoke in this way because the first family, that of Adam, long antedated the foundation of the state.

The family, moreover, is a "natural society", in the Aristotelian sense of having self-contained goals and purposes. As such it is a part of the Providence of God. This is a part of the reason for the strong Roman Catholic stand against divorce and abortion—these are not only sinful in themselves, they also undermine the sanctity of the family. Accordingly, it makes eminent good sense to protect the family against the corrosive effects of dire poverty and runaway industrialization. It is a Christian duty to work against any and all trends that undermine the place of the family in social life.

While Pope Leo suggested possible state action to improve the lot of the poor, in no way did he attack the institution of private property as such. Here too the basic theory goes back through St. Thomas to Aristotle. Once again private property is understood as a "natural" institution. It allows us to mix our personalities with material things and thus to make them part of ourselves. Thus to eliminate private property as collectivist doctrines demand would be to commit the highest injustice.

However, Leo's defense of private property has another Aristotelian property that separates it from the traditional liberal notion. In classic liberalism the right to property is virtually absolute: the owner is free to use or dispose of his property as his free choice determines. Pope Leo did not deny this outright but adds a dimension of duty and responsibility inherent in the possession of wealth. Though wealth should be privately owned, the owner should make public use of it. He should so employ his wealth as to benefit the community. Most important, given the Church's concern with the poor, is the duty of charity. The more fortunate members of the community should extend themselves to succor the less fortunate. Such helping should involve neither condescension on the one side nor embarassment on the other.

Both Pope Leo and modern-day Christian Democrats offer a defense of social diversity that accepts a certain amount of social *inequality*. Once more there is an appeal to what is "natural." It is by nature, writes Pope Leo, that "people differ in capacity, skill, health, strength, and unequal fortune is a necessary result of unequal condition. Such inequality is far from being disadvantageous either to individuals or the community. Social and public life can only be maintained by means of various kinds of capacity for business or the playing of many parts."[4] Instead of pitting class against class, these differences should result in a spirit of collaboration and mutual respect. The doctrine of inevitable class struggle is a falsehood spread by doctrinaire socialists.

In addition to defending religion and traditional social institutions, Leo XIII advanced a broad program aimed at improving the condition of the working class. Owners and workers should assume mutual obligations roughly in the sense of "an honest day's pay for an honest day's work." Beyond this Leo advocated a massive expansion of associations in the world of labor. Not just trade unions, but all sorts of mutual aid societies should be developed to cushion workers against the bumps of economic and working life. Moreover, the leisure time of workers should be channeled into uplifting pursuits.

In all of these measures Pope Leo called for the strong leadership of Catholics, both lay and clerical. Those who responded to the challenge were "worthy of all praise" for they "have taken up the cause of the working man, and have spared no efforts to better the condition of both families and individuals; to infuse a spirit of equity into the mutual relations of employers and employed; to keep the eyes of both classes on the precepts of duty and the laws of the Gospel."[5]

Toward the end of his pontificate (1901) Leo addressed himself to the nascent Christian Democratic movement, though at that time it had not yet assumed its future political form. Thus, he used the term "Christian Democracy" to designate the concerns and commitments we have just surveyed. Accordingly, he denied that approval of the term meant exclusive preference for "democracy" as a form of government. He hoped that "Christian Democracy" would be used "without any political significance, so as to mean nothing else than this beneficient Christian action in behalf of the people."[6]

Though Christian Democracy both as a doctrine and a movement would advance beyond this apolitical framework of Leo's, his guiding themes still reverberate in the speeches of Christian Democratic politicans and the writings of Christian Democratic thinkers. The religious and moral basis of society, the need to modify laissez-faire, the importance of the masses and their welfare, the defense of social institutions— these notions are alive and well in broad areas of Europe and Latin America.

JACQUES MARITAIN

Building upon the Thomistic foundations of the middle ages and the social teachings of Popes like Leo XIII and Pius XI (1922–39), Christian Democratic movements emerged after 1945 with renewed vigor. After the cataclysm of World War II, which saw the destruction of the Nazi and Fascist regimes, the times seemed ripe for a political movement that rejected the neopaganism of the extreme right and the atheism of the extreme left. For many, spiritual solace was to be sought in a return to religious orthodoxy. Though "democracy" had apparently defeated "dictatorship" in the late war, some thought that the totalitarian challenge had been so grave partly because prewar democracy lacked a firm religious-moral foundation.

This was the conviction of Jacques Maritain, a French Roman Catholic philosopher, who more than anyone else can be considered the "philosopher" of modern Christian Democracy. Three overarching themes developed by Maritain find reflection in Christian Democratic programs and pronouncements. These are "personalism," "pluralism," and the "religious basis" of democracy.

Personalism

Personalism was a doctrine closely associated with Maritain. He chose the term as a contrast to the "individualism" of the great liberal tradition. For Maritain—and most Christian Democrats—the individualism of liberalism is one-sided and incomplete. It is basically materialistic and sees man as a social atom ready either to profit from society or, if unlucky, to suffer from it. The motto of this sort of individualism seems to be "Watch out from number one."

Personalism, on the contrary, views the human being not just as a matrix of material wants and needs, but as an essentially spiritual creature. The person thus has a higher vocation and closer relationship with the Divine than a crude individualism can embody. It is not so much that material individuality is bad, but that it is incomplete. To focus on it exclusively or excessively would bar man from reaching the higher levels of his personal development. On the other hand, when the "development follows the direction of *spiritual personality*, then it will be in the direction of the generous self of saints and heroes that it will be carried. Man will really be a person, in so far as the life of spirit and freedom will dominate in him that of passion and the senses."[7]

Moreover, a personalist conception of man avoids the counterpoised pitfalls of social anarchy and social despotism. Personalism can admit that man can realize his human potential only in the framework of the social order. This does not mean, however, that the "aim of society" is simply the good of discrete individuals who compose it: "This formula would dissolve society *as such* for the benefit of its parts, and would lead to an 'anarchy of atoms.' "[8] On the contrary, "the end of society is its *common good*, the good of the body politics."[9]

Of course, antiliberal doctrines like communism and fascism also claim to enshrine the common good. Against such views, Maritain makes a strong disclaimer that "if one fails to grasp the fact that the good of the body politic is a common good of human persons—as the social body itself is a whole made up of human persons—this formula may lead in its turn to other errors of the collectivist or totalitarian type."[10] In his book *Man and the State*, Maritain makes the point more forcefully yet:

> The State is not the supreme incarnation of the Idea, as Hegel believed: the State is not a kind of collective superman; the State is but an agency entitled to use power and coercion, and made up of specialists in public order and welfare, an instrument in the service of man. Putting man at the service of that instrument is political perversion.[11]

Pluralism

The way to avoid the despotism of totalitarianism and the rigidity of collectivism is with a strong sense of *pluralism*.[12] Such pluralism can also avoid the defects of "atomistic" individualism. The general theory of pluralism asserts the importance of the group in the social order. The Christian Democratic pluralism of Maritain looks to two aspects of pluralism: vertical and horizontal.[13] Vertical pluralism represents a significant shift away from the dogmatism of the days of Pius IX. At that time Catholic doctrine questioned the right of non-Catholic "spiritual families" to exist. In the modern doctrine of vertical pluralism, however, there is a clear recognition that Protestant and certain secularist outlooks are essential parts of modern culture.

Instead of simply opposing or dismissing these trends, cordial and even cooperative relations between them and the "Catholic world" should be fostered whenever and wherever possible. As Maritain himself formulates this issue, we find that " men belonging to very different philosophical or religious creeds and lineages could and should cooperate in the common task and for the common welfare of the earthly community, provided they similarly assent to the charter and basic tenets of a society of free men."[14] Indeed, the German Christian Democratic Party, with its strong Protestant contingent, would be unthinkable without the rapprochement proclaimed by vertical pluralism.

"Horizontal pluralism" responds to the more standard concerns of political pluralists. These latter have always maintained that neither society as a whole nor the isolated individual is the proper focus of political thinking or social policy. Instead it is the social group. Left-wing pluralists are preoccupied with trade unions; right-wing pluralists with traditional groups like the family, the locality, and the church. Christian Democrats try to find a place for all these structures. Though some pluralists are inclined to depose or denigrate the state, Christian Democracy, we have seen, favors a strong, though limited state.

Thus, Christian Democratic pluralism criticizes liberal individualism for seeing specific individuals but not the body politic and the common good, while it attacks socialistic collectivism for seeing the whole but not the parts. In the Christian Democratic rendition of pluralism there is more than the individual, but the collectivity is not the whole story either. In other words, a vibrant society is made up of a myriad of social groupings. Maritain, in particular, envisaged a process, which, allowing a certain role for the state, would culminate in a social order honeycombed with autonomous yet cooperative groups. In the end,

> all organic forms of social and economic activity, even the largest and most comprehensive ones, would start from the bottom, I mean from the free initiative of and mutual tension between the particular groups, working communities, cooperative agencies, unions, associations, federated bodies of producers and consumers, rising in tiers and institutionally recognized . . . . And the state would leave to the multifarious organs of the social body the autonomous initiative and management of all activities which pertain to them.[15]

Naturally, the pluralism of religious thinkers like Maritain and of Christian Democrats is generally designed to maximize the Church's sphere of autonomy.

This application of "horizontal" pluralism is related to the vertical aspect. Because the latter recognizes that the Church cannot occupy the same privileged position it held universally in the middle ages, horizontal pluralism ensures that the Church will not be further dispossessed. Naturally, it is not just the Church that receives special solicitude in Christian Democratic pluralism. We know that the family is one of the "natural" communities dear to religious thinkers. The solidity of the nuclear family, recall, explains part of the historical stance of the Church against divorce, abortion, and birth control. Accordingly, Christian Democracy favors special policies designed to maintain and subsidize the traditional family.

Among these policies would be public support of religious education. In the Christian Democratic view, this does not really violate the now-established principle of separation of church and state, but merely allows parents the right to direct the overall spiritual development of their children. This issue has often been a bone of contention with moderate political groups who otherwise share many policy positions with Christian Democratic parties.

The Religious Basis of Democracy

Christian Democrats favor democracy as the only possible and just form of government suitable to the modern world. And yet, as we implied above, Christian Democratic thinkers like Maritain feel that democracy requires a more solid moral foundation than its traditional defense. One sore point is the doctrine of "popular sovereignty" so prevalent in traditional democratic theory.[16] According to this notion the whole people is sovereign (i.e., the highest power) and the unique legitimate source of law and policy.

Some doctrines of popular sovereignty even hold that *vox populi vox dei:* the voice of the people is the voice of God. Such thinking seems blasphemous to the Roman Catholic teaching, which maintains that God alone is truly sovereign and that in matters of faith and morals the Pope is the highest authority. For these and other reasons Maritain has advised the abandonment of the very notion of sovereignty—a bugaboo for virtually all varieties of pluralists. Sovereignty seems to suggest a power that is not only "highest" but virtually unaccountable to anyone. In this sense, however, neither the state not the people can be sovereign. In the case of the power wielded by the people "either by mass reflexes and extra-legal means, or through the regular channels of a truly democratic society," it is "in no way a power without accountability. For they are the very ones who fit the bill. They are sure to account to their own sweat and blood for their mistakes."[17]

To make matters worse, certain doctrines of popular sovereignty seem to undermine the Roman Catholic concept of natural law. Recall that natural law is the set of moral guidelines established by God to govern social relations. While the precepts of natural law often have to be modified to fit special circumstances, it always stands in judgment over the actions and policies of political regimes. If popular sovereignty means that any policy is legitimate provided that the people approves, there would be little place for a transcendent standard such as natural law. Christian Democracy would not accept such a rudderless "democracy."

Over the centuries there have been expressions of democratic doctrines that have been hostile or indifferent to traditional religion. Though modern Christian Democracy accepts separation of church and state and vertical pluralism, this does not entail complete public noninvolvement in religious matters. Indeed, the strongest basis for a democratic polity is a moral cohesion ultimately deriving from religion. Thus, separation of church and state means neither conflict nor mutual isolation, but rather *cooperation*.

The state has its mission and goals and so does the Church. In the peculiar province of each, the other should not impinge upon its rights and competence. But there are areas of overlap where an amicable collaboration is both feasible and desirable. With education and welfare, for example, more will be accomplished for all by an association between church and state, that is neither a fusion nor an isolation.

In all this it must be remembered that the Christian Democrat is serious about his Christianity. In a certain sense, therefore, he sees the Church as superior to the state or any other temporal institution. This "superiority" does not mean that the Church can dictate to the state as it sometimes did in medieval times. Rather the Church's superiority comes from its mission of saving and safeguarding souls. This mission is even higher than the state's promotion of the common good. The Church's mission is to be measured against eternity; the state's against the here and now. While there can be no question of theocracy, the autonomy of the Church to pursue her mission is of the utmost importance.

Here again, a strong sense of social pluralism will be enough to protect the Church from assaults upon its proper sphere of activity. The role of the state is important here. To some groups the state will simply grant freedom within the broad frame of the law. For groups that abuse this freedom and pose a threat to security and order, the state may have to act as an organ of social self-defense. But there is a third category of groups, for which the state should go a step further. Thus, it should "grant institutional recognition to those religious communities—as well as to all associations, religious or secular, educational, scientific, or devoted to social service, whose activity is of major importance for the common welfare." [18]

CONCLUSION

At the start of this chapter we noted that some people might question the consideration of Christian Democracy as a true and proper ideology. They would argue that the undoubted political success of Christian Democratic parties was due more to their middle-of-the-road policies and the outstanding adroitness of their leaders than it is to anything "Christian" about them. Naturally, almost any political party will show a mixture of "true believers" and career-minded opportunists, and Christian Democratic parties are certainly no exception to this rule.

Nevertheless, there are certain policy areas where the "Christian" mark of Christian Democratic parties is clear and strong. For example, we would assume that the Christian "universalism" based on Natural Law and the "ultramontane" (i.e., transnational) character of the Roman Catholic Church itself would act as a damper on the passions associated with extreme nationalism. We are not disappointed if we look to one of the most momentous developments of recent European history. Our test case is the evolution of the European Economic Community from a glorified customs union to a serious attempt to integrate the economies of member countries like Great Britain, France, Italy, Germany, Belgium, Luxembourg, the Netherlands, and Portugal. In the 1950s when the foundations of the European Economic Community were being laid, Christian Democratic leaders such as Konrad Adenauer in West Germany, Alcide DeGasperi in Italy, and Robert Schumann in France were instrumental in overcoming deep-seated national animosities and mistrust. There is little doubt that the ideological affinity based on Christian Democracy was a critical variable in the shaky early days of this "grand experiment."

More broadly, the notions of vertical and horizontal pluralism have given rise to policies such as family support and labor legislation which have proven quite popular. Even the apparently more philosophical notion of "personalism" undergirds the Christian Democratic attempt to avoid the extremes of pure laissez-faire capitalism on the one and pure socialistic collectivism on the other. Such a middling position also corresponds with the political center of gravity in many European countries, thus allowing Christian Democratic parties to reap electoral and political advantages. Christian Democracy does appeal to certain concerns in the modern world.

NOTES

1. Pius IX, "A Syllabus of Errors," in *The Papal Encyclicals in Their Historical Context*, ed. A. Fremantle (New York: Mentor Books, 1956), p. 152.
2. St. Thomas Aquinas, *Aquinas: Selected Political Writings*, ed. A. P. D'Entreves (Oxford: Basil Blackwell, 1954), p. 31.
3. Pope Leo XIII, "Rerum Novarum," in *The Church Speaks to the Modern World*, ed. E. Gilson (New York: Image Books, 1962), p. 211.
4. Ibid., pp. 213-14.
5. Ibid, p. 234.
6. "On Christian Democracy," in Ibid., p. 318.
7. Jacques Maritain, *Scholasticism and Politics* (New York: Image Books, 1960), p. 69.
8. Ibid., p.72.
9. Ibid.
10. Ibid.
11. Jacques Maritain, *Man and the State* (Chicago: University of Chicago Press), p. 13.
12. See Michael J. Fogarty, *Christian Democracy in Western Europe 1820–1953* (South Bend, Ind.: University of Notre Dame Press, 1966), esp. Ch. 4.

13. On the specifically religious plane vertical pluralism is the preparatory step to the ecumenical movement for closer relationships among the chief branches of Christianity launched by Popes John XXIII and Paul VI.
14. Jacques Maritain, *The Social and Political Philosophy of Jacques Maritain*, ed. J. W. Evans and L. R. Ward (South Bend Ind.: University of Notre Dame Press, 1976), p. 117.
15. Maritain, *Man and the State*, p. 23.
16. This comes out most clearly in doctrines influenced by Rousseau's "general will" as we saw in Ch. 2.
17. Maritain, *Man and the State,* p. 53.
18. Ibid, p. 174.

SUGGESTIONS FOR FURTHER READING

Fogarty, Michael J. *Christian Democracy in Western Europe 1820–1953.* South Bend, Ind.: University of Notre Dame Press, 1966.
Gilson, Etienne, ed. *The Church Speaks to the Modern World.* New York: Image Books, 1962.
Irving, R.E.M., ed. *The Christian Democratic Parties of Western Europe.* London: Allen & Unwin, 1979.
Maritain, Jacques. *The Social and Political Philosophy of Jacques Maritain.* Ed. by J. W. Evans and L. R. Ward. South Bned, Ind.: University of Notre Dame Press, 1976.
Menczer, Bela, ed. *Catholic Political Thought 1789–1848.* South Bend, Ill.: University of Notre Dame Press, 1962.

12

LIBERALISM

This chapter emphasizes the political aspects of liberalism. Certain economic aspects were covered in Chapter 4 in discussing the neoclassical approach to capitalism. The neoclassical approach comes right out of classic liberalism, whereas theorists of managerial capitalism lean more toward modern liberalism. Such debates, whether today, or a hundred or two hundred years ago, represent a basic tension in all forms of liberalism: the balance between liberty and equality. All liberals cherish both, but their meaning and connection are highly controversial.

CLASSIC LIBERALISM

Classic liberalism stresses laissez-faire and has doubts about democracy. In other words, freedom is understood as basically "negative" and requires that the role of government be kept to a minimum. Democracy is threatening because it may bring undue expansion of the role and powers of government. This would be at the expense of liberty. We will see later on that modern liberalism has a different conception of freedom and a more favorable estimate of democracy and the expanded role of government.

Natural-Rights Liberalism: John Locke

Classic liberalism has several major forms. These reflect specific national traditions as well as divergent philosophical backgrounds. Our treatment will stress the latter differences. One version is the natural-rights liberalism epitomized—some say founded—by John Locke in late seventeenth-century England. Given our earlier discussion of Locke in Chapter 2, we will now only elaborate his doctrine that government is inherently limited and that arbitrary government forfeits its legitimacy. Let us recall that for Locke the purpose of government is to protect the three basic rights of life, liberty, and private property. When government systematically and persistently violates these rights, the people can rightfully depose it.

In Locke the basic themes of classic liberalism are evident. His defense of property, individualism, representative and limited government, and separation of church and state sets the stage for the evolution of liberal thought in the eighteenth and nineteenth centuries. This is especially so in the United States, for, as Louis Hartz has shown, Lockean liberalism early became the dominant current in the mainstream of the American political tradition.[1]

Natural-rights liberalism animates the American Declaration of Independence of 1776, for example. Its author, Thomas Jefferson, wrote of the "inalienable rights" with which the Creator endowed all men, who were thereby "created equal." His only departure was to encompass "life, liberty, and the pursuit of happiness" in those rights, whereas Locke said "life, liberty, and estate."

Jefferson also referred to the equality and rights of men as "self-evident" truths. Earlier Locke himself seconded the views of a still earlier thinker, who taught that "this equality of men by nature" was *"so evident in itself* and beyond all question" that it served as the foundation of political and moral obligation.[2] In natural-rights liberalism, the "natural" and the "rational" are difficult to separate. Since government is instituted to protect the God-given rights of men, its functions are inherently limited. Jefferson's dictum that "that government is best which governs least" is Lockean in spirit, if not in direct inspiration.

Utilitarian Liberalism: John Stuart Mill

The liberal political philosophy of John Stuart Mill (1806–73) represents a type of liberalism that gives up much of the Lockean baggage of natural law, state of nature, and social contract. Mill began his intellectual career as a disciple of Jeremy Bentham, the founder of utilitarianism, whom we discussed in Chapter 2. There we saw that Bentham had evolved a defense of democracy based on staunch individualism and the idea of "the greatest happiness of the greatest number."

For Bentham, happiness was the same thing as pleasure, and the balance of pleasure over pain was the foundation of both ethics and public policy. In the Benthamite perspective all pleasures were equal in value in the sense that only quantity (i.e., intensity or duration) makes a real difference. No categories of pleasures are inherently higher or nobler than others.

This is where Mill, a man of greater breadth and sensitivity than his teacher, disagreed. He expressed this most forcefully by arguing that "it is better to be a human being dissatisfied than a pig satisfied; better to be Socrates dissatisfied than a fool satisfied. And if the fool, or the pig, is of a different opinion, it is because they only know their own side of the question. The other party to the comparison knows both sides."[3] With this reservation Mill felt comfortable with the "greatest happiness" principle as the essence of "social utility." And social utility is the guide for public policy.

Mill, however, shares the basic egalitarianism we found in both Locke and Jefferson. Thus, his conception of justice will try to balance the claims of individual equality and social utility:

> the equal claim of everybody to happiness in the estimation of the moralist and the legislator, involves an equal claim to all the means of happiness, except in so far as the inevitable conditions of human life, and the general interest, in which every individual is included, sets limits to the maxim.[4]

Somewhat more simply, this means that equal access to the means of happiness can be overridden only when the "general interest" i.e., social utility, demands it. In order for social inequalities to be just, they must be necessitated by the general social utility.

A similar interplay between social utility and the rights of individual personality is found in Mill's defense of liberty. He argued that maximum individual liberty is demanded both on the grounds of individual personality and the good of society. Let us separate these arguments. While Mill rejected the notion of "natural rights" which were somehow antecedent to human society, he nevertheless does appeal to some primordial right of personality. There is an inherent dignity to man that goes beyond a Benthamite equal claim to pleasure or happiness. Indeed, Mill's defense of individuality is so strong that pain and unhappiness may be the cost of letting the individual rule his own life freely.

Mill's individualism, however, does not make him an anarchist. Public law and social pressure, under certain conditions can rightfully limit what the individual can do. The rule governing these conditions comes from Mill's distinction between "self-regarding" and "other-regarding" actions. The former affect only ourselves, the latter affect other members of society as well. With self-regarding actions, as we will see, Mill's rule is "hands-off!" The public, formally or informally, cannot *forcibly* interfere with the individual's free actions. With other-regarding actions, however, the public may coerce the individual to stop. Laws with appropriate sanctions can be used to deter some types of behavior.

So, it is only those other-regarding actions that are harmful to others that can be legitimately stopped or punished.

Self-regarding actions are another story altogether. They constitute an inviolable realm that the public must not enter coercively. There the individual must be left free to sink or swim on his own. Accordingly Mill feels that

> the only purpose for which power can be rightfully exercised over any member of a civilized community, against his own will, is to prevent harm to others. His own good, either physical or moral, is not a sufficient warrant. He cannot rightfully be compelled to do or forbear because it will be better for him to do so, because it will make him happier, because in the opinions of others, to do so would be wise or even right.[5]

In a word, "over himself, over his own mind and body, the individual is sovereign."[6]

This means that social or political power cannot be used to coerce the individual even for his own personal welfare. Thus, certain forms of self-damaging, self-corrupting, or even self-destructive behavior would have to be tolerated. On the other hand, Mill does allow us to plead with the individual to mend his ways or save himself. But we cannot actually force him to do so, unless his behavior is clearly harmful to designated others.

This is a strong doctrine, but it follows from Mill's essentially "negative" conception of liberty, which is characteristic of most types of classic liberalism. This view of liberty is "negative" because liberty is seen as an *absence* of restraints. The individual is free when there are no hindrances or barriers to his action or expression. The imagery is of an object moving through space wholly unaffected by other cosmic objects. Of course, it is up to the individual how well or ill he will use his freedom.

While maximum individual freedom is demanded by the rights of mature personality, it also serves the public interest. Here what is good for the individual and what is good for the collectivity coincide. The nub of Mill's argument is congenial to all forms of liberalism: *truth is socially useful.*

> The truth of an opinion is part of its utility. If we would know whether or not it is desireable that a proposition should be believed, is it possible to exclude the consideration of whether or not it is true? In the opinion, not of bad men, but of the best men, no belief which is contrary to truth can be really useful . . . .[7]

Thus, the public interest requires the discovery and advance of truth.

The question then becomes: how do you get the truth? Mill did not believe in the absoluteness of truth. No one can legitimately claim that he monopolizes final, finished truth. Over time we might get closer to ideal truth without ever really reaching it. Given the fraudulence of any claim to monopolize truth, the only resort in Mill's eyes is to free competition of ideas. Here he seems to embrace the notion of a "marketplace of ideas," borrowing from economic liberalism for political liberalism.

According to the market-place idea, ideas must stand up to the test of competition. The apparent strangeness or silliness of ideas is no warrant to suppress them. Most ideas that now seem commonplace truths were once condemned as bizarre, alien, or just stupid. Time proved differently, however. Thus, we cannot be utterly certain that an apparently wrong idea will not eventually turn out to be right. *Maximum individual freedom, therefore, is the guarantee that all ideas will be ventilated so as to show their worth or worthlessness.* Mill was convinced that over the long haul the more valid ideas will drive out the weaker ones, just as in the economic market place quality goods will eventually outsell shoddy ones at the same price.

But there is still more to Mill's defense of liberty than this. He was also concerned with the manner in which true beliefs are held. There is a profound difference between dead dogma and living truth. In the first case, we hold a belief passively and unquestioningly. In the second, however, we have earned the right to hold it. Mill clearly prefers earning the living truth for "truth gains more even by the errors of one who, with due study and preparation, thinks for himself, than by the true opinions of those who only hold them because they do not suffer themselves to think."[8]

The competition of ideas that individual freedom promotes forces us to rethink our convictions. This process may lead us back to our original position, but now it is better, more alive and vibrant. Our ideas have won their spurs in a genuine contest. Thus, Mill defended what later liberals have called the "open society," both in terms of the dignity of the individual and the social utility of allowing free expression of ideas, no matter how unorthodox.

Social Darwinist Liberalism: Herbert Spencer

Herbert Spencer (1820–1903) brought the Social Darwinist school of classic liberalism into the twentieth century. Social Darwinism attempted to apply the notion of evolution to history, society, and public policy. The movement took its name from Charles Darwin, whose book *The Origin of Species* (1859) brought the concept of evolution scientific respectability. However, Darwin was not a "Social Darwinist"; nor was Spencer, in strict biological matters, a true Darwinist.

Spencer was a grand theorist, who saw evolution at work in astronomy, geology, biology, sociology, and psychology. Evolution was one of the fundamental laws of nature. Whenever and wherever it operated, we would find "along with an advance from simplicity to complexity, there is an advance from confusion to order, from undetermined arrangement to determined arrangement."[9] This overall principle explains the development of galaxies, the solar system, the earth, organic life, and human society.

In most of his writings Spencer simply assumed that evolution and progress were synonomous. He was thus confident that progress was "not an accident, but a necessity."[10] In the near perspective, progress was evident in the transition from "militant" to "industrial" society. The former, epitomized by the warrior societies of the past, featured a rigid, coercive, and hierarchical social order. It wholly subordinated the individual to a culture of violence. The coming of industrial society was bringing greater individual freedom, more prosperity, social equality and popular government, and eventually the abolition of war.

In a longer perspective progress would result in a society, in which egotism and altruism, the needs of the individual and those of the collectivity, completely coincided. Such a highly-evolved humanity would come, however, only in the far-off future.

Spencer's concern was to ensure that this beneficial evolutionary mechanism be allowed to work without obstruction. Social progress depended on the basic principle of biological evolution, the "survival of the fittest." "Fittest" referred to those organisms best "adapted" to the environment. Only these could survive the "struggle for existence" that reigned throughout nature. Only if the fittest survived would their offspring in the next generation be superior to the present generation. Over time, the average level of humanity would rise, until man would enter that utopian end-state where egotism and altruism are one.

In actuality, Spencer's concern was more with the "non-survival of the unfit" than with the survival of the fittest. These lesser specimens of humanity had to meet their unpleasant fate; otherwise the evolutionary process would fail. For this reason, any public attempt to aid the unfit (i.e., the poor and indigent who presumably failed in the struggle for existence) was worse than useless. The harsh competition of laissez-faire capitalism thus reflected the basic laws of nature. Those who prospered were "fit," and those who fell were "unfit." Government intervention to aid the latter was hateful to Spencer. Besides fouling up the evolutionary selection process, it ensured that the unfit would more heavily burden later generations.

In Spencer's day the welfare state and modern liberalism were already showing themselves. In his famous book, *The Man Versus the State*, he deemphasized evolutionary ideas in a defense of laissez-faire based more on individual freedom. He was shocked that some liberals were beginning to favor extending the functions of government. He asked,

How is it that Liberalism, getting more and more into power, has grown more and more coercive in its legislation? How is it . . . Liberalism has to an increasing extent adopted the policy of dictating the actions of its citizens, and, by consequence, diminishing the range throughout which their actions remain free.[11]

New public policies of aiding the weak, regulating business, and providing certain services were condemned by Spencer. Liberalism in his eyes was horribly becoming its opposite.

With Locke, Mill, and Spencer we see that individualism and individual freedom are the choice commodities of classic liberalism. There is a fear of the state, which means that any growth of governmental power beyond a certain minimum necessary to defend order comes at the direct and proportionate loss of individual freedom. Since Liberalism is not anarchism, the problem is to mark out that line beyond which public power constitutes an illegitimate infringement of freedom.

Locke draws this line in terms of certain procedures—taxation and representation, delegated legislation, legal fairness, etc. Mill does this by maintaining that all self-regarding actions lie beyond the state's coercive intervention. Spencer sees anything beyond extreme laissez-faire as noxious to progress and destructive of freedom.

MODERN LIBERALISM

Modern liberalism naturally preserves many aspects of its classic parent. Individualism, reformism, parliamentarism, and separation of church and state retain an importance. Differences in emphasis stem from modern liberalism's full acceptance of democracy and the welfare state. While the ultimate cause of the changes is liberalism's response to the coming of industrial mass society, there are some philosophical grounds as well. Not surprisingly, much follows from the transition from a "negative" to a "positive" conception of freedom.

Negative freedom, the absence of restraints, considers the individual to be free when governmental or social pressures do not block his thought and action. On the other hand, "positive" freedom deems the individual to be free only when he has achieved a certain state of mind. The mere absence of restraints is thus no assurance that he is truly free. Indeed, the ability to float around, buffeted this way and that by certain inner forces, is the opposite of freedom.

The freedom-creating state of mind varies according to the particular doctrine involved. Sometimes it is the ability to make objective moral decisions; sometimes it is the ability to act rationally; sometimes it is the ability to participate intelligently and effectually in those decisions that affect our lives; sometimes it is all of these things together.

Some theories of positive freedom assume a sort of duality in the human mind. There is a "lower self," in which passions, instincts, animal needs, and the like predominate. There is also a "higher" or "true" self, in which reason and morality govern how we think and act. We are free only when the higher self has the upper hand over the lower self. Thus, true freedom realizes the true self and is "self-realization."

Idealistic Liberalism: T. H. Green

T. H. Green (1836–82), an English philosopher and disciple of Hegel, is a bellwether of modern liberalism. His vision of positive freedom moved him to re-examine the traditional liberal hostility toward the state. Freedom is not random movement in a social vacuum as the earlier liberalism imagined. To become a mature human being thinking rationally and acting ethically is impossible outside a social context. Civil and social institutions are neither a barrier to freedom nor even a necessary evil. They are absolutely essential for the individual "to realize his reason, i.e., his idea of self-perfection, by acting as a member of a social organization in which each contributes to the better-being of all the rest."[12]

With Green therefore we find no necessary man-versus-the state dichotomy. Indeed, he points out that "the realization of freedom in the state can only mean the attainment of freedom by individuals through influences which the state . . . supplies."[13] True freedom then is to be sought in and through the state and not outside and against it as classic liberalism sometimes seems to suggest. Green sees man as free only within the orbit of a genuine social community. As the community is a part of us as we of it, a similar reciprocity governs man and the state.

But Green is a liberal: there are limits to what the state can and ought to do. Contrary to Spencer, he assumes that the state may move to help those individuals whose poverty or ignorance prevents a mature exercise of freedom. This very important conclusion heralds the birth of the welfare-state idea within the framework of liberal ideology. However, the limits of the state's welfare activities are implied by Green's conclusion that "the effectual action of the state, i.e. the community acting through law, for the promotion of the habits of true citizenship, seems necessarily to be confined to the removal of obstacles."[14] This obstacle-removing involves "much that most states have hitherto neglected."[15]

This means that the state can raise the individual up to a certain point, beyond which moral growth is up to him. To go further would be to endorse "paternal government," which robs the individual of that personal responsibility which is the emblem of his freedom. Green shows us here that while modern liberalism can support a broader scope for government, especially in the areas of economics and education, it must stop short at some point.

Just as freedom runs counter to paternal government, it runs toward democratic government. The freedom of a mature personality requires political participation along democratic lines. The individual should either serve in a public capacity or vote for those that do. "Only thus will he learn to regard the work of the state as a whole, and to transfer to the whole the interest which otherwise his particular experience would lead him to feel only in that part of its work that goes to the maintenance of his own and his neighbor's rights."[16]

With Green we cross the bridge between the old liberalism that fears both the state and democracy as threats to freedom, and the new liberalism that sees both an expanded state and expanded democracy as enhancing freedom. But too much of a good thing can become a bad thing: neither paternalism nor blind majoritarianism is a solution to the problem of politics for the modern liberal.

Pragmatic Liberalism: John Dewey

Setting out from rather different philosophical premises the great American pragmatist philosopher John Dewey (1859–1952) reached conclusions similar to Green on liberalism, democracy, and the state. Dewey, along with William James and C. S. Peirce, was one of the trio of great thinkers who developed the philosophy of pragmatism, which many consider America's unique contribution to philosophy. Some understanding of pragmatism must precede our look at how Dewey tried to bring liberalism up to date.

Pragmatism mistrusts absolutes. Important truths are not fixed once and for all. The rationalist faith in "self-evident" truths and deductive reasoning is a superstition. Pure logic and reason assume a world that is constant, coherent, and consistent.

The pragmatist very differently sees the world as dynamic and evolving. The pieces of its reality are ever-changing and often do not fit together neatly at all. Such a view has important consequences for truth. For the pragmatist truth cannot be a static relation between ideas (rationalism) nor a static relation between ideas and outside objects (empiricism). Truth must be related to the multifarious processes which make up our world.

This means that questions of truth must be related to practical problems of real flesh and blood persons. This acid test can also be applied to complex philosophical issues. As William James pointed out:

The pragmatic method . . . is to try to interpret each notion by tracing its respective practical consequences. What difference would it practically make to anyone if this notion rather than that notion were true? If no practical differences whatever can be traced, then the alternatives mean practically the same thing, and all dispute is idle.[17]

Truth thus cannot be absolute: it must change as the world changes; as the times change; and as people's problems change. For John Dewey this was the true message of Darwin, not Spencerian "Social Darwinism." Accordingly, he maintained that the qualities that originally gave value and relevance to certain ideas, practices, and institutions prove largely to be "the very grounds that deprive them of their 'actuality' in a world whose features are different."[18]

Ideas therefore are condemned to obsolescence. Change is the law of life and no constellation of ideas or attitudes can hope to live beyond its time of relevance. Dewey saw this principle confirmed by the very history of liberalism itself. In the two centuries from Locke to Spencer, the classic liberal ideas of laissez-faire and natural rights went through the three stages of revolution, reform, and reaction. Once these ideas played a revolutionary role overturning largely feudal institutions. Then later they inspired attempts to reform old and new abuses. Finally, as with Spencer, they worked to halt attempts to deal with the shortcomings of the now established capitalist order.

For Dewey, one reason why liberalism now retarded change stems from the "earlier liberals" lack of "historic sense and interest." Though once helpful to advance the liberal cause, this unhistorical method

blinded the eyes of liberals to the fact that their own special interpretations of liberty, individuality, and intelligence were themselves historically conditioned, and were relevant only to their own time. They put forward their ideas as immutable truths good at all times and places; they had no idea of historical relativity. . . .[19]

This short-sightedness condemned the principles of classic liberalism eventually to become outworn cliches.

The vulnerable points of classic liberalism were its doctrines of individualism and social progress. To the classic liberal, individuality was "something ready-made, already possessed, and needing only the removal of certain legal restrictions to come into full play. It was not conceived as a moving thing, something that is attained only by continuous growth."[20] This involved a negative, man-versus-the state conception of freedom.

Classic liberalism was also defective through its "atomistic" view of society. Individuals were seen as social atoms with only a limited involvement in the social whole. Rejecting any dichotomy between the individual and society, Dewey's rendition of "positive" freedom includes a strong social dimension. Liberty thus becomes "that secure release and fulfillment of personal potentialities which takes place only in wide and manifest association with others: the power to be an individualized self making a distinctive contribution and enjoying in its own way the fruits of association."[21] Dewey's dual stress on "association" plunges the individual deeply into the social firmament. Society is a precondition, and not a threat, to our freedom.

In another vein, classic liberal doctrines of social progress also seemed to Dewey to retard true social advance. These theories, exemplified by Spencer's iron-clad laws of evolutionary change, acted to discourage truly constructive reform efforts. Dewey complained that the culprit was any philosophy "which trusts the direction of human affairs to nature, or Providence, or evolution, or manifest destiny—that is to say, to accident—rather than to a contriving and constructive intelligence."[22]

Appeals to nature and the rest struck Dewey as an abdication of human responsibility for human destiny. By assigning such responsibility to mythical cosmic forces, they condemned society to drifting and back-sliding. True progress is not a gift of the cosmos; rather, it is an achievement that men must earn. In Dewey's opinion, the "only genuine opposite to a go-as-you please, let-alone philosophy is a philosophy which studies specific social needs and evils with a view to constructing the special machinery for which they call."[23]

Modern liberalism must thus reject any do-nothing view of progress. All that Spencerian "social evolution" can do is to break down barriers and clear the way for true progress. Progress itself requires "social action," which may well mean using government in ways alien to classic liberalism and its contemporary defenders. Accordingly, Dewey argues that modern liberalism must take on a "radical" cast, which assumes the "necessity of thorough-going changes in the set-up of institutions and corresponding activity to bring the changes to pass."[24] On this score, however, Dewey's pragmatism rejects both the extremes of pure capitalism and pure socialism. Instead, specific reform programs, whose sum-total equals the modern welfare state, would reflect the "experimental" attitude of the pragmatist.

Quite naturally, Dewey dispelled any classic liberal doubts about the compatibility of democracy with liberty. Like Green he considered the modern democratic idea simply an extension of a truly liberal notion of individuality. A true belief in individuality involves a sense of human equality that rejects old-fashioned ideas of superiority and inferiority. Individuals, morally speaking, are unique—not identical, not superior, and not inferior to each other. A valid concept of democracy captures the very essence of liberalism, because "no matter how great the quantitative differences of ability, strength, position, wealth, such differences are negligible in comparison with something else—the fact of individuality, the manifestation of something irreplacable.[25]

In Dewey's eyes, this convergence of the liberal concern for individuality and the democratic concern for equality did not mean following any specific recipe for institutions. Thus democracy is as much or more a "way of life" than it is a rigid structure of elections, parties, and parliaments. The heart of the democratic faith is that the individual should have an equal chance to contribute whatever he can to the total social will.[26]

CONCLUSION

The complexities of the ideology of liberalism reflected by our covering several representatives, results from its long and broad history. Emerging in Great Britain in the middle and late seventeenth century, liberalism spread to Europe and America where strong movements flourished and often came to power in the course of the nineteenth century. While the eruption of communism and fascism in the middle of the twentieth century threatened liberalism's very survival, it came through World War II with renewed vigor, especially in the United States and Western Europe.

While explicitly liberal parties never recovered their former strength in Europe, this is not the only test of liberalism's impact and resilience. Liberal ideas have influenced social democratic and Christian Democratic parties, and even in some cases conservatives, to such an extent that these ideologies contain far more originally liberal notions than was true fifty or a hundred years ago.

Basic liberal principles such as individualism, parliamentary government, limited government, separation of church and state, equality of opportunity, and social reformism have been defended on a wide variety of philosophical foundations. Indeed, this chapter dealt with the natural law philosophy of Locke, the modified utilitarianism of Mill, the Social Darwinist evolutionism of Spencer, the Hegelian idealism of Green, and the American pragmatism of Dewey. Any synthesis of even classic or modern liberalism alone, which leaves out this diversity, would produce a simpler and more consistent picture of liberalism than ours, but one that was historically far less accurate.

We can nevertheless be sure about the contrast between classic and modern liberalism in general. All varieties of classic liberalism tend to dichotomize liberty and authority. Individual liberty must be maximized and the chief threat to it comes from the state. The sense is clear that when government authority expands (rules, regulations, interventions) beyond a certain necessary minimum, individual freedom contracts. The classic liberal reasoning for defending individual freedom differs substantially among Locke's three primoridal rights of life, liberty, and property; Mill's romantic sense of human personality and his linkage of truth and social utility; and Spencer's analogy between laissez-faire capitalism and evolutionary survival of the fittest.

This concern for individual freedom also inspires classic liberalism's fear that "popular government" is dangerous. The masses of people, whose lack of education and property make them unreliable, will use their power to despoil the wealthy and imperil freedom. Thus, classic liberals favored property and educational qualifications for voting to ensure that only those with a "stake" in society voted for those who made public policy.

Modern liberalism, we have seen with Green and Dewey, entertains a more "positive" notion of freedom—one which requires action, perhaps governmental action, in order to being to as many members of society as possible into full citizenship. The state, provided that things did not go as far as "paternal government," is seen less as the inevitable foe of freedom than as its possible friend. Hopefully, with the welfare state's policies, the general moral and intellectual level of the masses will be raised so high as to make classic liberalism's fears of tyranny of the majority "obsolete." Democracy and liberty have become inseparable, not incompatible.

NOTES

1. Louis Hartz, *The Liberal Tradition in America* (New York: Harcourt, Brace & World, 1955).
2. John Locke, "Second Treatise," in *Two Treatises of Government* (New York: Hafner, 1969), sec. 5.
3. John Stuart Mill, *Utilitarianism,* in *John Stuart Mill: A Selection of His Works,* ed. J. M. Robson (New York: St. Martin's, 1966), p. 161.
4. Ibid., pp. 225–26.
5. Mill, *On Liberty,* in *Works,* p. 13.
6. Ibid., p 14.
7. Ibid., p. 30.
8. Ibid., p. 45.
9. Herbert Spencer, *First Principles* (New York: P. F. Collier and Sons, 1905), p. 361.
10. Herbert Spencer, *Social Statics,* quoted in Jay Rumney, *Herbert Spencer's Sociology* (New York: Atherton, 1966), p. 269.
11. Herbert Spencer, *The Man Versus the State* (Baltimore: Penguin Books, 1969), p. 67.

12. T. H. Green, *Lectures on the Principles of Politcal Obligation* (London: Longman, 1960), sec. 7.
13. Ibid., sec. 6.
14. Ibid., sec. 209.
15. Ibid.
16. Ibid., sec. 122.
17. William James, *Pragmatism* (New York: Meridian Books, 1959), p. 42.
18. John Dewey, *Reconstruction in Philosophy* (Boston: Beacon Press, 1964), p. vii.
19. John Dewey *Liberalism and Social Action* (New York: Capricorn Books, 1963), p. 32.
20. Ibid., p. 39.
21. John Dewey, *The Public and Its Problems* (Denver: Allen Swallow, 1954), p. 150.
22. John Dewey, *Characters and Events*, vol. II (New York: Octagon Books, 1970), p. 827.
23. Ibid.
24. Dewey, *Liberalism*, p. 62.
25. Dewey, *Characters*, p. 854.
26. John Dewey, *Problems of Men* (New York: Philosophical Library, 1946), p. 60.

SUGGESTIONS FOR FURTHER READING

De Ruggiero, Guido. *The History of European Liberalism*. Boston: Beacon Press, 1959.
Girvetz, Harry K. *The Evolution of Liberalism*. New York: Collier Books, 1963.
Hartz, Louis. *The Liberal Tradition in America*. New York: Harcourt, Brace, World, 1955.
Hobhouse, Leonard T. *Liberalism*. New York: Oxford University Press, 1964.
Manning, D. J. *Liberalism*. New York: St. Martin's, 1976.
Macpherson, C. B. *The Political Theory of Possessive Individualism*. New York: Oxford University Press, 1964.

13

CONSERVATISM

TWO VIEWS OF CONSERVATISM

If we call someone "conservative" we generally mean that he prefers things as they are and is reluctant to change them. This sort of conservatism is based on the belief that present arrangements or methods are really better than novel ones, or even on a simple emotional level on caution or laziness. In such cases, the conservatives, say in industry or education, do not wish to disrupt a satisfactory and stable state of affairs. Why take chances?

Our ordinary use of "conservatism" thus suggests caution and reserve. The conservative in this sense takes the line of least resistance and prefers to risk little, even if he gains little. These senses of conservatism are reflected in the "situational" theory, which sees it as

> that system of ideas employed to justify any established social order, no matter where or when it exists, against any fundamental challenge to its nature or being, no matter from what quarter. The essence of conservatism is the passionate affirmation of the value of existing institutions. This does not mean that conservatism opposes all change. . . . No person, however, can espouse the conservative ideology, unless he is fundamentally happy with the established order. . . .[1]

If we follow this interpretation, the ideas of Edmund Burke in eighteenth-century Britain, Barry Goldwater in twentieth century America, neo-Stalinists in the USSR of the 1950's, defenders of Confucianism in early twentieth century China, the Ayatollah Khomeini in recent Iran, and the signers of the Magna Carta all represent conservatism. Like the Greek god, Proteus, conservatism can dramatically change its shape, depending on the circumstances.

Such a protean theory of conservatism, however, has two fatal weaknesses. First it virtually ignores the tremendous variety of ideals and ideologies used to defend so many different established orders. Second, it begs the question whether all conservative thinkers are really enamored with the given status quo. Although somewhat one-sided, the theory of "transcendent" conservatism will head us in the right direction.[2]

Correctly viewing conservatism as a recurrent perspective on man and society that goes beyond (i.e., transcends) any particular status quo, the transcendent theory considers Plato the true founder of the conservative tradition of the West.[3] In direct contrast to the situational approach, the transcendent theory maintains that "to define Conservatism as the defense of existing institutions is to define it by it most congenial technique *but to omit the whole foundation.*"[4] (Italics added.)

What then is this "whole foundation" of conservative ideologies? In one interpretation "the transcendent value of Conservative ideology" is vested in "the Platonic idea of harmony," which "has assumed a wide variety of historical forms."[5] Thus, the test to determine if a thinker is a conservative is his adherence to the "conservative ideal," which involves

> harmonious personality, made possible by a harmonious society in which social cohesion is maximized and economic needs minimized—a society in which coercion is unnecessary because each keeps his place and learns the supreme beauty and rationality of harmony from an integrated cultural tradition, a society in which conflict is minimized because economic power is isolated and all other is rooted in the social realm of affection and cohesion, where the happiness of the individual and the needs of the community coincide.[6]

Critics, of course, consider this ideal an "illusion" because it assumes a stagnant society and tries to eradicate social conflict.

While the transcendent approach is superior to the situational approach, it tries to squeeze too much out of Platonic harmony. It is eminently correct to see defense of the status quo as a "technique" of conservatism and not its pith and marrow. Accordingly, we will distinguish between "affirmative" and "critical" conservatism. This first term means that the theorist is defending the existing order of his society. But his very defense implies a set of principles, which seems to him more or less faithfully embodied in that society. He is affirmative because of the match-up between principles and polity.

Another thinker or ideologist might find himself in the diametrically opposed circumstance. He will see little or no connection between his cherished political principles and the social and political institutions around him. His conservatism therefore cannot be affirmative and must be *critical* (i.e., it must find serious fault with the status quo). Now, if our transcendent theory is correct, those background principles of the affirmative and the critical conservative are basically the same. The affirmative conservative uses them to undergird his basically favorable estimate and judgment upon the status quo. The critical conservative employs them to undergird his basically unfavorable judgment of his own society. Conservatism itself thus has a meaning that "transcends" any and all situations.

A transcendent theory of conservatism should be able to identify those principles common to conservatism thinkers regardless of time and place. Taken together, these principles constitute a system, which includes ideas like *organicism, aristocracy, authority, traditionalism, social pessimism, and clericalism.* These are the earmarks of conservative thought for at least two centuries past. After a brief survey of them, we will look at Edmund Burke, "the father of modern conservatism," as an example of affirmative conservatism, and closer to our own day, George Santayana, as an example of critical conservatism.

Organicism

Organicism refers to the "organic" theory of the state (or society) characteristic of most conservative thinkers and ideologists. Conservatives are fond of the organic analogy. By comparing state or society to a living organism, they suggest that a healthy society is a harmonious cooperating whole, whose parts are subordinate to and contribute to the welfare of the whole. Just as an organism flourishes when its various organs are functioning properly, each doing its job and thus supporting the rest, the state flourishes when its various elements (individuals, groups, or whole classes) collaborate in this way.

Society or the state therefore consist of real entities. They have a place in reality and thus have a high and distinct moral purpose. No real society can be a mere collection of atomized individuals. It is the chief vice of liberalism to think that way. As Samuel Taylor Coleridge (1772–1834), English poet and philosopher, put it

> the true patriot will reverence not only whatever tends to make the component individuals more happy . . . . ; but likewise whatever tends to bind them more closely as a people; that as a multitude of parts and functions make up one human body, so the whole multitude of his countrymen may, by the visible and invisible influence of religion, language, laws, customs, and the reciprocal dependence and reaction of trade and agriculture, be organized into one body politic.[7]

Unity then is the capstone of the conservative doctrine—unity that involves both diversity and hierarchy. The conservative cherishes unity, but not by social homogenization.

Aristocracy

Aristocracy is the second principle of conservative ideology. This is understood in the literal sense of "rule of the best." The conservative thus believes that social and political leadership should be placed in the hands of a distinct elite. In this sense, conservatism is "antidemocratic," at least in its classic expressions. It doubts the capacity of the common people to govern themselves successfully. Democratic systems are likely to degenerate into mob-rule or one-man despotism.

While the conservative extols aristocracy, he does not consider that group as an end-in-itself. Aristocratic rule is justified because it benefits the whole society, not just the aristocracy itself. Here aristocracy is linked to the organic doctrine of the good of the whole. With respect to the masses, conservatives endorse a frankly "paternalistic" conception, with aristocrats playing the father and the masses the children. However, this notion of aristocracy does not necessarily mean a hereditary, closed nobility. We can see this is Edmund Burke's eloquent defense of "natural aristocracy":

> A true natural aristocracy is not a separate interest in the state, or separate from it. It is an essential integrant part of any large body rightly constituted . . . . To be bred in a place of estimation; to see nothing low and sordid from one's infancy; to be taught to respect one's self; to be habituated to the censorial inspection of the public eye; to look early to public opinion; to stand upon such elevated ground . . . to take a large view of the widespread and infinitely diversified combinations of men and affairs [Burke further mentions leisure and contact with the wise and intelligent, military responsibility, concern for fellow citizens, political and judicial duties, intellectual and commercial talent, and high personal virtue]: these are the circumstances of men that form what I should call a *natural* aristocracy, without which there is no nation.[8]

While Burke's natural aristocracy includes titled noblemen, it is a more composite formation that draws from the cream of a nation's various occupations.

Authority

Authority is the third main principle of conservative thought. Conservatism teaches the basic compliance with and obedience to constituted authorities. The citizen's basic duty is to obey the laws and the just commands of the authorities. Even in the family, the school, and the church, subordinates are to remain essentially passive. Leaders should be allowed to lead; followers should follow. The right of leaders to lead and rulers to rule is not unconditional. Authority is not merely personal or charismatic.

Rather, authority devolves upon a person because he or she occupies a role that is part of an organic social whole that is presumed to be just and legitimate. While the role gives the incumbent rightful authority over others, the role itself has obligations. Authority has definite limits, and there are conditions when the subject or citizen is absolved from obedience. The person in authority can overstep his rightful bounds, but then it is he who is the true rebel, not those who refuse him obedience. Indeed, this principle has been invoked in many revolts: the rebels proclaim their adherence to the established system of authority—it is the corrupt clique in power who broke with tradition!

So impressed with defending authority are many conservatives that they give it a divine sanction. In other words, existing societies (of the right type, of course) reflect God's purpose or intent in this world. Since the powers that be are "ordained by God", and since we "should render unto Caesar those things which are Caesar's and unto God those things which are God's," an attack on established authority would be as blasphemous as it is impolitic. An extreme version of this notion was given by the philosopher Joseph De Maistre (1753–1821), who argued that

> every *theist* would no doubt agree that whoever breaks the laws sets his face against the divine will and renders himself guilty before God, although he is breaking only human ordinances, for it is God who has made *man* sociable; and since he has *willed* society, he has *willed* also the sovereignty and laws without which there would be no society.[9]

While there is, to be sure, a man-made element in the laws, De Maistre is at pains to point to the underlying divine purpose.

Traditionalism

Traditionalism is such an important component of modern conservatism that students have been misled into virtually equating the two. But to take the part for the whole is a mistake. Traditionalism, as it figures in conservatism, is the presumption that tried and true practices and institutions are generally the best. What has become traditional has survived the test of time and has shown itself truly expressive of the needs and spirit of a given people.

From this standpoint, the burden of proof is most heavily upon those who counsel drastic reformation or wholesale abandonment of traditional practices. As a twentieth-century conservative put it,

Modification of the rules should always reflect, and never impose, a change in the activities and beliefs of those who are subject to them, and should never on any occasion be so great as to destroy the ensemble . . . .]The [The Conservative] will be suspicious of proposals for change in excess of what the situation calls for . . . .[10]

Somewhat the same sentiment was captured in the last century by Lord Falkland's aphorism: "when it is not necessary to change, it is necessary not to change."

The conservative defense of tradition admits of change, but it is a change that suggests "growth" and "renovation" rather than "construction" and "innovation." The conservative doubts man's capacity to reshape institutions to his own liking and design. The power of human reason to fathom what really makes society work is limited. A radical departure from existing practices is thus a most risky gamble. Tradition provides a framework for those more limited experiments that fall within the range of human understanding.

Social Pessimism

Social pessimism is partly the grounds for reliance on tradition, but it involves another problem as well. The conservative emphatically denies the radical's or the utopian's claim that social evils are primarily due to defective social institutions, which can be improved or exchanged for better ones. Such "optimism" crashes upon the shoals of "human nature." For the conservative, institutions do not just shape man, they also reflect him. Their shortcomings thus come largely from man himself. Modern utopias, especially anarchical or egalitarian ones, are hopeless, and sometimes harmful, delusions. They promise what it is impossible to deliver.

Crime, poverty, oppression, cruelty, agression, and unhappiness may be alleviated; they will not be easily eliminated. Conservatives feel this way because of their pessimistic view of human nature. This human nature, which changs slowly if at all, has basic flaws, which are partly responsible for crimes of man against man and for the weaknesses of human society. As a British Conservative politician put it in 1947, "The Conservative does not believe that the power of politics to put things right in this world is unlimited. This is partly because there are inherent limits on what may be achieved by political means, but partly because man is an imperfect creature with a streak of evil as well as good in his inmost nature."[11]

Certain conservatives go further and ground their pessimism about man in the Christian doctrine of "original sin." According to this idea man is a fallen, imperfect creature condemned to a certain amount of suffering because the first man Adam sinned by rebelling against God in the Garden of Eden. This accounts for the radical flaw in human nature and justifies strong rule as well as social pessimism. De Maistre as usual represents the extreme by proclaiming that "there is nothing but violence in the world; but we are tainted by modern philosophy which has taught us that *all is good*, whereas evil has polluted everything and in a very real sense *all is evil*, since nothing is in its proper place."[12]

Clericalism

Finally, we have clericalism, the idea that complete separation of church and state is undesirable. One reason for this stand is the conservative's belief in the "religious basis" of society. Many of them would agree with the nineteenth-century British statesman, Benjamin Disraeli, that "the most powerful principle which governs man is the religious principle . . . . A wise government allying itself with religion, would as it were consecrate society and sanctify the state."[13] Church and state are parts of an organic social whole so that completely separating them would be like dismembering a living organism. The conservative views politics, morality, and religion as flowing into each other so that church and state overlap and intersect without losing their separate identities. Without this latter reservation conservatives would come close to advocating full priestly rule or "theocracy."

Conservatives thus favor an "established" or official national church, though they generally allow some toleration of other religions. Those with a special interest in art and culture such as T. S. Eliot (1888–1965) have found a national church highly beneficial in a country like England. It is once more the desire for organic unity that infuses Eliot's notion of a "Christian society." This involves "the existence of one Church which shall *aim at* comprehending the whole nation. Unless it has this aim, we lapse into that conflict between citizenship and church membership, between public and private morality, which today makes moral life so difficult for everyone."[14] Eliot reflects the view of many conservatives that a certain basis of religious orthodoxy is essential to form and continuity in a cultural tradition.

These six principles—organicism, aristocracy, authority, traditionalism, social pessimism, and clericalism serve as a rough test of conservative ideology. This opens the door for a closer examination of two noted thinkers as "test cases" of the contrast between affirmative and critical conservatism.

AFFIRMATIVE CONSERVATISM

Edmund Burke's staunch defense of the British Constitution and the social and political institutions of his time is sometimes offered as proof that the conservative message is always and only defense of the status quo. Our interpretation is different. Burke is a classic example of an "affirmative" conservative, one of those whose principles allow them to look with favor at the society and polity of their time and place.

Burke, however, clearly understood that basic principles underlay his passing political judgments, even though his rhetoric sometimes attacked "abstract" ideas as harmful and misleading. Burke was not a professional philosopher, but a professional politician who served for many years in the House of Commons as a member of the Whig "party." For this reason his political ideas are strewn out in a large number of speeches and occasional political tracts. However, many of his key political ideas are concentrated in his book, *Reflections on the Revolution in France.*

The nature of Burke's political career meant that his thought was often reactive and defensive. In other words, while a reformer on many specific issues, he was often provoked into defending British institutions against their detractors. Indeed, even his *Reflections,* an impassioned attack on the French Revolution of 1789, warns against any imitation of such mischief in the British side of the Channel. Despite this narrow focus, this book has been called the "bible of modern conservatism."

The British Constitution, so revered by Burke, was, of course, no written document. It was simply the set-up of British political institutions in the 1700s. At that time the monarch was far more than the figurehead he is today. His ministers were free of the simple and direct control that we find in modern parliamentarism. The House of Lords, which today has far less power than the House of Commons, was at least its full equal. It was composed exclusively of hereditary noblemen.

The Commons, in which Burke served for decades, was chosen by an extremely narrow electorate. Many of its seats were filled by the "rotten borough" system, whereby a small number who were the agents of the rich and powerful "elected" members of parliament. In that day, as today, both church and state were headed by the monarch. The difference is that two centuries ago membership in the Church of England was often a condition for exercising certain rights and privileges. Catholics and "nonconformist" Protestants were in many ways second or third class citizens.

Burke was not unaware or unmoved by certain specific shortcomings of the British Constitution. His point was always that the whole is good and that serious tinkering with the parts could well disrupt that whole.

> Our constitution stands on a nice equipoise, with steep precipices and deep waters upon all sides of it. In removing it from a dangerous leaning towards one side, there may be a risk of oversetting it on the other. Every project of a material change in a government so complicated as ours, combined at the

same time with external circumstances still more complicated, is a matter full of difficulties . . . .[15]

Burke was thus willing to allow certain weaknesses or abuses to remain in the Constitution, if the price for removing them was to create new and perhaps worse evils.

More broadly, Burke counseled moderation in any attempt to reconstruct social and political institutions, for "it is with infinite caution that any man ought to venture upon pulling down an edifice which has answered in any tolerable degree for ages the common purposes of society, or on building it up again without having models and patterns of approved utility before his eyes."[16] It is in this light that Burke extolled what he called "prudence" and "prejudice." Prudence was an instinct beyond pure logical reasoning that allowed one to "size up" a situation and take the appropriate action. In politics Burke considered prudence "the first of the virtues" which would "lead us to acquiesce in some qualified plan that does not come up to the full perfection of the abstract idea, than to push for the more perfect, which cannot be attained without tearing to pieces the whole contexture of the commonwealth."[17]

While prudence relates mainly to the political elite, "prejudice" is more general in scope. Burke naturally did not mean "prejudice" in our contemporary sense of religious or ethnic bias. Instead he had in mind a kind of presumption, without much deliberation, in favor of what exists. Prejudice would suggest the strongest benefit of the doubt in behalf of traditional institutions and ways. Contrasting the British to the "abstract" French mentality, he points out that "instead of casting away all our old prejudices, we cherish them to a very considerable degree. . . . Many of our men of speculation, instead of exploding general prejudices, employ their sagacity to discover the latent wisdom that prevails in them."[18] For Burke prejudice is not pure irrationalism: reason operates in collective practices and institutions more reliably than in the individual human mind.

Clearly, Burke favored appreciation of tangible existing institutions to abstract speculations about the ideally best polity. Cast in immature minds such wish-dreams could unleash the passions of revolution. Some have seen this aspect of Burke as part of the "revolt against reason," which would produce the romanticism of the early nineteenth century. A more accurate account sees Burke "revolting" not so much against reason as against the rationalist philosophy of the Enlightenment and the French Revolution. To avoid this confusion, Burke himself made the disclaimer that

> I do not vilify theory and speculation—no, because that would be to vilify reason itself . . . No, whenever, I speak against theory, I mean always a

weak, erroneous, fallacious, unfounded, or imperfect theory; and one of the ways of discovering that it is a false theory is by comparing it with practice."[19]

Although selecting one-sided quotations might make Burke no more than a "situational" defender of the status quo, there is clearly a second dimension to his thought. Indeed, we could easily pick out the various principles of conservatism discussed above. He spoke to his time and our own time, regardless of whether we agree with him or not. He defended traditional institutions not only because of prudence and prejudice, but also because he saw many of his principles at work in the British social and political order of his time.

CRITICAL CONSERVATISM: GEORGE SANTAYANA

George Santayana (1863–1952) was a critical conservative in our own century. He was a philosopher and an academic, who came to America at an early age and left it for good in middle age. While Santayana admired many things about his adopted country, the sense of his writings reflects the alienation and frustration of the critical conservative. His problem was a simple one: he was a man of conservative beliefs and inclinations who grew to maturity in the most liberal of countries. Thus, he could not like Burke defend and extol the existing society; instead he had to criticize it.

Santayana's critical conservatism is most evident in his critique of the ideals and institutions of twentieth-century liberal democracy. While he does not share the usual conservative organic concept of society, he nevertheless felt that liberalism preached a false and self-destructive sort of liberty and individualism. As he once mused biographically, "the liberal age in which I was born and the liberal circles in which I was educated flowed contentedly towards intellectual dissolution and anarchy."[20]

In Santayana's eyes liberalism is based on a kind of skepticism, the idea that no ultimate moral or general truths can be found. Liberal policy then is to reject any orthodoxy, to reject any definitive answer. This results in generalized tolerance and free competition of ideas. For a long time through the nineteenth century this free-and-easy liberal tolerance produced no major disaster. This was largely because liberalism implicity assumed middle-class "respectability" and the survival of pre-liberal institutions like the family, the church, and the local community. This things retarded the corrosive impact of the liberal doctrine of freedom.

However, in the twentieth century the results of liberal policy have come home to roost. Santayana thus asked: "how long, if all moral codes are tolerated, those who hold those vir̄ws can be restrained from putting them into practice?" Such tolerance ǝventually undermines the "dominant morality," though "it is only in recent years that the Russian Revolution, Madame Caillaux, D. H. Lawrence, and Andre Gide, have openly and conscientiously written down robbery, murder, adultery, and sodomy among the inalienable rights of man."[21] It is not so much that liberalism actually advocates these manifestations of moral anarchy; it simply has no strong argument against them. Its very suspicion of dogma and authority prevents liberalism from imposing a system of moral absolutes.

Another weakness of liberalism and the modern age is infatuation with change. Modern society virtually worships change and modern liberalism—such as with John Dewey—simply reflects this idolatry. For Santayana, it is the idea of progress that sustains our modern and liberal love of change. But the liberal doctrine of progress is built upon sand in so far as it assumes general improvement or amelioration over time. Against this, Santayana protests that "in fact, something better does not always follow, but often something worse; and yet, in spite of history and experience, many believe in a Law of Progress."[22]

There is no "law" of progress, and the things adduced as evidence of it—rapid technological change, population growth and urbanization, economic interdependence, social complexity, and the spread of liberalism itself—do not necessarily mean a better life for man. Moreover, this very illusion of steady progress in history carries a heavy price-tag. It promotes a negative and cavalier attitude towards timeless truths. In Santayana's words, "the habit of regarding the past as effete and as merely a stepping stone to something present or future, is unfavorable to any true apprehension of that element . . . which was vital and remains eternal."[23]

In addition, since the progress doctrine denigrates the past in general, history is robbed of any tutelary value. Since our own era is so much higher, better, or nobler than its predecessors, we feel that there is nothing to learn from history. But such historical arrogance has its own ironical penalty, for modern folk "prefer to repeat the old experiment without knowing that they repeat it."[24]

As a conservative, Santayana naturally looks askance at modern democracy. Its denial of the "aristocratic" principle dramatically lowers the level of political leadership. Indiscriminate social levelling has even more disastrous results for culture because civilization has moved from the top down, not from the bottom up: "What we have rests on conquest and conversion, on leadership and imitation, on mastership and service. To abolish aristocracy, in the sense of social privilege and sanctified authority, would be to cut off the source from which all culture has hitherto flowed."[25]

While the movement toward democracy has brought some needed reforms, Santayana was alarmed by the trend to what he termed "social democracy." This is runaway egalitarianism, that is hostile to social hierarchy and individual distinction. Such an attempt to impose complete equality would mean that "social democracy at high pressure would leave no room for liberty."[26] Liberty then is important, but it is a "positive" and not a negative or classic liberal conception that Santayana has in mind.

In Santayana's view the individual is free, not when he does what he feels like doing (negative freedom), but rather when he does what is best for himself in terms of his innermost nature. However, for Santayana it is quite possible that someone else may do a better job at promoting his good than the individual himself. Strong leadership may be crucial to make some people truly free. Since democracy mistrusts strong leadership and suggests that the individual is the best judge of his own interest, it may actually reduce freedom in the guise of increasing it.

In a broader social context, Santayana's "liberty" would be best realized in a social order of distinct classes, that reflected the basic inequality of men. Here as well modern democracy's passion for equality would prove hostile to genuine liberty. At any rate, even our brief account should show that the principles of Santayana's critical conservatism would make him find fault with liberal democratic societies on a variety of fronts.

CONCLUSION

This chapter's first task, in a sense, was to justify its inclusion in this text. This was necessary because defining conservatism simply and solely as defense of the status quo hardly makes it an ideology. Rejecting the "situational" approach for a more "transcendent" one, we envisaged conservatism as a set of principles—organicism, aristocracy, authority, traditionalism, social pessimism, and clericalism—that allowed given thinkers either to defend or attack their actual societies. An affirmative conservative such as Edmund Burke, finds a reasonable similarity between his guiding principles and values and the status quo. The critical conservative such as George Santayana, uses the same principles and values to point out the defects of the status quo.

Conservatism reached its maximum influence as a political ideology in the early nineteenth century. It was then a political and intellectual reaction to the "ideas of 1789," i.e., the liberal and democratic ideas that spread in the wake of the French Revolution. Since then it has grown considerably weaker, though retaining more strength in southern Europe than most other places. What then about the resurgence of conservatism that ultimately brought Ronald Reagan to the White House? Our answer must be that this resurgent "conservatism" is not really and fully conservatism at all. It is more a restatement, with suitable modifications, of nineteenth-century (classic) liberalism. More precisely, as a study of the postwar "conservative intellectual movement" in America points out, what goes by the name of "conservatism" is a complex movement that blends together a strong anticommunist militancy, a "libertarian" revulsion against "big government," and a traditionalism that does recall the ideas of Burke or Santayana.[27] Thus, the most we can say is that *some* contemporary American conservatives are under *some* influence from the genuine conservative tradition. In most cases, however, classic liberalism seems the more basic force.

NOTES

1. Samuel P. Huntington, "Conservatism as an Ideology," in *Political Thought Since World War II*, ed. W. Stankiewicz (New York: The Free Press, 1964), p. 357.
2. M. Morton Auerbach, *The Conservative Illusion* (New York: Columbia University Press, 1959).
3. Among the many figures discussed by Auerbach are St. Augustine, John of Salisbury, Edmund Burke, Russell Kirk, and Peter Drucker.
4. Auerbach, *Illusion*, p. 6.
5. Ibid.
6. Ibid., p. 11.
7. Samuel Taylor Coleridge, in *The Conservative Tradition*, ed. R. J. White (New York: New York University Press, 1957), p. 46.
8. Burke, in *The Philosophy of Edmund Burke*, ed. L. I. Bredvold and R. G. Ross (Ann Arbor: University of Michigan Press, 1967), pp. 60–61.
9. Joseph DeMaistre, *The Works of Joseph DeMaistre*, ed. J. Lively (New York: Macmillan, 1965), p. 94.
10. Michael Oakeshott, *Rationalism in Politics* (New York: Basic Books, 1962), pp. 190–91.
11. Quentin Hogg, in White, *Tradition*, p. 31.
12. DeMaistre, *Works*, p. 64.
13. Benjamin Disraeli, in White, *Tradition*, p. 107.
14. Eliot, in ibid., p. 113.
15. Burke, in Ross and Bredvold, *Edmund Burke*, p. 176.
16. Edmund Burke, *Reflections on the Revolution in France* (New York: Liberal Arts Press, 1955), p. 70.
17. Burke, in Ross and Bredvold, *Edmund Burke*, p. 38.
18. Burke, *Reflections*, p. 99.
19. Burke, in White, *Tradition*, p. 35.
20. George Santayana, "A General Confession," in *The Philosophy of George Santayana*, ed. P. A. Schillp (Menasha, Wisc.: Banta Publishing Co., 1940), p. 21.

21. George Santayana, *The Idler and His Works* (New York: George Brazilier, 1957), p. 40.
22. George Santayana, *Dominations and Powers* (New York: Charles Schribner's Sons, 1951), p. 334.
23. George Santayana, *Interpretations of Poetry and Religion* (New York: Harper & Row, 1957), p. 172.
24. Ibid., p. 170.
25. George Santayana, *Reason in Society* (New York: Collier Books, 1962), p. 99.
26. George Santayana, *Character and Opinion in the United States* (Garden City, N.Y.: Anchor Books, n.d.), p. 101.
27. George H. Nash, *The Conservative Intellectual Movement in America Since 1945* (New York: Harper & Row, 1979).

SUGGESTIONS FOR FURTHER READING

Auerbach, M. Morton. *The Conservative Illusion.* New York: Columbia University Press, 1959.

Epstein, Klaus. *The Genesis of German Conservatism.* Princeton: Princeton University Press, 1966.

Hearnshaw, F. J. C. *Conservatism in England.* New York: Howard Fertig, 1967.

Kirk, Russell. *The Conservative Mind.* Chicago: Regnary, 1961.

Nash, George H. *The Conservative Intellectual Movement in America Since 1945.* New York: Harper & Row, 1979.

O'Sullivan, N. K. *Conservatism.* New York: St. Martin's Press, 1976.

14

POPULISM

Because the term "populism" is sometimes used in a wider sense than the one governing this chapter, we must briefly examine the social basis of populist movements. Such movements draw their main support from the "petty bourgeoisie." This group is composed of *small* farmers, *small* businessmen, *small* craftsmen, and inhabitants of *small* towns and villages in general. In the past these people were the pillars of the old middle class. Recently, however, industrialization and modernization have imperiled the social and economic position of these groups. The defensive posture and past-orientation of most populists is one key reason for placing them on the "right" side of the political spectrum.

Small, family-run farms have been challenged by huge "agro-businesses," whose size enables them to use the latest technology. The small farmer can hardly compete with the big modern farms and is threatened with bankruptcy. Small businessmen for their part are confronted by huge retail chains and supermarkets, which can undersell them and perhaps drive them out of business. Artisans and craftsmen, who make things by hand, find their wares too costly to compete with mass-produced goods. More generally, small-town notables lose their clientele in these groups because of the overall decline of the petty bourgeoisie. In a parallel development big-city life increasingly sets the tone and pace for national life, and the old small-town types lose their sense of self-importance.

Thus, populist movements are protests against the impact of industrialization and urbanization upon these petty bourgeois groups. Populist ideologies accordingly reflect frustration over a deplorable state of affairs and a certain aggression against those held responsible for it.

Despite the reformist tenor of their programs and proposals, populist ideologies situate their "golden age" in the past instead of the future. They wish to restore a condition that ostensibly existed in a bygone era, when the petty bourgeoisie was economically secure and socially esteemed.

This chapter examines six principles of populist ideology. To this end we use three populistic movements separated in time and space to illustrate the general ideas. The six common principles we find in the three movements are: (1) the attack on bigness; (2) nativism; (3) ruralism; (4) financial-monetary reform; (5) rugged individualism; and (6) conspiracy theory. The movements involved are American Populism of the 1890s, French "poujadism" of the 1950s, and the Social Credit movement in England and Canada in the 1920s and 1930s.

American Populism was a phenomenon of the 1890s and reached its high point in 1896 when the Populist Party nominated William Jennings Bryan as its presidential candidate. As the Democrats also nominated Bryan in that same year, it is a question of which party swallowed the other? While their rise was truly meteoric, the constitutional weakness of the Populists was their singular lack of appeal in the northern and eastern portions of the United States. The Social Credit movement emerged in Europe, especially England, after World War I and was championed by one Major Douglas, its foremost theorist. While Douglas had disciples the world over, it was in western Canada that Social Credit became a serious political force. For many years it was the third largest party in that country. French poujadism was a short-lived political movement of the late 1950s. Its animating force, Pierre Poujade, began as the leader of a protest movement and pressure group to champion small business in France. In 1956 a poujadist political party—Union and French Fraternity—did rather well in the parliamentary elections. However, with the coming of the French Fifth Republic in 1959 poujadism rapidly receded.

THE ATTACK ON BIGNESS

Movements of revolt generally have a shakier ideological basis than do revolutionary movements, and populism is only a partial exception to this rule.[1] However, most movements of revolt have a clear of idea of what they are against, even if what they are for is sometimes hazy. One of the things most hated by populists is bigness itself. This animosity, of course, is towards social, economic, and political bigness.

We can begin with big government.[2] According to the populist, who after all is not an anarchist, government does have certain legitimate functions. However, the massive growth of government in our century exemplifies the growth of organization in general, which seems ominous and incomprehensible to the populist. The complexities, rules and regulations are put there just to stymie the "little guy," who by populist reckoning is the very backbone of the nation.

The growth of government has not happened by accident—the populist is convinced that none of the things he deplores happen by accident. No, there is a reason for it. Some group or groups profit from situations so harmful to the little man. In populist thinking the guilty parties are the bureaucrats and their allies, the politicians. Former presidential candidate, George Wallace, was echoing populism when he said to the Democratic National Convention in 1972:

> when I go to Washington, . . . all the Governors themselves sometimes wonder what all the hundreds of thousands of bureaucrats do. The hundreds of thousands of bureaucrats that draw twenty-five and forty thousand dollars a year of the workingman's money, looking after matters that ought to be looked after by those elected in the local states and local political subdivisions.[3]

Big government is not only cumbersome and meddlesome; it carries a huge price-tag. To finance needless services at exorbitant cost and to support a superfluous and parasitical bureaucracy requires a tax base, whose constant expansion crushes the little man who is the populist's concern. The French poujadists of the 1950s pounded unceasingly on these themes. One leaflet asserted, "The vampire-state is killing France." According to their program of July 1955, "the common enemy of all classes is constituted on the one side by finance and big capital, on the other by certain governmental reforms at the service of a minority privileged class."[4]

The poujadists' "vampire-state" has been foisted on the little people through an unholy alliance of bureaucrats, politicians, and intellectuals. The first live directly off the largesse of the state; the second get patronage-plums and the support of the beneficiaries of big government; and the third beat the propaganda drums for ever new ways to spend the people's hard-earned money.

Big business—the precise terminology can be "the vested interests" or the "money power," for example—is also a bogey in the populist demonology. Does this mean that populism is anticapitalist along the lines of socialism and communism? One might get that impression from some of the blistering rhetoric of certain populist manifestoes and treatises. Indeed, in the novel *Caesar's Column* by the American Populist writer Ignatius Donelly, one of the characters complained of certain economic changes "in the shape of subtle combinations, 'rings,' or 'trusts,' as they called them, corporations, and all the other cunning devices of the day . . . which transferred the substance of one man into the pockets of another, and reduced the people to slavery."[5]

But despite the rhetoric, populism is neither socialistic nor genuinely anticapitalist. What galls the populist are the special privileges and prerogatives of *big* business or parts of it. Only rarely is capitalism itself—capitalism in the classic sense of Chapter 4—called into serious question. Populism does not object to the private ownership of the means of production and exchange or to the market economy if it is truly free or to production for the sake of profit. It is the perversion of these things by the special interests that it loathes.

Rather than taking the capitalists or the bourgeoisie as the enemy along Marxist lines, the populists attack the "plutocracy."[6] In the populist lexicon plutocracy means that the rich few have captured the state and employ corruption to get laws and policies favorable to their selfish interests. The plutocracy has bribed or otherwise induced public officials so that an originally democratic political system is perverted to do their bidding. Thus, neither the original versions of capitalism or democracy is at fault, just their corrupt versions. Populism teaches the necessity of getting back to pure democracy and pure capitalism.

Less important in populist ideology is the nemesis of big labor. Indeed, populism often looks to industrial workers for allies against the common enemy of the day. And yet, there is a problem here. There is a certain basis for populist resentment towards organized labor and the trade union bosses. First, modern labor unions are massive, often bureaucratic organizations, which as such arouse populist suspicion. Second, unions have successfully pushed for economic gains that have raised workers to the level of petty bourgeois groups. As economic status is relative, the rise of workers might be seen as the decline of other groups.

In a more concrete vein, many petty bourgeois employ hired labor in their shops, workshops, and small farms. Since unionization often leads to higher wages for these employees, the survival or profitability of small enterprises may be endangered. The usual populist response will be to criticize the leaders of organized labor, while trying to maintain a conciliatory attitude toward rank-and-file workers.

NATIVISM

Populist ideologies are nativistic. We described nativistic movements in Chapter 5 as "any conscious organized attempt [of a group] to revive or perpetuate selected aspects of its culture."[7] In the nativistic response, cultural change has taken place, which rightly or wrongly is attributed to foreign or alien influences. Though nativism usually characterizes groups dominated by outsiders, it also occurs when the dominant group itself feels threatened. In this second, subtler form of nativism, the older group reacts against the unwelcome presence of newer groups, possibly of recent immigrant background.

Given the backward glance of populist movements, we can understand their disposition toward nativism. The nativistic response is a defense mechanism against past and future socioeconomic changes. The members of the populist movement can now fight back, since nativism has identified the source of their discontents. They can now "restore or perpetuate" those elements of traditional culture most congenial to the petty bourgeoisie.

There is a somewhat darker side to this nativism, however. On the one hand, we have defense of the in-group and its culture; on the other we have an attack on foreigners, outsiders, or aliens, who are transforming the traditional culture. Since the malaise of the petty bourgeoisie is both cultural and economic, Jews have often received rough treatment at populist hands. Jews are culturally distinct and have often been forced to play an economic role that competes with or clashes with the small businessmen and farmers that figure in populist movements.

This sort of nonracist anti-Semitism filters into most populist ideologies. In American Populism, for example, the Jews are linked with the financial and business groups who have supposedly exploited the farmers. Once again, *Caesar's Column* is a good indicator, when a chief character declaims that "the nomadic children of Abraham have fought and schemed their way . . . to a power higher than the thrones of Europe. The world today is Semitized. The children of Japheth lie prostrate slaves at the feet of the children of Shem . . . ."[8]

As a historian further points out, Populist nativism took the form that "anti-Semitism and Anglophobia went hand in hand."[9] One populist complained of the dealings between Baron James Rothschild and the United States Treasury, because it signalized "the resignation of the country itself *INTO THE HANDS OF ENGLAND,* as England had long been resigned into the hands of her Jews."[10]

The poujadist movement also had undercurrents of nativism and anti-Semitism. In France in the mid-1950s there was a fear that the Americans and the Germans would dominate the country. The poujadist fear of the foreigner favored a kind of isolationism. Much that the poujadists found wrong with France they attributed to the alien (*l'etranger*). This was often accompanied by thinly-veiled allusions to the Jews.

The Jewish background of Pierre Mendes-France, a leading politician of the day, is a case in point. At one meeting a poujadist speaker asked "by whom are we governed?" and answered his own question by saying "by people who do not even dare to say their own name: Mendes-Portugal, of a family of Portuguese Jews, who is married to an

Egyptian Jew. . . ."[11] The poujadists were also fond of speaking of the "metics" in their midst, thereby alluding to the resident aliens of the ancient Greek city-states. The message was that these alien elements were not bona fide Frenchmen.

Criticism of the social and economic role of the Jews is also found in the writings of Major Douglas, the founding father of Social Credit. In his theories, economic woes and poverty are due to wrong ideas about economic life and human activity. These wrong ideas, however, served certain groups very well, even though they hurt the majority. Douglas went so far as to say that "the Jews are the protagonists of collectivism in all its forms, whether it is camouflaged under the name of Socialism, Fabianism, or 'big business.'"[12]

Since the Jews "exhibit the race-consciousness idea to an extent unapproached elsewhere," their success results from "their adaptation to an environment which has been moulded in conformity with their own ideal."[13] Since the rules of the political and economic game are by and large Jewish, it is no surprise that the Jews play so well. Douglas's anti-Semitism had definite limits, since he qualified that "it is the Jews as a group, and not as individuals, who are on trial, and that the remedy, if one is required, is to break up the group activity."[14]

RURALISM

Populist movements flourish in small towns and rural areas. Modern political science makes much of the contrast between the "center" and the "periphery" of a country. The center comprises the capital city and other areas where cultural and economic affairs are clustered. The periphery is made up of areas remote from such epicenters of modernization. Some resentment usually prevails between people in the two zones and this can be reflected in movements and ideologies in both settings.

Populism grows best in the periphery. This is certainly true of our three focal movements. While George Wallace, in many ways a throwback to classic Populism, had considerable success among industrial workers and city folk, this part of his support seems closely tied with the "white backlash" against the Black movement in the United States. When his support went beyond this single issue, it was based on traditional populist themes and surfaced in peripheral areas.

The ruralist motif presents itself in populist ideologies in various ways. One social scientist has characterized this as combining

a rebellion against the alienated human condition, the idea that integral personality was maimed by the social division of labor, a belief in the sacredness of the soil and those who tilled it, a belief in the equality of status of all cultivators, a faith in belonging to a local, fixed, virtuous and consensual community, and a belief that this virtue could perish only by usurpation, conspiracy and the working of active, alien, urban vice.[15]

This notion of "rustic simplicity," (i.e., of the moral superiority of rural life over urban life) goes back to Greek and Roman thought, if not earlier.

Rustic simplicity means that farmers and peasants work hard for their livelihood and are situated remote from the corrupting luxuries and hedonism of the city. The city is viewed as a seductive temptress that slowly destroys the moral fortitude of those caught in her wiles. Rural life is clean and free of the twin dangers of the debauched rich and the debased poor that makes cities a sinkhole of moral turpitude.

Tilling the soil implies that one is close to nature and thereby close to God. While the farmer or small-town dweller lack the pseudo-sophistication and caginess of the big-city denizen, they have something far more important—character. This character comes from the simple piety and moral uprightness nurtured by the rural milieu. Modern-day populists have done little more than paraphrase the sentiments of Thomas Jefferson, who felt that "cultivators of the earth are the most valuable citizens. They are the most vigorous, the most independent, the most virtuous, and they are tied to their country, and wedded to its liberty and interests, by the most lasting bonds."[16]

American Populism, if anything, out-Jeffersoned Jefferson. William Jennings Bryan, in his famous "cross of gold" speech of 1896, stated that the "great cities rest upon our broad and fertile plains. Burn your cities and leave our farms, and your cities will spring up again as if by magic; but destroy our farms and the grass will grow in the streets of every city in the country."[17] Twentieth-century populism tones down, but does not silence this strident ruralism.

With the poujadists ruralism comes out less as a simple defense of French farmers than as a conviction that small-town people in peripheral France are the country's strength. Despite the need for Parisian political support, poujadists see Paris as the point of origin of many evil influences. As one study points out, "Poujadism feels that the power it has lost has been confiscated by Paris and those who, thanks to their schooling, have been able to occupy first place in the state and the economy."[18]

In the 1930s, in the province of Alberta in western Canada, a government headed by William Aberhart and inspired somewhat loosely by Social Credit doctrines came to power. Aberhart and the Social Credit movement were the direct heirs of the traditional farmers' movement there. Moreover, general populist ideas had seeped into western Canada from the American Northwest. This was a highly favorable environment for the growth of Social Credit populism because

> the complaints of the prairie farmers were essentially directed against the economic and political power of central Canada, concentrated in Montreal and Toronto, and served by Ottowa. . . . The defeat of reciprocity in 1911 convinced the farmers that both Conservatives and Liberals were subservient to eastern manufacturing and mercantile interests. . . . Finally, there was the subtle unmeasurable reaction arising from the distance between east and west which led many prairie pioneers to feel they were outsiders in the national polity.[19]

Here again we see the constellation of economic, political, and cultural discontents that so often mobilizes the periphery to accept the populist message of self-vindication and counter-attack.

FINANCIAL-MONETARY REFORM

Populist proposals for financial and monetary reform cover a wide area, though there is a sort of common diagnosis of what is wrong and a set of similar remedies. In the populist mentality, the economic troubles of farmers, tradesmen, and artisans are not simply the side-effects of the modernization of society. The core problem is that the economy is not working up to full capacity. The populist explanation of this poor showing contrasts sharply with that of economic orthodoxy, however. The conventional economic wisdom teaches that the downward turn of the business cycle, which results in recession or depression, is a necessary adjustment to over-production. Supply has exceeded demand and some time is needed to bring them back together. That some groups suffer excessively is unfortunate but unavoidable.

Populist economic theory sees things very differently. In the first place, the problem is with demand and not with an excess of supply. Major Douglas maintained that "it is not for lack of technical ability, but for lack of effective demand, that civilization to-day stands on the brink of irremediable catastrophe."[20] This situation exists because "the persons who want and cannot do without the goods which the productive and industrial system can, and is anxious to supply, have not . . . the tickets, the possession of which is essential before the goods . . . can be handed over."[21] That is, people do not have the money to buy what they want. Thus, under-consumption caused by low purchasing power is the endemic weakness of the present economic system.

Now, failure to acknowledge and correct this problem is not a chance matter. Given the populist penchant for conspiracies, definite groups are held responsible for the unfair economic performance. The general populist response then is two-pronged: (1) attack those groups who feed on the blood of the small people; and (2) find adequate solutions through political methods. For the old American Populists, the "trusts" were the enemy. Accordingly, regulation of industry and even government ownership of railroads, telephone, and telegraph were planks in the Populist platform of 1892.

Even more important for them was the cure-all of "free silver." As the United States gold monetary standard of the 1890s meant a restricted money supply, creditor groups like banks were favored. To bring back silver as legal currency would greatly expand the money supply and allow debtor groups like the farmers to pay off their debts in inflated dollars. Silver would not only ease the debt problem for many, it could expand the purchasing power of lower economic groups and solve the under-consumption problem.

The Social Credit movement likewise illustrates the populist search for financial-monetary solutions. Major Douglas long preached that the present version of the capitalist system is flawed by its adherence to an outmoded ethic of reward and punishment. The problem comes from the illusion that purchasing power is the reward for work done. According to this doctrine, if unemployment is high, very little can be done to restore the purchasing power thereby lost.

Social Credit strikes at the heart of this belief system. It argues that the national "cultural heritage" of knowledge and ecology is a far more important economic factor in the creation of wealth than the three classic factors of land, labor, and capital. According to economic orthodoxy these three things are the only basis for economic reward and hence for the granting of credit. In practical terms this means that banks and other financial institutions exercise a virtual monopoly over credit. This in turn drastically limits the number of people who can get credit. Since the masses are left high and dry, effective demand for goods is kept artificially low. The evident result is an economy well below its actual potential.

While the details of the Social Credit solution cannot be covered here, some general idea is essential. Because the cultural inheritance belongs to society as a whole and forms the true basis of credit, the Douglas system first demands a total assessment of the national capital. Upon this grand total there can be computed a share for each and every citizen. The government will have to freeze certain forms of property and supervise the transfer of others. As Douglas once put it: "As for the initiation of this scheme, the holding of any stock, share, or bond by a holding company to trustees will not be recognized."[22]

Shares of the total national capital will be allotted only to individuals and is called the "national dividend." Granting the national dividend is contingent upon following certain rules, such as wage restraint and staying at one's usual job. This system will pump enough purchasing into the economy to abolish under-consumption forever.

As poujadism was a more transient and frenetic movement than either American Populism or Social Credit, it had less time to formulate an elaborate economic program. Nonetheless, some familiar populist themes ring out in their various declarations. They hoped to reduce government expenditures so as to allow tax relief. This quite naturally led to a demand for an "administrative reform tending to limit the number of functionaries, notably at the upper echelons." They also demanded the return of unprofitable nationalized industries to private hands.

Yet another point was the formation of a second chamber of parliament to deal with economic affairs. Since high taxes are hateful to most populists, the poujadists demanded first a "fiscal amnesty" (i.e., for past tax evasion—which is widespread in France) and secondly a complete overhauling of the tax structure. This last reform was obviously intended to relieve the "unfair" burden on petty bourgeois groups.

RUGGED INDIVIDUALISM

A student of populism exaggerates only a bit when he maintains that it " is not about economics, politics, or even, in the last resort, society. It is about personality, and about personality in a moral sense. Populism claims that the individual should be a complete man."[23] We have already alluded to the populist fear of the large organizations characteristic of modern industrial society. The dilemma is that though one sort of organization is the problem, only another sort can relieve the populist malaise. The Populist Party in the 1890s, the poujadist shift from a pressure group to a full-fledged political party, and the growth of the Social Credit Party in Canada—these are all advances in political organization. Yet in this case the growing organization is not an end in itself. Instead, for the populist it is a means—perhaps a necessary evil— to counter the truly evil conspiratorial organizations that pose a lethal threat to individuality. The rationale is still defense of individuality.

We can see this in the theories of Major Douglas, who was implacably opposed to all forms of "collectivism." Whether socialism on the left, the monopolies in the liberal democratic center, or fascism on the right, these and other trends worked to "subordinate the individual to the group."[24] He complained further that idolization of various collective entities has become a pretext for crimes on a grand scale. Nevertheless, even Douglas admitted that some organizations could be beneficial: the problem was to distinguish between those that helped and those that harmed individuality.[25]

It is at this point that interpretations of populism as semifascist or protofascist go wrong. They only see its nativism and conspiracy theories, which do have a certain kinship with fascism. But they fail to discount such similarities in terms of the populist defense of individuality. To make a long story short, all our populist movements have a strong belief in civil liberties to protect the individual from the very state that fascists wish to expand and exalt.

CONSPIRACY THEORY

There is a clear tendency of populist movements and ideologies to produce conspiracy theories of history and politics. Certain political ideologies—classic Marxism is an example—argue that history is moved by social and economic forces largely beyond human control. Conspiracy theories are different. They maintain that discernable groups of people are behind what happens in the world. As a conspiracy, of course, these people take pains not to reveal their true identity or intentions. Nonetheless, they are the hidden manipulators, who control things from behind the scenes.

To prevent exposure the conspiratorial clique exploits naivete and corruption. In the first case they bank on the gullibility of the masses, for whom out-of-sight means out-of-mind. In the second, they can usually get somebody to do what they want for a price. We have seen that populism denies that the social and economic plight of the "small people" results from modernization. The sea of troubles comes rather from policies imposed by the conspiratorial clique and its minions. The problem thus is to take power away from the exploitative few and return it to the people, where it belongs.

Nowhere is the rhetoric of conspiracy plainer than in the Populist Platform of 1892, which proclaimed that "a vast conspiracy against mankind has been organized on two continents, and it is rapidly taking possession of the world. If not met and overthrown at once, it forebodes terrible social convulsions, the destruction of civilization, or the establishment of an absolute despotism."[26] When it came to naming the evil conspiracy, the American Populists spoke of the "trusts," the "money power," the "plutocracy," the "vested interests," the "monopolies," the "gold-bugs," and still other things. Somehow this hazy group had snatched power from the people in the course of the nineteenth century. Public officials at all levels had been bribed or otherwise seduced by the conspirators. Thus, political reforms were just as important to Populist leaders as financial-monetary schemes; these measures were to bring government back to the people.

While the writings of Major Douglas are generally more sedate than those of the Populists, he too resorts to conspiracy theory to explain why the simple truths of Social Credit have not been implemented. His favorite term was "the Invisible Government." This group was composed of those financial and banking interests who monopolized the granting of credit. This monopoly is the "most far-reaching and . . . valuable instrument of power and policy which the world has ever known, [and] it is in the hands of a comparatively small body of individuals and organizations, and . . . they are not going to give up that monopoly unless they are made to give it up."[27]

With poujadists as well we find the angry rhetoric of conspiracy theory. This comes out in one of their election bills, which runs:

> But if you do not accept France's becoming the land of the college graduates;
> if you rebel against the tyranny of the irresponsible, against fiscal strangulation, against the exploitation of man by man,
> Rouse yourselves
> Against the alien trusts who ruin and enslave you; the electoral trusts who cheat your votes.
> Against the gang of exploiters who live off your work and your savings; the gang of swine who fatten on the blood of your dead.[28]

Clearly, the populist ideology in any of its manifestations registers the anger and frustration of people who want to strike out against their enemies.

CONCLUSION

In this chapter we have tried to give shape and content to a distinct though somewhat elusive current of ideology called populism. The expression "populism," of course, can be used in a broad sense to describe any doctrine that defends or extols the "people." But we have found it far more useful to restrict the term to ideological manifestations that have expressed the distress of petty bourgeois elements in the face of "modernizing" trends that threaten their livelihood and culture.

We have surveyed what anti-bigness, nativism, ruralism, financial-monetary reform, rugged individualism, and conspiracy theory mean when viewed through the prism of populist ideology. While it would be dangerous to say that some of the principles are more important than the rest, it is helpful to stress the strategic relevance of ruralism and rugged individualism. This is the case because it is ruralism that gives rise to nativism and conspiracy theory. Ruralism implies a certain narrowness or parochialism that views the foreigner as hopelessly alien and fearsome. Likewise it is no accident that the "conspiracies" that threaten the samll folk are made by urban-based elites.

Rugged individualism can be seen as the reverse side of the anti-bigness theme in populist ideology. Bigness is bad largely because it smothers the individual and destroys his cherished freedom. Even the financial reform projects, such as Social Credit, are designed by populists to assure the economic viability of the small independent artisan, entrepreneur, or farmer. Degrading economic conditions might otherwise endanger individuality.

Populism is still with us though the classic movements we have used to explicate its ideology have passed their prime or disappeared. The resilience of populist ideology results from the lingering presence of the petty bourgeoisie and of the rural sector itself. Long ago condemned to extinction by certain social theories, the petty bourgeois mentality and distinctive rural perspectives remain important, if secondary, aspects of the political cultures of even the most "advanced" industrial societies.

In Europe, for example, the populist heritage is kept alive in parties like the Dutch Peasants Party or the Anders Lang Party in Norway in the 1970s. While modern-day populist parties rise and decline rather rapidly, their recurrent and fairly widespread appeal suggests that the conditions that give rise to populist thinking are still with us.

NOTES

1. For more on the revolt–revolution dichotomy, refer back to Chapter 6.
2. American populism would appear to contradict this because it called for an expanded role for government. But the 1890s were well before "big government" in the modern sense emerged. Latter-day populists have generally attacked the centralization of power in Washington.
3. George C. Wallace, "In Praise of the Average Man," in *American Populism*, ed. G. McKenna (New York: G. P. Putnam's Sons, 1974), p. 227.
4. Quoted in Stanley Hoffmann, *Le Mouvement poujade* (Paris: Colin, 1956), p. 232.
5. Ignatius Donnelly, "How the World Came to be Ruined," in *From Populism to Progressivism*, ed. L. Filler (Huntington, N.Y.: R. E. Krieger, 1978), p. 38.
6. Plutocracy means the rule of the selfish rich. Plutus was the Greek god of riches.
7. See Chapter 5, n. 16.
8. Donnelly, *Populism*, p. 36.
9. Richard Hofstadter, *The Age of Reform* (New York: Alfred A. Knopf, 1956), p. 78.
10. Quoted in Hofstadter, *Reform*, p. 79.

11. Quoted in Hoffmann, *Poujade,* p. 226.
12. Major Douglas, *Social Credit* (Hawthorne, Cal.: Omni, 1966), p. 30.
13. Ibid.; p. 29.
14. Ibid., p. 30.
15. Douglas MacRae, "Populism as an Ideology," in *Populism: Its Meaning and Characteristics,* ed. G. Ionescu and E. Gellner (London: Wiedenfield and Nicolson, 1969), p. 162.
16. Quoted in McKenna, *American Populism,* p. 12.
17. William Jennings Bryan, "Speech Concerning Debate on the Democratic Platform," in Filler, *Populism,* p. 61.
18. Dominique Bonne, *Petits Bourgeois en revolte: le mouvement poujade* (Paris: Flammarion, 1977), p. 196.
19. Lewis H. Thomas, "Introduction," in *William Aberhart and Social Credit in Alberta* (Toronto: Copp Clark, 1977), p. 10.
20. Douglas, *Social Credit,* p. 183.
21. Ibid., p. 80.
22. Ibid., p. 206.
23. MacRae, "Populism," p. 160.
24. Douglas, *Social Credit,* p. 28.
25. Ibid., p. 34.
26. "Populist Platform of 1892," in Filler, *Populism,* p. 92.
27. Major Douglas, in Thomas, *Aberhart,* p. 53.
28. Quoted in Hoffmann, *Poujade,* p. 144.

SUGGESTIONS FOR FURTHER READING

Canovan, Margaret. *Populism.* New York: Harcourt, Brace, Jovanovich, 1981.
Gellner, Ernest, and Ionescu, Ghita, eds. *Populism.* London: Macmillan, 1969.
Hicks, John D. *The Populist Revolt.* Lincoln: University of Nebraska Press, 1961.
Hofstadter, Richard. *The Age of Reform.* New York: Alfred A Knopf, 1956.
Shanin, Teodor, ed. *Peasants and Peasant Societies.* Baltimore: Penguin Books, 1971.
Thomas, Lewis H., ed. *William Aberhart and Social Credit in Alberta.* Toronto: Copp Clark, 1977.

15

FASCISM

THE NATURE AND SOURCES OF FASCIST IDEOLOGY

In analysing fascist ideology we reserve a special place for Italian fascism, since the very term "fascismo" comes from Italy. Fascismo was a political movement founded by the ex-socialist leader Benito Mussolini (1883–1945). Mussolini had been a revolutionary socialist but had broken with his party at the beginning of World War I. The Socialist Party favored nonintervention in the war, but Mussolini demanded Italian entry on the side of the Western allies.

After the war, in which he served as a corporal, Mussolini formed the *fasci di combattimento* or combat groups to protect returning war veterans and to oppose the "antipatriotic" efforts of the extreme left. Fascismo thus originally referred to Mussolini's paramilitary armed squads. In time many looked to his movement as a preventive to communist revolution and a cure for the political paralysis of moderate parties. In October of 1922, after the so-called March on Rome, Mussolini was appointed prime minister in a more or less legal manner. By 1928 the remnants of constitutional government had been extinguished in Italy and would remain so for the next decade and a half.

Mussolini's fascist dictatorship was a strong one, but it paled in comparison with the Stalin and Hitler regimes that emerged in the 1930s. Though the Italian fascists were fond of calling their takeover of power a "revolution" and their system a "totalitarian state," such terms were more bombast than realistic description. Nonetheless, the twenty years of fascism instituted a number of political and economic changes, which were justified by an ideology of reasonable coherence.

By the 1930s various movements and theoreticians outside Italy were identified as "fascist." Although Mussolini himself initially described fascism as uniquely Italian, he later claimed a "universal" significance for the phenomenon of fascism. Though focusing on the Italian version of fascism, our account will try to capture the threads of ideology common to all fascists. First, let us look at three figures, aspects of whose thought had a role in preparing the intellectual landscape for the onset of fascist ideology: Friedrich Nietzsche (1843–1900), Georges Sorel (1847–1922), and Vilfredo Pareto (1848–1923). As we have touched on some of their views elsewhere in this text, we can now blend their ideas together on four "prefascist" themes: a critique of "progress," irrationalism, creative minorities, and force and violence.

Nietzsche, Sorel, and Pareto launched many a broadside against the western liberal idea of progress. They were far more impressed by the tragic aspect of life and by the circular or cyclical aspect of time. They ridiculed the notion that the spread of liberal ideas or democratic institutions betokened the universal advance of the human race. Nietzsche considered liberalism and democracy as "nihilism" and "decadence." Instead of universal progress he spoke of the "eternal recurrence" of the self-same events in a universe devoid of purpose and guiding intelligence.

Sorel wrote caustically of the "illusions" of progress and ridiculed both liberals and radicals who felt that history necessarily advanced to "higher" forms of society. History would only have the meaning that heroic mass action imposed on it. Even if such action failed, there was a certain tragic glory and nobility in having fought the good fight. Pareto came to regard the "religion of progress" as frothy sentiment outside the pale of science.

Our three pre-fascists thus rejected any notion of progress that envisages liberalism and democracy as benevolent historical necessities. If history instead was devoid of overall meaning or simply registered the ups and downs of successive civilizations, then liberal democracy might not be the wave of the future. Authoritarianism or dictatorship could take its place.

Nietzsche's, Sorel's, and Pareto's doctrines have been called "irrationalist" and so has fascism. There is some justification for this, but also some need for caution. "Irrationalism" really encompasses two things. The first questions the ability of human reason to understand the world about us. The categories of human reason are too limited and static to comprehend the dynamic processes of reality. The second sense of irrationalism does not despair of the intellectual powers of human reason, but simply doubts that most men can make use of the little reason they possess. Such views as these thus undermine cardinal points of liberalism and democratic theory.

Nietzsche was most adamant in denying the rationality of the world. In his unfinished work *The Will to Power* he argued that "the faith in the categories of reason is the cause of nihilism. We have measured the value of the world according to categories that refer to a purely fictitious world."[1] Reason is thus impotent to establish a system of values, which depend instead on the will-power and instincts of the human animal.

Sorel's irrationalist doctrine that social movements must be inspired to enthusiasm by nonrational "myths," we will see reflected in several elements of fascist ideology. Pareto also gave reason a rather marginal role in man's mental economy and thus in his social and political behavior. He taught that "non-logical conduct" far outweighed "logical conduct." Reason was restricted to a few economic and scientific activities, while nonrational factors dominated everyday life and politics.

In Pareto's social psychology man was controlled by six basic nonrational needs called "residues." These were "sentiments" or "near-sentiments" and included the need to manipulate men and affairs, loyalty to the group, the need for self-expression, self-defense, the need for belongingness, and sexual drives. But men do not openly declare that their words and deeds really reflect the residues. Instead they "rationalize" their behavior by invoking "derivations," i.e., religious principles, moral codes, aesthetic ideals, political doctrines, and so on.

In the third place, our three pre-fascists spoke glowingly of the value and historical role of small creative minorities. They were almost bursting with condescension and contempt for democratic values and institutions. These antidemocratic notions had a definite formative influence on fascism. According to Nietzsche the "democratic movement is . . . a deteriorated form of political organization, that is to say, a depreciation of a human type, a mediocritizing and lowering of values."[2]

Democracy thus is a modern-day rendition of "slave morality" designed to exalt the "herd-animal" majority over the superior elite. In place of this, Nietzsche demanded a new aristocratic "order of rank" that would bring back meaning to a world otherwise condemned to nihilism. His call for a new elite of "supermen" beyond "good and evil" resounds in the fascist fascination with charismatic leaders and bellicose minorities.

Sorel also viewed democracy as the essence of mediocrity and its institutions as a pious fraud. Democracy allowed politicians and intellectuals to befuddle the masses and swindle their way to power and its fringe benefits. In the workers' syndicates alone could there arise a new elite capable of leading us toward a revitalized order. The fondness of some fascists for "national-syndicalism" clearly recalls Sorel.

Pareto's theory of elites earned him the rather inappropriate label of "the Karl Marx of fascism" in the 1930s.[3] His teachings about the impossibility of democracy and the foolhardiness of parliamentary government found echoes in fascism. One of these echoes is his pet idea that decadent elites composed mainly of weak-willed "foxes" would be ousted by forceful "lions" from below. Indeed, it has been pointed out that as early as 1908, Mussolini "referred to 'Vilfredo Pareto's theory of elites' as the 'most ingenious social conception of modern times. History,' Mussolini maintained, 'is nothing more than a conception of dominant elites.'"[4]

Another theme that marked off our three theorists from the liberal circles before World War I was a belief in the positive, possibly redemptive, role of force and violence. Nietzsche's thought is permeated with metaphors of war and bellicosity. Peace, safety, tranquillity epitomize the mediocre life-force of herd animals with their slave morality. "Master morality," which Nietzsche associated with his coming caste of supermen, revels in danger, risk, and combat. He called his new rulers "beasts of prey." With his usual verve he asserted that "A society that definitely and instinctively gives up war and conquest is in decline: it is ripe for democracy and the rule of shopkeepers."[5] In a more positive vein he found that the "maintenance of the military state is the last means of all of acquiring or maintaining the great tradition with regard to the supreme type of man, the strong type."[6] Such rhetoric as this was a growth industry in the Europe of the inter-war years.

We have already discussed Sorel's view of the morally purifying function of violence in earlier chapters. Though Pareto did not extol raw violence in the same way as the other two pre-fascists, he made willingness to use force for self-defense the acid test of an elite's fitness to rule. A decadent elite is one so corrupted by "humanitarian sentiments" that it is unable to fend off challenges from below. Such an elite deserves its fate, which will be to be toppled, not by the masses, but by a new and more vigorous elite.

We will find influences flowing from our three pre-fascist thinkers in much of our treatment of fascist ideology. For convenience sake we will treat six basic themes that recur in all genuine expressions of fascism: statism, voluntarism, corporativism, dictatorship, anti-Marxism, and integral nationalism.

STATISM

Fascist ideology greatly emphasizes the state. Countless fascists have expressed the same sentiments as Alfredo Rocco, theorist and Mussolini's Minister of Justice, for whom the state "which is the legal organization of society, is for Fascism an organism distinct from the citizens who at any time form part of it; it has its own life and its own superior ends, to which the ends of the individual must be subordinated."[7]

According to this "organic" view, the state is a real entity that transcends the individuals who compose it. All individuals need the state, but the state needs no particular individual. The fascist state thus aims to be comprehensive and all-pervasive. It includes all and has the right to control and interfere with all. However, the state is not an alien force that fastens upon individuals and groups and sucks out their vital energy. The state and its component parts are not in an adversary relationship.

Indeed, for fascism, individuals and groups like unions find their completion only within the orbit of the state. To explain this, the philosopher Giovanni Gentile (1875–1944) maintained that the state *"is* the syndicate in the same sense that it *is* the individual: for the effective will of the individual who is conscious of his own real complex individuality is the State."[8] As the part (individual or group) gains significance only through relation to the whole, there can be no intrinsic conflict between what is good for man and what is good for the state.

The state thus should be an activist or "totalitarian" state because no realm of social activity is closed to it. We can illustrate this statism in several ways. For example, though fascism is extremely nationalistic, it reverses the relationship between nation and state found with most ideologies. As Gentile put it, "it is not nationality that creates the state, but the state which creates nationality, by setting the seal of actual existence on it. It is through the conquest of unity and independence that the nation gives proof of its political will, and establishes its existence as a state."[9]

An even stronger ideological reflex of statism appeared in the 1932 statute of the Italian Fascist Party, which asserts that "the National Fascist Party is a civil militia under the orders of the DUCE, *in the service of the Fascist State.*"[10] (Italics added.) While this statement is partially the result of Mussolini's desire to limit the autonomy of the party, it clearly defines the party as a service institution to the state. No such statement could have appeared under Hitler in Germany or Stalin in the USSR. In those countries there was no basis for placing state over party—quite the contrary.

Not surprisingly, statism also figures in the fascist view of economics. Fascism decisively rejects the laissez-faire notion that economics stands outside the scope of the state. In November, 1933, Mussolini himself laid down the conditions of the corporative system that was to replace old-fashioned capitalism. The first condition was the single party system to make sure that economic discipline was "accompanied by political discipline." The second condition was "the totalitarian State, that is to say the State which absorbs all the energies, all the interests, all the hopes of a people in order to transform and potentiate them."[11]

We might conclude from all this talk of a "totalitarian" state that fascism's economic ideal was state socialism with government ownership of basic industries. This would be wrong, however. In the Labor Charter of 1927, which was a sort of general economic program for the fascist regime, it states that "the corporative state considers that private enterprise in the sphere of production is the most effective and useful instrument in the interest of the nation."[12] This meant further that "State intervention in economic production arises only when private initiative is lacking or insufficient, or when the political interests of the State are involved. This intervention may take the form of control, assistance, or direct management."[13]

In the fascist scheme of things "politics" ranks higher than "economics." This would suggest that prudence and pragmatism rather than rigid principle would guide the shape of economic arrangements in a fascist state. Conceivably, a fascist state could assume greater economic functions and reduce the private sector considerably. Mussolini did precisely this in 1945 when he was installed in a small puppet state by Hitler called the Italian Social Republic, after being ousted from power in the rest of Italy.

VOLUNTARISM

In our discussion of communism we noted that the deterministic framework of Marx was modified by people like Lenin, Stalin, Trotsky, and Mao. Because these thinkers stressed such things as minorities, the state, and collective enthusiasm, communist ideology evolved in a more voluntaristic direction. The voluntaristic aspect of fascist ideology comes out in two ways. First is the philosophical claim that thought and action go together, i.e., that thought without action is impotent and action without thought is hysterical. Second is the more political notion that history can be made by strong-willed elites.

Some sense of fascist voluntarism is captured by William Y. Elliott's phrase "the pragmatic revolt in politics." Pragmatism, of course, is a broad philosophical movement, which influenced a number of twentieth-century ideologies in addition to fascism.[14] One target of the pragmatic revolt is rationalism because it understands reality essentially as a logically interdependent system or whole. As we saw in an earlier chapter, the pragmatist holds that reality is problematic rather than systematic. This means that truth is not preestablished; it emerges in and through our dealing with the everyday world. History, for example, is what we make of it and cannot be a predetermined schedule of definite stages and transitions.

A link between such ideas and fascism can be seen in Mussolini's early statement that one of the foundation stones of "Fascismo is represented by anti-demagogism and pragmatism. We have no preconceived notions, no fixed ideas. . . ."[15] Upon assuming power in 1922 he further pointed out that "it is not, alas, programs that are lacking in Italy. Rather men and the will to apply programs. All the problems of Italian life, all I say, have been solved on paper, but what has lacked has been the will to translate them into facts."[16] Mussolini shows here the pragmatist impatience with logically impeccable plans and programs remote from the world of practical action.

Indeed, such fine-sounding programs and plans may actually serve as a substitute for real achievement. Only by diving head-on into action will genuine solutions to problems be found. Activism, moreover, is not just a means to get things done. For fascism it is an end in itself, a state of being that is virtually its own reward. In action the individual is at the height of his powers and feels a sense of exhilaration. Where fascism differs from other doctrines influenced by pragmatism is its tendency to view "action" as forceful, perhaps violent political combat. Pitched battles with opponents and wars of conquest are not just necessary political strategies; they raise existence to a higher, nobler plane.

Mussolini's voluntarism fit in with Sorel's teachings about the political myth. Will, not reason, is at the heart of strong movements and regimes. To evoke mass will-power Mussolini says, "we have created a myth. This myth is a faith, a noble enthusiasm. It does not have to be a reality, it is an impulse and a hope, belief, and courage. Our myth is the nation, the great nation which we wish to make into a concrete reality."[17] Though utterances like this seem to embrace pure irrationalism, philosophical fascists tried to limit this tendency.

For Alfredo Rocco it was certainly true that fascism was "above all, action and sentiment." Only in this manner could it generate the "force to stir the soul of the people, and to set free an irresistible current of national will." Nevertheless, he was quick to point out that fascism was also "thought" and possessed a "theory."[18] Gentile similarly wished to avoid pure irrationalism. Instead he preferred to describe fascism as "eminently anti-intellectual . . . if by intellectualism, we mean the divorce of thought from action, of knowledge from life, of brain from heart, of theory from practice."[19]

Fascism, according to Gentile, aims to heal the breach between these things. Though fascism is neither a "system" nor a "doctrine" in the usual sense, this does not mean that it is a "blind praxis or purely instinctive method." Indeed, if we redefine "system" or "philosophy" to suggest a "living thought, a principle of universal character . . . then

Fascism is a perfect system, with a solidly established foundation and with a rigorous logic in its development."[20]

CORPORATIVISM

Although fascism claims to raise politics over economics, this does not mean that economic policy loses ideological importance. Fascist ideology rejects both laissez-faire capitalism and statist socialism. The first, with its economic individualism, left the masses defenseless against the vagaries of the business cycle. On the other hand nationalization of the economy is likely to be a cure worse than the disease it was supposed to remedy. With statist socialism comes a massive bureaucracy, whose rigidity and caution clash with the fascist preoccupation with will, dynamism, and charisma.

The much-heralded "corporative state" of fascism was offered as the golden mean between laissez-faire and bureaucratic ossification. The idea of a corporative state has both an economic and a political dimension. Economically, the hope was to overcome the conflict between labor and capital through a new harmonious relationship. The relations between employers and employees should be regulated by collective "contracts, which have binding force over all those who belong to the same categories whether they are in the syndicates or not. All labor conflicts "must be settled in a conciliatory manner by the recognized associations of superior grade,"[21] and if this fails by the government itself.

Fascism considers strikes and employers' lockouts impermissable. Both groups are morally bound to work for the interest of the whole community. Conflict between them is incidental, not intrinsic. To divide the nation along the lines of class is tantamount to treason.

On the more political side the corporative state will tear down the barriers between economics and the state in still other ways. Now, fascism did not invent the corporative idea. French and German theorists, especially of religious or conservative inclinations, had long dreamed of resurrecting aspects of medieval social organization to moderate the disruptive impact of the Industrial Revolution. Strengthening professional, occupational, and other associations while assigning them new political functions was thought of as an alternative to liberal individualism and left-wing syndicalism.

Despite this historical background, the theory and practice of fascist corporativism developed with surprising slowness.[22] As it turned out, a fascist "corporation" was a large economic association that grouped labor and management together as the responsible units for various sectors of the national economy. There were a total of twenty-two corporations for grains, construction, metallurgy, textiles, and other industries. Each corporation had a council that was supposed to have an equal number of labor and management members. Together all these councillors made up the National Council of Corporations.

Due to the huge size of the National Council, it chose a smaller Corporative Central Committee to handle the regular work of the vast corporative structure. Here too, however, it was clear that Mussolini was of no mind to grant vast independent power to corporative institutions. In theory at least, the 1934 law on corporations decreed that the corporations could regulate certain types of production, wages, and working conditions as well as give general economic advice to the governmen'. But advisory bodies, and not only those found in dictatorships, have the often fatal weakness that the advisee is not obliged to heed the advice received.

But there is more than Mussolini's personal dictatorship to explain the ultimate weakness of fascist corporativism. Statism, after all, represents an organic view demanding the unity and sovereignty of the state. Fascist corporativism, on the other hand, derives from more "pluralistic" currents that focus on "functional" groups as with Guild Socialism and syndicalism. The problem here is that a powerful, truly autonomous corporative system is hardly compatible with any monolithic, let alone "totalitarian," conception of the state. Indeed, in Italy and elsewhere, the debate between statists and corporativists could be acrimonious.

In the more political aspect of corporativism, the Italian fascists needed seventeen years to phase out traces of the liberal and democratic past. Before 1922 and Fascism, Italy had a popularly elected Chamber of Deputies and an appointed Senate. While the Senate remained more or less intact, the fascists began to tamper with the Chamber early on. First, they passed a law that gave the party with twenty-five percent of the votes a two-thirds share of the seats. Clearly there was nothing corporative about this so that in 1928 the Italian electorate was presented with a list of 400 nominees, which they had to approve or reject in toto. These final 400 nominees were chosen by a top party committee out of a list of 1000 names. A sort of semicorporatism was involved in so far as the large list was provided by, among other groups, thirteen National Confederations, which were weak forerunners of the corporations.

The final step towards a fuller corporativism came in 1939 with the Council of Fasci and Corporations. This new group included the National Council of Corporations and two high party organs: the Grand Council of Fascism and the National Council of the party. Even if this was an imperfect corporativism, it finally did away with all trace of popular elections and geographical representation.

From all this we can conclude that the "corporative state" in Fascist Italy was a somewhat watered-down version of the theoretical one. It was sabotaged by elements from business, the party, the bureaucracy, and even by Mussolini himself. As we shall see, an ideology that defends the substance, if not the name, of dictatorship will inevitably downgrade corporative institutions.

DICTATORSHIP

Fascism envisages a political order dominated by one strong leader. This relates to its repudiation of liberal democracy and parliamentary government. Indeed, these two points hang together since fascists maintain that the "evils" of parliamentarism stem from the practice of liberal democracy. In all of this we must bear in mind the fascist near-obsession with *unity*. Indeed, the radical defect of parliamentarism and democracy is that they promote social disunity and ultimately disintegration.

The basic fascist charge is that majorities that liberal democracy produces and uses to legitimize itself are "artificial." The counting of heads in a liberal state that encourages individual and group selfishness produces a hopelessly incoherent result. These majorities at best reflect the lowest common denominator of base interests, not the common interest of a unified state. For fascists,

> Democracy vests sovereignty in the people, that is to say, in the mass of human beings. Fascism discovers sovereignty to be inherent in society when it is juridically organized as a state. Democracy therefore turns over the government of the state to the multitude of living men that they may use it to further their own interests; Fascism insists that the government be entrusted to men capable of rising above their own private interests and of realizing the aspirations of the social collectivity, considered in its unity and its relation to the past and future.[24]

Fascist elitism is seen clearly here, since the ability to rise above personal interests in "favor of the higher demands of society and history is a very great gift and the privilege of the chosen few."[25]

Sometimes fascists argue that their attack on democracy relates only to the "formal" democracy of the liberal state. Indeed, fascism, they say, practices a higher-order or "organic" democracy because it fully and truly integrates the masses into the state. As the "real" will of the masses is now inseparable from that of the state, fascism embodies the truly positive elements of the democratic ideal. Moreover, as we saw earlier with the Chamber of Deputies under Mussolini, fascism can resort to plebiscitory votes to generate or demonstrate popular support. Even rigged elections are testimony of the power of the democratic ideal in the modern world. The purest dictatorships are forced to go through the motions of democratic elections, even though the results are a fraud.

Since liberal parliaments are for fascism simple talk-shops where cynical vote-trading prevails, the common good gets lost in the shuffle. The fascist remedy for liberal-democratic "chaos" is the single-party to replace the many conflicting parties and the one great leader to restore the fractured unity of the state. If the state is a unity then a single party and a single leader should guide public policy. There are points of contact between the fascist defense of personal dictatorship and some traditional theories of monarchy. Both maintain that one single mind can best serve the unified interest of the state.

However, fascism depends more on *charisma* than traditional monarchy, when dealing with special leaders like Mussolini (or Hitler).[26] Such a theory of the charismatic hero was applied to Mussolini by a fascist ideologist, who stated that

> The man was simply the mouthpiece chosen by destiny to utter what needed to be uttered at a crucial time of human history; what he said all people were longing to say; what he did many people, perhaps, were trying to do. . . . Alone he could do nothing, as a leader he could change, and is changing the aspect of the world.[27]

Mussolini's tremendous role is explained by a typically fascist account. After listing sincerity, courage, and self-confidence as essential traits of the hero-leader, the ideologist adds that "within the soul's deepest recesses," there must also exist "a mystic power of immediate knowledge of the truth through the supreme gift of intuition, if the action of a man must share the finality of an act of God."[28]

This "supreme gift of intuition" means that the fascist leader possesses a kind of sixth sense that allows him to see further and faster what is truly good for the nation he leads. Since the leader knows what he knows, true patriotism demands unconditional obedience to his will. How can you quarrel with someone who has "a mystic power of immediate knowledge of the truth?" If the twists and turns of the leader's policy seem openly contradictory or rankly opportunistic, this simply reflects one's own lack of insight. There was even a slogan in Fascist Italy that ran "*Mussolini ha sempre diritto*" (Mussolini is always right!)

While communist regimes have had serious "succession crises" after the death of great leaders such as Lenin, Stalin, and Mao, these are to some extent outside the pale of ideology. However strong the idolization of the former communist leader, sooner or later it will be criticized as the ideological deviation of the "cult of personality." When Lenin, Stalin, and Mao died, the party carried on and new leaders emerged. But one wonders how a new charismatic leader could come forth in a fascist succession crisis. Membership in the club of those with "the supreme gift of intuition" may be limited to one every generation.

ANTI-MARXISM

Opposition to Marxism is an important component of fascist ideology. It figures in the intellectual and political background of fascist movements in Italy and elsewhere. Let us recall that as a young socialist leader Mussolini himself was exposed to Marxist ideas. He naturally rejected certain of these when ousted from the Socialist Party in 1915. While some claim that he never fully shed these early Marxist influences, it is less debatable that the ideological development of fascism responded in many ways to questions posed by and about Marxism.

In practical politics, the Fascist movement in Italy (and to a degree elsewhere) was a direct counterblast to leftist advances in the wake of the Russian Revolution of 1917. Fascism attacked Marxism as an anti-patriotic, alien ideology. These attacks came mainly in the issues of internationalism, class struggle, materialism, and egalitarianism.

Marx, we have seen, was a staunch internationalist, convinced that nationalism was on the wane. He and later communists championed "proletarian internationalism" and the solidarity of the working class of all nations. For fascism this thinking was a case of "rootless" cosmopolitanism.Thus, the Marxist idea that workers in a country are closer to workers elsewhere than to their own bourgeoisie is the rankest heresy to the fascist. Indeed, any doctrine that places any ties whatsoever above national solidarity is to be combatted.

Also treasonable is the Marxist idea of class struggle. While fascists claim to understand specific causes for class antagonism, they deny that it is inevitable. The root of class conflict is the liberal state's exclusion and neglect of the workers. However, if the masses are welcomed into the state as fascism promises, class struggle should disappear. Rather than irreconcilable adversaries, owners and workers should equally be servants of the national interest.

Marxism not only misunderstands modern society; it is a doctrine spawned and spread by elements implacably hostile to the nation. If the specific version of fascist ideology involves anti-Semitism, Marxism will be blamed on the Jews. Perhaps the most general defect of Marxism is its *materialism*. Fascism rejects materialism both as a general philosophy and as a view towards life. It claims to be a "spiritual" conception opposed to materialism and determinism. Mussolini once maintained:

That the vicissitudes of economic life—discoveries of raw materials, new technical processes, scientific inventions—have their importance, no one denies; but that they suffice to explain human history to the exclusion of other factors is absurd. Fascism believes now and always in sanctity and heroism, that is to say, in acts in which no economic motive—remote or immediate—is at work.[29]

Fascist "spiritualism" means that states of mind and moral factors play an important role in history and politics. The spread of any form of materialism thus saps the vital energies that fascism promises to unleash. Morale, will, force—such factors make human greatness and history in a way no materialism can fathom. The fascist motto "believe, obey, fight!" symbolizes a view of life that opposes the doctrines of the French Enlightenment, many of which survive in Marxism.

INTEGRAL NATIONALISM

Fascism is perhaps the most stridently nationalistic of all ideologies. This may reflect the paradox that fascism was generally strongest in countries like Italy or Spain where national identity was tardy or shaky. The term "integral nationalism" has been applied to nationalist movements that are especially intense, militant, intolerant, and encompassing. The goal of all fascist movements and regimes is to create and protect, and promote and expand the nation. Indeed these purposes are invoked to justify the strongest authoritarian aspects of fascist theory and practice.

Integral nationalism figures prominently in the rhetoric of fascist leaders and ideologists. Their nation is special, and is called to perform some special mission in the world. While some ethnocentrism is found in most nationalist movements, in fascism it reaches a fever pitch. In Italian fascism, Rome assumes tremendous symbolical significance, both in terms of the imperial idea of ancient Rome and in terms of Rome as the focal point of Roman Catholicism. In the words of one enthusiast, "A spiritual power generated from those great Italian spirits who have been in the past the asserters of Rome's immortal and eternal right to Empire, and the prophets of Rome's third form of Empire, is the leaven which has brought about that fermentation of spiritual forces called Fascism."[30]

An interesting issue is the relationship between fascist integral nationalism and racism and anti-Semitism. In the first case, there does not appear to be any necessary connection between fascism and racism. While the Italian Fascists became ever more racist as Mussolini came more under Hitler's influence, their earlier unconcern with racist theories seems closer to the intent of their ideology. This, however, does not mean that there is any logical incompatibility between fascism and certain forms of racism. And yet, as we will see in the next chapter, the rigid biological determinism of extreme racism is hard to reconcile with the statism and voluntarism of fascism.

The connection with anti-Semitism is still more complicated. Italian Fascism started out relatively free of anti-Semitism, while fascist movements elsewhere in Europe thrived on it. Anti-Semitism can accompany integral nationalism, provided that Jews are considered an unassimilable minority. The most we can say is that the integral nationalism of fascism can lean toward both racism and anti-Semitism, but how far this goes in any country depends on specific conditions.

CONCLUSION

In our discussion of fascist ideology in terms of statism, voluntarism, corporativism, dictatorship, anti-Marxism, and integral nationalism we have relied strongly on sources from Fascist Italy in the 1920s and 1930s. By doing so we have avoided a rather hotly debated issue on the "nature of fascism." There are two extreme viewpoints on this matter, each with several important variants. The first viewpoint includes broad theories of "generic fascism." However different, these interpretations somehow contend that fascism was characteristic of a whole era in recent political history.

One such approach to generic fascism sees it mainly as the "highest" or "final" stage of capitalism. Popular among communists and certain Marxists in the inter-war years, it maintains that as capitalism enters its "general crisis" it is forced to set aside parliamentarism and democracy and rule through naked force and repression. With the rise of the workers' movement and socialism and the lethal threat they pose to the capitalist system, the "monopoly capitalists" are forced to look for a repressive counterforce. Following the adage "any port in a storm" the leaders of big business discover in the vulgar thuggery of nascent fascist movements after World War I an instrument they can use against the workers and socialism. Thus, fascism is not serious as an ideological system, but only as a movement or regime that is clearly counterrevolutionary.

Still another general theory stresses the crucial role of "mass society."[31] In a simplified version, this theory suggests that with the coming of industrialization and modernization, traditional social groupings like the clan, the status group, the church, and the local community tend to weaken. If things work out well, the individuals set adrift by modernization regroup into a vast network of voluntary associations such as unions, business associations, professional organizations, farmers groups, and a whole host of cultural, sportive, and charitable associations. Thus there emerges a "pluralist" society, where individuals are firmly embedded in group relationships.

However, sometimes the traditional groups decline without the rise of a strong modern pluralism. Individuals are left on their own. When this happens society becomes a "mass society" of isolated, atomized individuals. Now they are psychologically vulnerable to the ministrations of the next would-be messiah that comes on the scene. Often he is religious, but in our century he is just as often the charismatic leader of a mass movement that tells the atomized individual just what he wants to hear. The message is that he is important, that enemies are keeping "us" down, and that he will find redemption and brotherhood in the caderies of the movement. Fascism is simply the form that mass movements sometimes take.

In stark contrast to the "generic" theories are those that maintain that fascism in the strict sense was a limited Italian phenomenon. In this approach Italy at the close of World War I presented a unique set of cultural and political conditions that allowed the political adventurer Mussolini and his movement to come to power. The glory that was Rome, the contrast between Northern and Southern Italy, the disappointment with the victory of World War I, the estrangement between Catholics and the state, serious problems of overpopulation, etc.—these and other factors that could not be precisely duplicated elsewhere placed an indelible stamp on the theory and practice of Italian fascism. Alleged resemblances with right-wing movements elsewhere cannot outweigh serious differences due to historical background.

Resolving these issues is not possible here; we can only stipulate that fascism was something of a general phenomenon and certain of its ideological tenets found a ready response in a variety of countries. Nonetheless, as our next chapter will show, historical differences between Italy and Germany make it difficult to call Nazism purely and simply "German fascism."

NOTES

1. Friedrich Nietzsche, *The Will to Power* (New York: Random House, 1967), p. 13.
2. Friedrich Nietzsche, *Beyond Good and Evil* (Chicago: Regnery, 1955), p. 203.
3. Quite simply, there was no figure comparable to Karl Marx in the history of fascist ideology. Pareto's qualified sympathy for Fascism and Mussolini did not extinguish his traditional liberal ideas.
4. Quoted in A. James Gregor, *The Ideology of Fascism* (New York: The Free Press, 1969), p. 106.
5. Nietzsche, *Power*, p. 728.
6. Ibid., p. 729.
7. Alfredo Rocco, "The Transformation of the State," in *What is Fascism and Why?*, ed. T. Sillani (New York: Macmillan, 1931), p. 18.
8. Giovanni Gentile, *The Genesis and Structure of Society* (Urbana: University of Illinois Press, 1960), p. 129.
9. Ibid., pp. 121–22.

10. "Statute of the National Fascist Party," in Benito Mussolini, *Fascism: Doctrine and Institutions* (New York: Howard Fertig, 1968), p. 198.
11. Mussolini, *Fascism*, p. 60.
12. "The Labor Charter," in Ibid., pp. 135–36.
13. Ibid., p. 136.
14. See Chapter 11 for pragmatism's impact on liberal thought.
15. Quoted in William Y. Elliott, *The Pragmatic Revolt in Politics* (New York: Howard Fertig, 1968), pp. 341–42.
16. Benito Mussolini, *Discorsi di Benito Mussolini* (Verona: Monadori, 1937), p. 13.
17. Quoted in Karl Mannheim, *Ideology and Utopia* (New York: Harcourt, Brace, 1936), p. 139.
18. Alfredo Rocco, "The Political Doctrine of Fascism," in *Communism, Fascism, and Democracy*, ed. C. Cohen (New York: Random House, 1966), p. 335.
19. Giovanni Gentile, "The Philosophic Basis of Fascism," in Ibid., p. 365.
20. Ibid., p. 366.
21. Giuseppe Bottai, "The Corporative State," in Sillani, *What is Fascism?*, p. 35.
22. Ironically, though a Ministry of Corporations was created in the early 1920s, the Corporations themselves were not formed until 1934 and their full conflation into the corporative state was delayed to 1939. This is a rather typical example of the gap between theory and practice in Mussolini's Italy.
23. The presence of these two top party groups strongly suggests that Fascist Italy did not represent a real experiment with a corporative state—a fact often forgotten by those who try to discredit the idea by references to Fascism.
24. Rocco, in Cohen, *Communism*, p. 345.
25. Ibid.
26. According to Max Weber, charismatic authority relates to a leader who for religious or other reasons is considered an extraordinary, perhaps superhuman, figure by his followers. To such a leader, the follower owes obedience without debate or hesitation.
27. Mario Palmieri, "Fascism and the Meaning of Life, " in Cohen, *Communism*, p. 389.
28. Ibid., p. 387.
29. Mussolini, "Political and Social Doctrine," in Mussolini, *Fascism*, p. 20.
30. Palmieri, in Cohen, *Communism*, p. 385.
31. William Kornhauser, *The Politics of Mass Society* (Glencoe, Ill.: The Free Press, 1963).

SUGGESTIONS FOR FURTHER READING

Ashton, E. B. *The Fascist: His State and His Mind.* New York: William Morrow, 1937.
Elliott, William Y. *The Pragmatic Revolt in Politics.* New York: Howard Fertig, 1968.
Gregor, A. James. *The Ideology of Fascism.* New York: Free Press, 1969.

Joes, James. *Fascism in the Contemporary World: Ideology, Evolution, Resurgence.* Boulder, Colo.: Westview Press, 1978.

Laquer, Walter, ed. *Fascism: A Reader's Guide.* Berkeley: University of California Press, 1978.

Payne, Stanley G. *Fascism: Comparison and Definition.* Madison: University of Wisconsin Press, 1983.

16

NAZISM

NAZISM AND FASCISM

The theory and practice of German National Socialism (Nazism) bear certain family relationships to Italian and other forms of fascism.[1] Thus we must avoid two opposite errors: the first which sees no major differences between Nazism and generic fascism, and the second which sees no connection whatsoever between them. Certainly there can be no question of a simple German imitation of an Italian model. While Hitler was appointed chancellor over a decade after Mussolini became prime minister—January 1933 as opposed to October 1922—the two political movements were born almost simultaneously right after World War I. Each, moreover, had ideological roots both in its own country and in the general European milieu. Indeed, Hitler's *Mein Kampf*, begun in 1924, was as ambitious a statement of ideology as any Italian Fascist could produce at that time.

A look at the major ideological similarities and contrasts between Nazism and fascism will surely help to orient our discussion. Similarities stand out most regarding the leadership principle and the attack on Marxism. Chapter 15 spoke of how the fascist obsession with unity led to an exaltation of a charismatic hero-leader with extraordinary powers of intuitive political judgment. The will of the leader was a remedy for the cynical machinations of parties and parliaments. The Nazi "leadership-principle" (*Führer-prinzip*) so closely resembles fascism that we need not cover the same ground once more.

Nazi anti-Marxism was even more intense than the Italian variety. There was a similar rejection of "materialism," "internationalism," and

229

"class struggle" of Marxist doctrine. Materialism was replaced by a more idealistic or "vitalistic" view of the world.[2] Internationalism in the usual sense was hateful to Nazism. Like the fascists the Nazis denied the inevitability of class struggle and maintained that true social unity and discipline could be restored in a racially purified "folk community" (*Volksgemeinschaft*).

However, the Nazis added a dimension to their anti-Marxism. They charged that Marx's Jewish background guaranteed that his ideology was a ready-made weapon for the "Jewish world conspiracy" in its drive to divide and rule non-Jewish peoples. The class-struggle idea pitted members of the same nation against each other and thus eased Jewish domination.

We hope to show that in the final analysis it is racism and anti-Semitism that causes certain divergencies between fascist ideology and Nazi ideology. Two important cases of divergency come out in the notions of the state and of history in the two ideologies.

THE NAZI VIEW OF THE STATE

Both before and after 1933, there was some contrast of opinions in the Nazi theory of the state. There was a "fascistizing" trend that was enamored of the term "total state" and sought to give the state the same ideological eminence it enjoyed in Italy. This departed sharply from the orthodox Nazi position on the state formulated by Hitler in 1925 and was pretty much squelched by the mid-1930s.

If we recall the fascist rhetoric about the higher nature, comprehensiveness, and activism of the state, Hitler's doctrine provides a sharp contrast. Indeed, he even said in a speech in 1930: "Men do not exist for the state, the state exists for men."[3] Behind this liberal-sounding utterance is, of course, a racist idea, as the long formulation of *Mein Kampf* some years earlier shows:

> The state represents no end, but a means. It is, to be sure, the premise for the formation of a higher human culture, but not its cause, which lies exclusively in the existence of a race capable of culture . . . .

> The fact of human state formation would not in the least exclude the possibility of the destruction of the human race, provided that superior intellectual ability and elasticity would be lost due to the absence of their racial bearers.[4]

While Hitler demotes the state from end to means, it can still assume vital importance.

It is the state, for example, which will implement the Nazi program, particularly its racist and anti-Semitic aspects. The state will administer selective breeding in terms of race and impose an education dedicated to racist and *volkish* values. If the Nazi state is not exalted as "total" or "totalitarian" as with the Italian Fascists, it is eminently activist and authoritarian in areas that liberals would consider beyond its competence.

Instead of "totalitarian state" the Nazis' own concern with unity is captured in the slogan *Ein Reich, Ein Volk, Ein Führer* (one reich, one people, one leader). "Reich" (empire) is preferred to "state", and when President von Hindenburg died in 1934, Hitler did not bother to formally assume that title and office. His title as Führer of the German People was considered more legitimate than the constitutional position of president. All this reflects a definite de-emphasis of the role of the state.

Alfred Rosenberg (1893–1946), probably the chief ideologist of Nazism after Hitler, likewise emphasized the instrumental or subordinate nature of the state. He warned Nazis "not to speak any more of the total state, but of the *completion of the National Socialist Weltanschauung*, of the (Nazi Party) *as the embodiment of this* Weltanschauung, *and of the National Socialist State as the means by which National Socialism* . . . secures soul, intellect and blood."[5] Thus, in Nazi ideology the mission of the party outranks that of the state. First, the party organizes the elite elements of the people. Second, the party has special ties to the Führer himself. Given the Nazi emphasis on personalism, these ties are more important than the bureaucratic relationships associated with the state.

On the economic role of the state, Nazi ideology was rather vague. While some Nazis took the *socialism* of National Socialism quite literally and demanded nationalization of industry, they were outside the mainstream of Nazi ideology. Generally, the Nazis tried to downplay economics, though there were some strong economic planks in the original party program of 1920. There we find some radical-sounding, if hazy, economic notions. After asserting that the common interest must precede individual interest—the way most Nazis understood "socialism"— the program demanded such things as "the abolition of incomes unearned by work, and emancipation from the slavery of interest charges," "the complete confiscation of all war profits," "the nationalization of all business combines (trusts)," "the great industries," it said "shall be organized on a profit-sharing basis."[6] Such "socialistic" ideas were balanced by more "populist" ones about strengthening small farmers, small businessmen, and the "creation and maintenance of a healthy middle class."[7]

That the Nazis never really delivered the goods on the economic part of the 1920 program is often cited as proof of their cynical opportunism. Indeed, one theory defines Nazism as a "revolution of nihilism."[8] Before we accept such interpretations, let us bear in mind that Hitler in 1922 did point out that "economics is a secondary matter.

World history teaches us that no people became great through economics: it was economics that brought them to their ruin. A people died when its race was disintegrated. Germany, too, did not become great through economics."[9]

This negative estimate of economics allowed whatever Nazi "anticapitalism" that existed to be vented largely against the Jews. Moreover, when Hitler began to woo elements of German big business after 1930, the very vagueness of the Nazi economic program helped him to win them over. The Nazis henceforth could pose as defenders of capitalism against the threat of the Marxist left.

Still another difference between Nazism and Italian Fascism concerns the corporative state. While right-wing thought in pre-Nazi Germany produced its share of "corporative" theorists, their impact on Nazi ideology was surprisingly slight.[10] The Nazis reorganized German business and industry into a plethora of "estates" and "chambers" but no corporations. These estates and chambers were organs of "social self-government" and were not brought into the state structure like the Fascist corporations. Hitler's distaste for bureaucracy was apparently even stronger than Mussolini's.

The Nazi vision of utopia was not cast in terms of a state, but of the "folk-community." Hitler naturally opposed this to the "Jewish-Marxist" idea of class struggle:

> The splitting up of the nation into groups with irreconcilable views systematically brought about by the false doctrines of Marxism, means the destruction of the basis of a possible communal life . . . . It is only the creation of a real national community, rising above the interests and differences of rank and class, that can permanently remove the source of nourishment of these aberrations of the human mind.[11]

Since such a folk-community was blessed with total unity, alien racial types would have to be extruded. While the new order was not exactly a "classless society," a new elite would rule a society where "folk-comradeship" would outweigh traditional social differences.

RACISM AND ANTI-SEMITISM

The racism of Nazi ideology differs sharply from the "racism" Americans have heard about for two decades. This latter sense of racism incorporates the meaning of earlier terms such as "discrimination," "bigotry," "prejudice," and "bias." Such racism means simply that some poeple look down on others on the basis of certain differences they relate to skin color. It does not involve a grandiose philosophy of history and life as do the classic forms of racism represented by Nazi ideology.

Classic racism maintains that cultural differences between peoples are ultimately traceable to biological (or as we say today "genetic") differences. The classic racist explains higher and lower cultures in history by pointing to "superior" and "inferior" races. Higher cultures are the handiwork of superior races. Thus, the decline of a higher culture means that the racial composition of the "culture-creating" group has been "corrupted" by racial intermingling.

Count Gobineau

While racial doctrines have a long pedigree, Count Joseph-Arthur de Gobineau (1810–82) has been labeled the "father of racist ideology."[12] He expounded his racist ideas in his massive *Essay on the Inequality of the Human Races* (1854). Like other thinkers of conservative inclinations he was fascinated by the spectacle of the "rise and fall" of civilizations. The prelude to his own racist theories was a minute examination of traditional doctrines about the cyclical pattern of past civilizations. He found wholly inadequate theories that tried to attribute the fall of civilizations to a decline in morals. Such theories, he argued, put the cart before the horse by mistaking effects for causes. In addition, they forced the facts to fit the theory because virtue and vice are found in all societies regardless of upward or downward movement.

"Misgovernment" has also been blamed for the decline of civilizations. But here again misgovernment is found too often in flourishing centers. The same with theories about the decline of religion: the correlation between decline of civilization and slackening of religious faith is much too loose. There can thus be no question of cause-effect relationships.

The missing factor in these theories for Gobineau is race. A decline in the level of civilization is simply the outer side of inner racial degeneration. This is caused by intermarriage of different racial groups, which modern racists call "miscegenation." Gobineau thus voices the fears of race mixture that haunted racists for the next century. Actually, Gobineau distinguishes between two types of race mixing. One type of mixing raises the level on the "new" racial strain; the other lowers the level and may in the long run destroy the original civilization. Racial purity is something relative: the real question is the quality of the resulting group.

Gobineau divided mankind into three broad racial families: the white, the yellow, and the black. Trying to reconcile his teachings with Christianity, he argued for the primordial racial unity of mankind. In other words, back in the mists of time there was a "primary" human race that was not white, yellow, or black as we understand them. Thus, the subsequent white-yellow-black division represents the emergence of "secondary" races. However, these too have gone and their place taken by mixed or "tertiary races." Though tertiary races in turn are nearly extinct, we might consider them relatively pure racial stocks. Beyond this are "quarternary" races that are mixtures of mixtures. At any rate, when mixing goes too far, the polyglot humanity that results cannot long support a high level of civilization.

Though no longer pure, Gobineau is willing to rank the three races. The black race is the lowest group because of their low intellect. Blacks, however, have certain aesthetic qualities due to powerful sensory faculties. Speaking of the "negro" in stereotyped terms, he maintains that "many of his senses, especially taste and smell, are developed to an extent unknown to the other two races."[13]

In the middle of the racial hierarchy comes the yellow race. A member of this race

> tends to mediocrity in everything; he understands easily enough anything not too deep or sublime. He has a love of utility and a respect for order, and knows the value of a certain amount of freedom. He is practical in the narrowest sense of the term . . . .
>
> The yellow races are thus clearly superior to the black. Every founder of a civilization would wish the backbone of his society, his middle class, to consist of such men. But no civilized society could be created by them.[14]

At the summit of the racial hierarchy stand the "white peoples." It is no surprise that Gobineau gives a list of very positive qualities of the white races. They have an "energetic intelligence" that includes a sense of utility that is "more courageous and ideal" than we find with the yellow races. Persistence, great physical power, as well as "an extraordinary instinct for order" and a "love for liberty" are among their virtues. In addition, their "extraordinary attachment to life" is balanced by a sense of "honor" which "together with all the civilizing influences connoted by it, is unknown to both the yellow and the black man."[15]

The white race's deficiencies in sensory-aesthetic matters seem minor in the light of his conviction that the "lesson of history" shows "that all civilizations derive from the white race, that none can exist without its help, and that a society is great and brilliant only insofar as it preserves the blood of the noble group that created it, provided that this group itself belongs to the most illustrious branch of our species."[16] Clearly, not so much the white race as a whole, but its Aryan branch, has founded the great world civilizations. The Aryans are the elite within the elite of the human family.[17]

Gobineau's Aryanism had the most potent influence on twentieth-century forms of racism, such as Nazism. They echo his thoughts on the civilizing role of the Aryan race. However, there is one important difference: Gobineau felt that racial intermingling had proceded beyond the point of no return. In other words, the "blood" of the white race in general and the Aryans in particular had been "corrupted" beyond reversal. The days of glorious civilization were in the past, and for the future we could anticipate "the declining march toward decrepitude."

For this reason, the depths of Gobineau's pessimism rule out the activist message of redemption necessary to a programmatic ideology. Hitler and the Nazis shelve this aspect of Gobineau's racism and preach instead that the *degenerative cycle can be reversed.* They argued, in short, what Gobineau could not: politics and public policy can "repurify" the Aryan race. Where Gobineau counseled despair, Hitler bizarrely preached hope.

H. S. Chamberlain

Houston Stewart Chamberlain (1850–1927) and his book *Foundations of the Nineteenth Century* (1899) represent a second major step toward Nazi ideology. A disciple of the great German composer, Richard Wagner, Chamberlain lived long enough to meet and admire Hitler himself. Though resembling Gobineau in some ways, Chamberlain disagreed with the Frenchman on issues such as "Aryanism," anti-Semitism, and social pessimism.

Chamberlain challenged the concept of a separate Aryan race. The notion of "Aryan" made a false linkage between language and the racial composition of peoples. Chamberlain charged that people who spoke Aryan (i.e., Indo-European) languages by no means constituted a single racial family. The so-called Aryans displayed sharp physical differences among themselves, and "even granted that there was once a common ancestral Indo-European race, what evidence can we offer against the . . . facts which make it probable that other absolutely unrelated types have also been . . . richly represented in our so-called nations of today?"[18] Understandably, Chamberlain found his own substitute for the Aryans as the elite within the elite. He called them the "Teutonic peoples" or simply, the Teutons.

For Chamberlain the key to modern history is Europe since the fall of the Roman Empire. Rome "fell" from internal decay due to the hodge-podge racial mixture of the "chaos of peoples" (*Volkerchaos*). It was not brought down by "barbarian" Teutonic hordes. The latter were in no way barbarians and their conquest of degenerate Rome spared further decay and disintegration.

It is the "heirs of Rome" who determine the fate of Europe and hence of the modern world. The three main parties are the chaos of peoples, the Teutons, and the Jews. The chaos are a null quantity because their racial make-up prevents the specialization of qualities. This lack is crucial as "nothing extraordinary is produced without 'specialization'; in the case of men, as of animals, it is this specialization that produces noble races."[19]

The Teutons are clearly the heroes of Chamberlain's epic racial drama. The Teutons are defined as the "different North-European races, which appear in history as the Celts, Teutons (Germanen) and Slavs, and from whom—mostly through indeterminable mingling—the peoples of modern Europe are descended."[20] Chamberlain's broad conception of Teutonic peoples diverges sharply from later Nazi ideas because the Nazis excluded the Slavs from elite status. Indeed, the Nazis considered the Slavs an inferior race, nearly as dangerous as the Jews as a racial nemesis of true Aryans.

Having saved Europe from "Asiatic Barbarism" at the fall of Rome, the Teutons sometimes succumbed to self-destructive practices. Nonetheless, the basic qualities of the Teuton, "his mystical tendencies, his thirst for knowledge, his force of faith, his impulse to create, his high organizing abilities, his noble ambition, his need of ideals," place him far above the peoples of the chaos. The Teutonic peoples formed our modern western civilization from 1200 AD to 1800 AD and thus brought about the "creation of a new world, that is to say, of an absolutely new order of society adapted to the character, the needs, and the gifts of a new species of men. It was a creation brought about by natural necessity, the creation of a new civilization, a new culture."[21]

In addition to the Teutons only the Jews stand apart from the chaos. Chamberlain's anti-Semitism is neither religious nor cultural; it is racial. The Jews are not precisely an "inferior" race: rather, their inner nature is alien and hostile to that of the Teutons. An inevitable struggle rages between the two groups for mastery over the future. There will be no easy victory for the Teutons, for the Jews are a formidable foe. They even deserve a certain admiration because "they have acted with absolute consistency according to the logic and truth of their own individuality." Also, the Jews have understood the racial principle better than most and have never forgotten "the sacredness of physical laws because of foolish humanitarian day-dreams which they shared only when such a policy was to their advantage."[22]

It is not just that the Jews are a foreign body in Teutonic culture. Chamberlain sounds a note that Nazis raised to a deafening roar, when he charges that "our government, our law, our science, our commerce, our literature, our art . . . practically all branches of our life have become willing slaves of the Jew."[23] If the Teutons represent the spiritual principle in culture, the Jews embody materialism. Their religion, philosophy, and way of life reflect a narrow-mindedness that Chamberlain finds repugnant. In any case, the war is on and the stakes are control over the modern world.

Hitler and Rosenberg

With Adolph Hitler and Alfred Rosenberg the racist and anti-Semitic aspects of Nazi ideology reach their final form. Despite its erratic structure Hitler's *Mein Kampf* displays the racism and anti-Semitism that characterized the Nazi movement. Rosenberg's *The Myth of the Twentieth Century* purports to be more philosophical and is a more coherent racist statement based on Chamberlain as well as Hitler.

With these two ideologists we find programmatic statements and demagogic rhetoric, which are almost absent in Gobineau and rare in Chamberlain. The breeding program based on race emerges from the background. Gobineau's and Chamberlain's somewhat ironic respect for the Jews is replaced by the crudest stereotypes and unadulterated vitriol. Racism and anti-Semitism descend from armchair speculation and become sloganized in political warfare.

In terminology, we find Hitler rejecting "Teuton" in favor of Gobineau's "Aryan" so that he can drive the "Slavic sub-humanity" out of the charmed circle. Rosenberg, on the other hand, talks of a Nordic race, another concept popular with twentieth-century racists. Whether it is Aryans or Nordics—the Nazis did not distinguish sharply between the two—Rosenberg's dilemma remains similar to the one first posed by Chamberlain: "either we attain, through a re-experiencing and cultivation of primal blood combined with an elevated will to struggle, a new purifying level of achievement, or even the last Germanic-Western values of civilization and state discipline will vanish amidst filthy metropolitan crowds. . . ."[24] Inferior or alien elements must be excluded from the future state, which must use racial breeding.

And yet, it is the so-called "Jewish problem" that troubles both Hitler and Rosenberg. The Jew is the enemy and must be so. The only remedy is exclusion, though naturally in published works it is not spelled out that the "final solution" meant Auschwitz and Buchenwald. Before World War II one could even speculate that all the Nazis had in store for the Jews was forced exile or some sort of second or third class citizenship.

According to Nazi doctrine the Jews chop away at the Aryan cultural edifice in two main ways. The first is a sort of moral-cultural attack, which Hitler once expressed by saying that: "No, the Jew possesses no culture-creating force of any sort, since the idealism, without which there is no true higher development of man, is not present in him and never was present. Hence his intellect will never have a constructive effect, but will be destructive. . . ."[25]

On the political front the Jew is the hidden force behind two evil manifestations, which seem wholly unrelated. On the one hand, the Jew is the guiding force of left-wing movements—especially Marxism and Bolshevism. On the other hand, "Jewish international finance" seeks the economic bondage of free peoples. This two-pronged attack is a planned strategy to ensure Jewish world domination. To support such extreme allegations Hitler invoked the infamous forgery *The Protocols of the Elders of Zion*, which supposedly contained the secret master-plan for ultimate Jewish supremacy.

Hitler indeed comes very close to dumping responsibility for everything that offends him about modern society on the Jews.

> Whether we consider questions of general justice or economic life, symptoms of cultural decline or processes of political degeneration, questions of faulty schooling or the bad influence exerted on grown-ups by the press, etc., everywhere and always it is fundamentally the disregard of the racial needs of our people or failure to see a foreign racial menace.26

We have made racism and anti-Semitism the main focus of Nazi ideology, what distinguishes it from fascism and other right-wing doctrines. If there is anyone who doubts the power of ideals and ideologies, however fraudulent they appear, let him examine the history of the Third Reich.

VOLKISM

The body of thought we call *volkism* has a long history in modern Germany. It emerged in the early nineteenth century as a reaction to Napoleon's conquest of Germany and the penetration of the ideas of the French Revolution of 1789. A recent student defines volkism as an

> ideology which stood opposed to the progress and modernization that transformed nineteenth-century Europe. It used and amplified romanticism to provide an alternative to modernity, to the developing industrial and urban civilization which seemed to rob man of his individual, creative self, while cutting him loose from a social order that was seemingly exhausted and lacking vitality. Volkish thought revitalized the social framework by charging it with the energy of the Volk. It simultaneously gave new life to the possibility of individual self-fulfillment by making it a part of the creative process of a higher life force.28

Hitler devoted large sections of *Mein Kampf* to elaborating volkish views on art, race, and politics.

All authorities agree on the intimate connection between volkism and romanticism. Romanticism is not really a philosophy, but rather a body of ideas and attitudes relating to art, religion, morality, human relations, history, and politics. In the early nineteenth century, romanticism was a pan-European movement, probably stronger in Germany than elsewhere. Instead of seeing reason as the royal road to truth and authenticity, romanticism sees it as a long detour and possibly a dead-end street. Reason is neutral or negative in learning the really important lessons of human life. In fact, reason often leads to rules, conventions, and institutions that choke the truly creative, liberating impulses of man. These impulses come far more from feeling, passion, sentiment, and emotion.

Romanticism considers these aspects of mind as more natural and honest than reason. As the seventeenth-century French thinker Pascal put it, "The heart has reasons, of which reason is ignorant." Whereas rationalism exposes the "universal truths" of a common humanity, romanticism is enamored with the unique and the particular. These unique and particular things can be a specific individual or the culture of a specific people. Romanticism relishes what makes men and peoples different, no matter what binds them together. This outlook is well represented in the volkish nationalism and racism preached by the Nazis, as racism would make cultures unique on biological grounds.

A cardinal tenet of German romanticism is the contrast between *Kultur* and civilization. Kultur is the mode of life of an essentially agrarian people, and is based on an instinctive closeness to the earth and hence nature in general. Kultur furthermore expresses the nonrational bonds of an organic social community. It involves a religious view of life, even if it dispenses with formal rites and theological dogmas. The priest, the warrior, and the peasant are the typical people, the tone-setters of *Kultur.*

Civilization, on the other hand, is a rootless, urban way of life. It displays a rationalistic philosophy and a materialistic spirit. It has, on the one hand, a clique of money-grubbing plutocrats; on the other, a shiftless mob devoid of morals and tradition. Civilization promotes free-thinking and secularism and culminates in atheism. It is cosmopolitan in the worst sense, for it brings in ideas and practices from all over without any thought to how these things fit together or relate to home-grown traditions.

Volkish themes characterize many aspects of Nazi ideology. Ideas like "blood and soil" or "living space" (*Lebensraum*) reflect the mythical attachment to a peasant-oriented society. The Lebensraum doctrine means that the German people (*Volk*) need land to relieve overpopulation. "Thinking with the blood" combines the romanticist love for intuition with the racist notion that racial biology determines thought.

Volkish thought disputes many principles of the western liberal democratic tradition. Its rationalism, its (type of) individualism, its egalitarianism, its progressivism are considered superficial and mechanical conceptions. Volkism instead cherishes the heroic intuition of the great leader and the collective sense of the folk community. Peoples are not equal and a notion of progress that sees them all headed towards the same destiny is against nature. Any examination of *Mein Kampf* would confirm that for Germans imbued with these volkish ideas, "Hitler was not a stranger, not an innovator, but an adapter, a molder, who gave the prevailing Volkish theories a new edge, a more dynamic emphasis."[29]

ELITISM

While the Aryans are the elite of races, Nazi ideology also demands leadership and elites within the racial community itself. Hitler advanced these ideas in his general critique of liberal democracy. Indeed, his racist-volkish onslaught against internationalism seems tightly linked in his mind to rejection of equality and democracy in the state. Thus, he considers it logical that "democracy, which within a people denies the special value of the individual and puts in its place a value which represents the sum of all individualities—a merely numerical value—should proceed precisely in the same way in the life of peoples and . . . result in internationalism."[30] This noxious equality, once accepted, must work across the board.

For Hitler and Nazi ideology the notions of equality and democracy are opposed to both nature and history. Hitler embraced the "great man" view of history, espoused by a favorite author of his, the nineteenth-century British writer Thomas Carlyle. Like Carlyle he argues that the "whole edifice of civilization is in its foundations and in all its stories nothing else than the result of the creative capacity, the achievement, the intelligence, the industry of individuals: in its greatest triumphs it represents the great crowning achievement of individual God-favored geniuses."[31] It should be clear that this glorification of the "individual" is not a liberal defense of all and sundry individuals, but a romanticist defense of the exceptional, the hero or genius.

According to Hitler, democracy is thus doubly mistaken when it not only discourages the formation of the creative minority but also refuses to follow it when it reveals itself. The result is that "peoples with a great past, from the time when they surrender themselves to the unlimited, democratic rule of the masses slowly lose their former position: for the outstanding achievements of individuals . . . are now rendered practically ineffective through the oppression of mere numbers."[32]

To attract elements of German business to his own brand of elitism, Hitler asked that since private property produced economic inequality, how could the business community deny a similar principle in politics? To accept the strategic role of leadership in one area and deny it in the other was illogical. Indeed, egalitarianism would have the same results in both spheres, because "in the economic sphere communism is analogous to democracy in the political sphere."[33]

In *Mein Kampf,* Hitler pointed out that a "Weltanschauung" that rejected democratic rule and accepted the mission of advancing the higher races "must also apply that same aristocratic postulate to the individuals within the folk-community. It must take care that the positions of leadership are given to the best men."[34] Hitler's new elite is to be an "open" rather than a "closed" one, for the task of the volkish state is "not to preserve the decisive influence of an existing social class, but to pick the most capable kinds from the sum of all the national comrades and bring them to office and dignity."[35]

Although there is some similarity between Hitler's open elite and liberal "equality of opportunity," the differences are more prominent. We must bear in mind that selection of individuals is made by the volkish state, not by spontaneous social and economic processes as with traditional liberalism.

After 1933 the Nazi party became for a time the favored organ for producing the elite of the New Order. In 1934 Hitler declared that the Nazi party

> will for all time form the picked body of the leaders of the German people. It will develop a state of political apostles and combatants who then as obedient officers . . . will serve the Movement. . . . In it there will develop a tradition in the art of leading a people. . . .
>
> The aim must be that all decent Germans shall be National Socialists; only the best National Socialists shall be members of the Party.[36]

In these passages Hitler distinguishes between Movement and Party. The Movement was a rather unwieldy set of groups associated with the Party proper. Though theory made the Party the heart and soul of the Movement, practice showed that some of its groups enjoyed considerable autonomy.

In the late 1930s another contender for the elite-selector role arose. Beginning rather humbly as a body guard for Hitler in the 1920s, the SS (*Schutz-Staffel* = security squad) later expanded prodigiously in numbers, power and functions during the course of the Third Reich. Its leader Heinrich Himmler saw the SS as the source of the new elite that would run Nazi-dominated Europe. One of his lieutenants echoed such aspirations in the following terms:

> We, who must educate these young people into leaders, are aiming at a modern state which finds its inspiration in the city of the ancient Greeks. It is to those democracies led by an aristocracy and resting on the economic

foundation of a large class of helots that antiquity owes the finest master-pieces of its civilization. Five to ten percent of the population, the flower of its elite must have the command. The remainder have only to work and obey. . . . The choice of the new class of leaders will be made by the SS.[37]

To develop this new Nazi aristocracy, Himmler and company set up training and education centers. At the end of the Third Reich, the SS recruited among non-Germans provided certain racial standards were met. Half of SS membership was non-German at this final stage.

CONCLUSION

By placing racism and anti-Semitism at the heart of Nazi ideology, we take a stand on several important issues. First, we maintain that Nazi ideology or the National Socialist Weltanschauung is a serious matter. There are those, of course, who question this. Recall Hermann Rausch-ning's thesis that the Nazi "doctrine" was serious, but only at the level of mass consumption. In other words the leaders stand beyond ideology and only manipulate it to aid their unquenchable thirst for power and their intoxication with the pure experience of revolution.

Here we can only suggest that although Hitler and the other top Nazis showed great versatility in modulating the message to fit the intended audience, certain underlying principles were pursued with almost ruthless consistency. The systematic killing of countless Jews and other "racial inferiors" is proof that the relevant tenets of Nazi ideology were fundamental convictions of Hitler and his subalterns.

Those single-mindedly bent on maintaining and expanding their raw power under wartime conditions would hardly have engaged in gratuitous slaughter of human resources. On a lesser plane Nazi moves in foreign and domestic policy made little sense, unless a grand racial battle for the future was thought to be involved. Racism and anti-Semi-tism were ends, not means for the Nazi leadership.

The degree of commitment to these things is also what prevents us from lumping National Socialism together with Italian Fascism as key cases of a generic fascism. The similarities, of course, are there as in the attack on Marxist and democratic theories in the name of charismatic leadership and a militant elite. But our treatment shows that fascist statism has no true counterpart in Nazi ideology, and that the latter's grandiose philosophy of history coming from the likes of Gobineau and Chamberlain is quite different from the fascist stress on will power and the pragmatic openness of history.

Finally, the key issue of the relationship between the party and the state comes out quite differently in the two ideologies. Recall how the

Italian Fascists clearly subordinated the party to the state and compare that notion with Hitler's declaration at the party meeting of 1934 that "the state does not command us, but we command the state. The state did not create us; we created our state."

NOTES

1. The Nazis themselves would have rejected the expression "Nazi ideology." They preferred "National Socialist world-view" (*Weltanschauung*).
2. Vitalism in this context refers to a basic life-force, which moves man and the world. This force is neither mind nor matter, but works in and through both. Reason and science are not the best ways to fathom the operation of the life-force. Instead, a nonrational intuition is necessary to grasp it sympathetically from within.
3. Adolph Hitler, *My New Order* (New York: Reynal & Hitchcock, 1941), p. 89.
4. Adolph Hitler, *Mein Kampf* (Boston: Houghton Mifflin, 1943), p. 391.
5. Alfred Rosenberg, *Race and Race History*, ed. R. Pois (New York: Harper & Row, 1974), p. 192.
6. "The Nazi Program," in *Fascism: Three Major Regimes*, ed. H. Lubasz (New York: John Wiley, 1973), p. 78.
7. Ibid.
8. This was the title of a book by Hermann Rauschning, an ex-Nazi who defected to the West in the late 1930s. According to Rauschning: "National Socialism is action pure and simple, dynamics *in vacuo*, revolution at a variable tempo, ready to be changed at any moment. One thing it is not— doctrine or philosophy. Yet it has a philosophy. It does not base its policy on a doctrine, but pursues it with aid of a philosophy. It makes use of its philosophy, as it makes use of all things men have, and all they want, as fuel for its energy." *The Revolution of Nihilism* (New York: Alliance Book Corp., 1940), p. 23.
9. Hitler, *Order*, p. 45.
10. See Ralph Bowen, *German Theories of the Corporative State* (New York: Columbia University Press, 1947).
11. Hitler, *Order*, p. 152.
12. See Leon Poliakov, *The Aryan Myth* (New York: Basic Books, 1974). Gobineau is more properly the father of racist "thought" than of "ideology," since despair over the fate of civilization hardly qualifies as ideology in the sense of this text. For a somewhat different view, see Michael D. Biddiss, *Father of Racist Ideology: The Social and Political Thought of Count Gobineau* (New York: Weybright & Talley, 1970).
13. Count Gobineau, *Gobineau: Selected Political Writings*, ed. M. D. Biddiss (New York: Harper & Row, 1970), p. 205.
14. Ibid., pp. 206–07.
15. Ibid., p. 207.
16. Ibid., p. 210.
17. Indeed, Gobineau goes so far as to say that of the ten great world civiliza-

tions, six (the Indian, the Egyptian, the Chinese, the Roman, the Greek, and the Germanic) were created wholly or largely by Aryans. A seventh, the Assyrian, is basically the work of non-Aryan whites. The other three were the New World native civilizations of the Aztecs, the Incas, and the Alleghanians (i.e., various Indian groups of Eastern North America).

18. Houston Stewart Chamberlain, *Foundations of the Nineteenth Century*, vol. I (New York: John Lane, 1913), p. 264.
19. Ibid., p. 261.
20. Ibid., p. 257.
21. Ibid., vol. II, p. 187.
22. Ibid., vol. I, p. 331.
23. Ibid.
24. Rosenberg, *Race History*, p. 75.
25. Hitler, *Mein Kampf*, p. 303.
26. Ibid., p. 328.
27. See George L. Mosse, *The Crisis of German Ideology* (New York: Grosset & Dunlop, 1972); Fritz Stern, *The Politics of Cultural Despair* (Garden City, N.Y.: Anchor Books, 1965); and Peter Viereck, *Metapolitics: The Roots of the Nazi Mind* (New York: Capricorn Books, 1961).
28. Mosse, *Crisis*, pp. 16–17. *Volkisch* would be the German for "populist," and there are some similarities between volkism and populism (Chapter 14). The difference is that volkism appealed more strongly to intellectuals than populism usually does.
29. Ibid., p. 311.
30. Hitler, *Order*, p. 97.
31. Ibid.
32. Ibid., p. 98.
33. Ibid., p. 100.
34. Quoted in *The Third Reich*, ed. M. Baumont (New York: Praeger, 1955), p. 370.
35. Hitler, *Mein Kampf*, p. 431.
36. Hitler, *Order*, p. 293.
37. Quoted in Baumont, *Third Reich*, p. 657.

SUGGESTIONS FOR FURTHER READING

Biddiss, Michael D. *Father of Racist Ideology: The Social and Political Thought of Count Gobineau*. New York: Weybright & Talley, 1970.
Bullock, Alan. *Hitler: A Study in Tyranny*. New York: Bantam Books, 1961.
Mosse, George L. *The Crisis of German Ideology*. New York: Grosset & Dunlop, 1972.
Poliakov, Leon. *The Aryan Myth*. New York: Ballantine Books, 1974.
Rauschning, Hermann. *The Revolution of Nihilism*. New York: Alliance Book Corporation, 1940.
Viereck, Peter. *Metapolitics: The Roots of the Nazi Mind*. New York: Capricorn Books, 1961.

17

CONCLUSION

We have spent several hundred pages discussing a wide range of ideas that relate to political life. Yet such attention requires some final justification. What if political ideals and ideologies are mere effects rather than true causes of political events? What if they are simple cover-ups for the underlying motives of political leaders? If so, our analysis of "isms," such as liberalism, communism, fascism, nationalism, utopianism, and the rest would amount to little more than a parlor game. Far better to introduce students to the reality of politics by ignoring the ideological flotsam and jetsam and heading straight for the supposed "root causes" of political behavior.

Indeed, this sort of advice has been offered by diverse schools of thought and we can call their general disparagement of ideals and ideologies the *critique of ideologies*. We must first concede that each "critique" possesses a partial, though exaggerated, insight into the real world of politics. The exaggeration is apparent when the critiques deny serious independent force to ideals and ideologies.

The Realist Critique

Political realism, the notion that power is the prime mover of politics, is a widespread idea found even in the cultures of antiquity. It is well represented in classics of Indian, Chinese, and Greek thought. The strength of the realist current in fourth-century Athens can be seen Plato's dialogues. In the *Gorgias* Plato's alter ego and teacher Socrates is discussing the nature and advantages of both justice and injustice in human affairs. About half way into the dialogue one Callicles jumps into a discussion of the idea that it is worse to inflict injustice than to suffer it. To show the wrongness of such a notion he contrasts what people believe by mere *convention* and what is actually true according to *nature*. If something follows according to nature it has a firm foothold in reality, whereas something merely "conventional" is arbitrary, accidental, and superficial.

Why, however, do so many share Socrates's apparently naive and conventional belief that suffering injustice is somehow superior to inflicting it? Callicles answers that it is because

> the makers of laws are the majority who are weak; and they make laws and distribute praises and censures with a view to themselves and to their own interests; and they terrify the stronger sort of men, and those who are able to get the better of them, in order that they may not get the better of them.[1]

Politics in the Calliclean view is essentially a struggle for power, a contest which, if left alone, would see the strong dominate the weak. Indeed, in this there would be a sort of natural justice for nature shows that "among men as among animals, and indeed among whole cities and races, that justice consists in the superior ruling over and in having more than the inferior."[2]

If we agree with Callicles, we must conclude that commonplace notions of justice and morality, since they violate "nature," are simple conventions or fictions masking the power interests of the majority. Despite Callicles' example the realist doctrine of power over ideology is not the monopoly of aristocratic philosophies. Modern democratic thinkers have also argued that political power is the hard currency of politics. The contemporary realist warns against taking the professions of ideologists too seriously. He has seen leaders and politicians all too often switch ideological horses in midstream, and he is not taken in by the face-value of ideological utterances.

Ideologies for the realist are too vague and manipulable to support a valid understanding of political behavior. Indeed, he warns the friends of democracy to maintain a healthy scepticism of ideologies because, contrary to Callicles, it is usually minorities that use ideologies to bamboozle the majority.

The Marxist Critique

While we have discussed Marxism in Chapter 9, we must go a few steps further here to appreciate the Marxist conception of ideology. Let us recall that for Marx and his disciples every historical society has a "substructure" and a "superstructure." The substructure is the mode of production and exchange or the "economic base" of society. It includes

the "productive forces" of technology as well as the economic relationships of ownership and work. For most of history the minority "ruling class" has owned the main means of production. In antiquity slave
labor made the slave-owners the ruling class; in the middle ages land
made the land-owning feudal aristocracy the ruling class; and in modern
times capital has made the bourgeois capitalists into the ruling class.
This economically dominant ruling class is dominant politically and in
other ways as well.

The superstructure of society comprises the state, law, morals, art,
religion, and philosophy. The last five items on this list we generally call
culture, but Marx termed them "ideology." Such "ideology" functions
to preserve, protect, and defend the interests and overall dominant
position of the ruling class. The ruling class is not only economically
dominant but it rules as "thinkers, as producers of ideas, and regulate
the production and distribution of the ideas of their age: thus their ideas
are the ruling ideas of the epoch."[3]

Culture—with the notable exception of science—is basically ideology for Marx. Ideology consequently is a form of "false consciousness," since he saw the individual's consciousness as being determined
by his social being. In other words, the ideas in our heads are reflections
of the socioeconomic circumstances in which we are born, live, and
work. False or ideological consciousness means that we have become
victims of the distorted view of reality that serves the interests and
domination of the ruling class.

Such a conception underlies Marx's famous statement that religion
is the "opiate" of the people. Religion is ideological because it turns our
eyes away from this world and its injustices and towards the "other"
world. Moreover, religion preaches nonviolence and nonresistance—
"turning the other cheek"—which dampens protest and thus forestalls
revolution against the social order dominated by the ruling class.

Much controversy surrounds the exact relationship between the
substructure (economic base) and the superstructure (ideology). Some
Marxist writings suggest a sort of economic determinism insofar as the
substructure has a controlling influence over the superstructure. That
some exaggeration was indeed involved here was admitted by Engels
some time after the death of Marx. However, even though Engels con-
ceded a certain reciprocal impact of ideological factors upon society's
economic base, the latter in the final analysis was the more important
driving force in history.

From a Marxist perspective, therefore, ideals and ideologies have a
firm foundation in the realities of economic life. They reflect the economic position and interests of specific classes and sometimes of sub-
groups within those classes. Moreover, any sharp distinction between
political ideologies and other aspects of culture such as religion, philoso-

phy, art, law, or morality is invalid. These latter things play a political role even if in a somewhat subdued manner. Ideals and ideologies only make a headway in society because of their connection with definite social groups.

The Psychological Critique

A third outlook minimizing the independent role of political ideals and ideologies can be traced back to Sigmund Freud (1856–1939). While Freud himself did not devote all that much direct attention to modern politics or ideologies, he provided a theory of human behavior relevant to both. Freud viewed mankind as dominated by unconscious motivational factors. These are the sexual or erotic drives encompassed in the *libido*. The libido works mainly through the aspect of the mind known as the "id." Libidinal drives, if allowed a wholly free expression, would result in a saturnalia of sex and violence beyond the wildest dreams of Hollywood producers. Such untrammeled freedom would make civilization as we know it impossible.

All of this means that civilization requires a containment or "repression" of the primordial ferocity of the libido. Moreover, there are certain aggressive tendencies inherent in man to worry about. Repression can take a wide variety of forms, and the "ego"—the largely conscious and rational part of the human mind—acknowledges the need for some repression of erotic and aggressive impulses. As Freud put it, the "pleasure principle" (free expression of libido) must be counterbalanced by the "reality principle" (the need for restraint).

Nevertheless, such socially required repression can go too far with the overdevelopment of the third part of the mind or "super-ego." An overactive super-ego or conscience taps some of the reservoir of passion held in the id. It then becomes a tyrannical moral censor from within the individual and produces what Freud called an "unconscious sense of guilt."[4]

No form of repression is completely successful, which is why Freud considered all men, including himself, to be more or less neurotic. Disciples of Freud have applied this principle and some new ones to the study of political leaders and followers. Harold Lasswell provided the basic formula for this approach many years ago when he analyzed "the private motives, their displacement on to public objects, and their rationalization in terms of public interests."[5] The causal sequence would suggest that the private motives—Freudian drives and symptoms—are fundamental. These internal problems are then externalized into the realm of public affairs. Some form of ideological rationalization is then invoked to hide from the individual the fact that his public concerns and behavior are in reality the working out of psychological problems.

A disciple of Freud, Gustav Bychowski, applied this sort of analysis to the great leader of the French Revolution of 1789, Maximilien Robespierre. In Bychowski's interpretation, Robespierre's troubled childhood and youth produced in him "powerful feelings of hatred." The result was that "people whom he regarded as evil, unjust, or tyrannical served as objects against whom this hatred could be directed. His great capacity for sublimation made it possible for him to express these tendencies in *an ideological form that corresponded with the prevailing social and political ideas.*"[6] (Italics added.)

The psychological approach offers the basis for a critique of ideologies. In hard-line versions like Bychowski's, ideologies function as symptoms or manifestations of personality types or disorders. The latter things are the independent variable; the ideologies are the dependent variable. Modified Freudianism, however, allows for a more subtle interplay between the personality factors and the social and cultural factors of the given historical situation.[7]

The Sociological Critique

The sociological critique of ideologies combines elements of the previous three critiques. The pioneer figure in this critique is the German sociologist Karl Mannheim (1893–1947). For Mannheim too political ideals and ideologies lack an independent or objective basis in reality. It is thus misleading to study them as they are handed down from thinker to thinker over the generations. Rather we should study ideas as reflections of the competing political and social groups of a given time and place.

Mannheim sets out from the contrast between *ideology* and *utopia.* Both of these intellectual patterns distort social reality. They are forms of thought that deform and exaggerate certain aspects of the given historical situation. They do so, of course, purposely. Their distortions are structured to advance the political interests of one or another of the contending social groups in a given time and place. Some of these groups favor the status quo because they benefit so much from it. When their position is challenged, they respond by having an "ideology" created for them. Their ideologies are thus inherently conservative and work to impede social change, which would change their pleasant state of affairs.

Rising and underprivileged groups, on the other hand, need some doctrinal weapon to attack the existing order and highlight its evils. They want to contrast it to a future order that could and should replace it. Mannheim calls these futuristic visions "utopias." However, neither the higher groups on the defensive nor the lower groups on the offensive manufacture ideologies or utopias themselves. This role is perfromed by a distinct group called the "free-floating intelligentsia." Although, "situated between classes," the intelligentsia "does not form a middle class. Not, of course, that it is suspended in a vacuum into which social interests do not penetrate; on the contrary, it subsumes in itself all those interests with which social life is permeated."[8]

Mannheim then applies this theory to several of the leading ideologies of the modern age. He finds that "bureaucratic conservatism" functions as a kind of occupational disease of civil servants who attempt to "hide all problems of politics under the cover of administration."[9] Historical conservatism, on the other hand is linked to the nobility and certain intellectual groups of the bourgeoisie. Liberal democratic thought with its faith in human reason is the peculiar province of the middle class, while the "socialist-communist conception" reflects the rise of the modern working class. Finally, fascism is seen as the work of certain groups "led by intellectuals who are outsiders to the liberal-bourgeois and socialist stratum of leaders."[10] Ideologies and utopias have force only because they express and rationalize the interests and aspirations of distinct social strata.

In their different ways the four critiques of ideology deny or minimize the importance and independence of ideals and ideologies in political life. Each can adduce test cases to confirm its belief in power, economic, psychological, and sociological motives and factors. However, our survey of ideals from democracy to neo-individualism and ideologies from anarchism to Nazism supports a rather different conclusion. Though our job in this text has been more to expose ideas than to document their impact on politics, our chapter conclusions sometimes gave us the occasion to make some relevant suggestions.

We have pointed out the power of ideals and ideologies themselves in influencing political history and the policies of actual governments. Our argument has been that while sometimes ideological assertions are trotted out *post facto* to justify a course of action already determined upon, many times the ideological system influences the choices of political leaders by precluding some options and encouraging others.

Of course, political leaders do not simply take their current policies out of a manual of ideological "standard operating procedures." The actual process is both more complex and more subtle. In one sense an ideology helps to construct the political world that the leader (or the follower) sees around him. Students of public opinion, for example, have spoken of a sort of "perceptual screen," through which the individual lets certain messages enter his consciousness, but keeps other out.

The screening process, however, is not accidental. There is a principle of selectivity involved, which is constituted by the fundamental ideological beliefs of the individual. Because this is so, the individual's definition of the situation is strongly influenced by his ideological preconceptions.

This conclusion, perhaps, could be partially admitted by advocates of the realist, psychoanalytical, Marxist, and sociological approaches. They would simply deny that political actors are conscious of the true meaning and origin of the ideological beliefs they cherish. These beliefs, it is held, reflect economic, psychological, sociological, or power realities that the individual involved may only be dimly aware of.

Our assumption throughout this text has been that the human mind is flexible enough to rise above the pressures of power lusts, economic interests, youthful psychic traumas, and membership in social classes. The result is that many people do try to understand the world around them, the political world included. Some of us some of the time can break out of the confines and constrictions of our group affiliations and personal life histories. Ideals and ideologies thus gain some of their independent force from this flexible or open aspect of the human mind.

THE ELEMENTS OF IDEOLOGICAL THINKING

We have covered much ground in our discussion of ideals and ideologies. We are now in a position to distill certain points of contrast and controversy that give rise to the separate elements or baseline principles of distinct ideological systems. These elements or principles concern such issues as human nature, society, history, justice, and truth.

Assumptions in ideologies about human nature concern such questions as: Can human nature change? Is man good or evil? Peacable or aggressive? Rational or irrational? Selfish or generous? Equal or unequal? There is a connection between answers to these questions and the type of political program that an ideology advocates. For example, if an ideology promises to reconstruct society so as to cure all social problems and make everyone happy and content someday (anarchism, communism) this naturally assumes that man is or can be made good or cooperative enough to make such a society work. Such "optimistic" notions have been challenged by conservatives and other pessimists who consider most social evils as symptoms of a defective human nature.

Assumptions about society and the state, not just *this* society and *this* state, are in the background of political ideologies. Ideologies like liberalism, populism, and strains of anarchism are individualistic (i.e., they view society as a conglomeration of separate and distinct individuals). The state is simply the political association of these selfsame individuals. Ideologies like fascism and conservatism deny this, however, and see society or the state "organically" as real entities, with a life and moral status above and beyond their components. Pluralism, which is manifest at various points in the ideological compass, sees society neither as purely individualistic nor organic. Rather, society is the framework for the activity of groups.

An interpretation of history is a feature of most modern ideologies. Some like Marxism and pure racism teach that history is a concatenation of causes and effects largely beyond the control of man. Others like modern (pragmatic) liberalism or fascism portray history as both fathomable and susceptible to human action and planning. Sometimes the "actor" in the historical drama is the "great man" or "hero" and sometimes it is some human collectivity. Certain ideologies such as Maoist communism tread a middle path between a deterministic and voluntaristic approach.

Also important regarding history is the question of *progress*. As a historical and ideological term, progress means an increase in the well-being of society over the long span of history. Just what this well-being consists of is different in different ideologies. Possible choices are freedom, equality, justice, democracy, morality, prosperity, technology, knowledge, peace, social harmony, and so on. Progress thus involves the growth of any number of these things. Marxism is a good example of a theory of progress because all of these good things will be achieved in the classless society of communism.

Not only do different ideologies have different measures of what constitutes progress, they have a different image of its path. Will the path be gradual, smooth, and steady as in evolutionary progress? So says liberalism. Or will the path be erratic and stormy as in a "dialectical" progress? So says classic Marxism. Or, in a completely different vision, will progress be spurned as an illusion and history seen instead as the recurrent cycle of the "rise, decline, and fall" of civilizations—a favorite theme of certain conservatives and racists.

Rare is the ideology that fails to claim "social justice" as its highest concern. "Distributive" justice deals with the distribution of wealth, status, and power among groups and individuals in society. What then is the base principle of just distribution? Is it an absolutely equal share for all members of society? Or is it "to each according to his needs," as classic Marxism would have it? Is there some principle such as "social utility" (as in the classic liberalism of John Stuart Mill) that allows for some overriding of the basic principle of equality?

Perhaps, equality is not the place to begin. Perhaps we should emulate Plato's scheme in the *Republic*, where power and status, if not wealth, are unequally distributed to three basic levels of society: philosopher–kings, warrior–auxiliaries, and common people. A kindred principle of justice is defended by modern conservatives, for whom hierarchy is a natural and beneficial trait of a well-ordered society. Certainly, the rich and the well-born are very heavily overrepresented in Burke's "natural aristocracy." In any event, the relationship between justice and equality is differently viewed in different ideologies.

All of these points of doctrine assume some standard of truth. How do we know that our views of man, society, history, and justice are true? Though a full analysis is impossible here, a few suggestions might help us to understand the knowledge aspect of ideologies. In general terms, the four basic theories about how we gain truth and knowledge stress reason, intuition, revelation, and sense experience. For rationalism knowledge increases and truths multiply by means of logical deduction. Rationalism of this sort was common in classic liberalism. Intuition is a tricky concept that refers to a sort of sixth sense that gives us immediate knowledge of the truth. Intuitionist philosophers reject the claims of reason and logic to lead us to the truth. In any ideology influenced by romanticism there is likely to be a plea for intuition. Our best examples were Sorel's irrationalist theory of anarcho-syndicalism and the intuition of the charismatic leader in fascism and Nazism.

With the secularization of the modern western world appeals to divine revelation have become rarer in ideologies. Nonetheless, Christian Democracy has made explicit reference to it, and we must recall that Papal social theories so important in the origins of Christian Democracy come from one considered "infallible in matters of faith and morals." The infallibility comes from God. Of course, a non-western example would be the rise of so-called "Islamic fundamentalism" in parts of Asia and Africa. Whether in the extreme form represented by the movement of the Ayatollah Khomeini in Iran or some milder versions, these movements hope to reinstitute Islamic law as revealed by God through the Prophet Mohammed.

Sensory experience as the source of knowledge is the main tenet of the philosophy called "empiricism." Because all knowledge originates in the senses, empiricism rejects the common rationalist claim that universal truths or "innate ideas" have a timeless validity. While it is difficult to locate empiricism in one exclusive zone of the political spectrum, it does seem to gain strength as we move to the left of the spectrum and to weaken as we move to the right. It was especially strong in classic liberalism as Locke, Mill, and even Spencer could be considered "empiricists."

In the first part of this concluding chapter we surveyed various critiques of ideology that minimized its impact on the basis of sociological or psychological factors. The second part, which raised the broad issues contained within ideologies, suggests why ideologies have been influential in the past and will continue to be so for a long time. Despite the advances of the social and natural sciences and the technologies related to them, the issues of human nature, the state, the meaning of history, the essence of justice, or the nature of truth have not been definitively resolved. Rational men disagree about these issues and the social discontents of modern societies produce conflicts that fuel ideological movements.

This point was missed somewhat by theorists in the late 1950s and early 1960s who spoke of the "end" or "decline" of ideology. They mistook a temporary lull in ideological conflict as a fatal weakening of ideological passions. What had really happened was a short-lived remission of *extreme* ideologies of the right and the left in certain western countries as a by-product of the "affluent society."

The late 1960s saw a resurgence of ideological thinking that now ebbs and flows but shows no signs of disappearing. Those who wish to understand the politics of the future would do well to pursue further the study of those things we have called "ideals and ideologies of modern politics."

NOTES

1. Plato, *Gorgias*, in *The Dialogues of Plato*, vol. I, trans. B. Jowett (New York: Random House, 1937), p. 543.
2. Ibid., p. 544.
3. Karl Marx and Friedrich Engels, *The German Ideology* (New York: International Publishers, 1964), p. 39.
4. Sigmund Freud, *The Ego and the Id* (New York: W. W. Norton, 1962), p. 25.
5. Harold Lasswell, *Psychopathology and Politics* (New York: Viking Press, 1960), p. 124.
6. Gustav Bychowski, *Dictators and Disciples* (New York: International Universities Press, 1969), p. 112.
7. See Erik Erikson, *Young Man Luther* (New York: W. W. Norton, 1962)
8. Karl Mannheim, *Ideology and Utopia* (New York: Harcourt-Brace, 1936), p. 157.
9. Ibid., p. 118.
10. Ibid., p. 141.

SUGGESTIONS FOR FURTHER READING

Cox, Richard H., ed. *Ideology, Politics and Political Theory*. Belmont, Cal.: Wadsworth, 1969.

Erikson, Erik. *Young Man Luther*. New York: W. W. Norton, 1962.

Lasswell, Harold. *Psychopathology and Politics*. New York: Viking Press, 1960.

Mannheim, Karl. *Ideology and Utopia*. New York: Harcourt, Brace, 1936.

Plekhanov, George. *Fundamental Problems of Marxism*. New York: International Publishers, 1969.

Waxman, Chiam I., ed. *The End of Ideology Debate*. New York: Simon and Schuster, 1969.

NAME INDEX

Subject Index